ADVANCES IN TEACHER EDUCATION

ADVANCES
IN TEACHER
EDUCATION

EDITED BY
V. ALAN McCLELLAND
AND VED P. VARMA

ROUTLEDGE

First published 1989
by Routledge
11 New Fetter Lane, London EC4P 4EE

© 1989 V. Alan McClelland and Ved P. Varma

Printed and bound in Great Britain by
Billings & Sons Limited, Worcester

British Library Cataloguing in Publication Data

Advances in teacher education
   1. Great Britain. Teachers. Professional
   education
   I. McClelland, Vincent Alan
   II. Varma, V.P. (Vishwanath Prasad), *1924–*
   370′.7′10941

ISBN 0-415-01883-8

CONTENTS

Dedication

Contents

DEDICATION

Normally one is expected to be dead, retired, or at least approaching the biblical age-span of three score years and ten to be the recipient of a Festschrift. Bill Taylor is none of these, yet in an active professional career spanning over thirty-five years as schoolmaster, lecturer, researcher, writer, professor, administrator and, since 1985, university vice-chancellor, few have contributed more than he has done to the analytical examination of the theory and practice of education. His services and advice have been sought by government agencies and by academic bodies at home and abroad; his publications have constituted a rich resource for effective teacher formation. Honoured by several universities with the award of their highest doctorates and by the fellowships of learned bodies, he has been invited to lecture in many of the world's most important centres of teacher education. In 1982 he was awarded the CBE for his services to education. As chairman of the Council for the Accreditation of Teacher Education, to which office he was appointed in 1984, he has succeeded in carrying through a major change in the organization and conditions governing the provision and conduct of teacher-training courses in England and Wales with compassion and dedication. Throughout the vicissitudes of his career he has never lost the ability of being able to relate to all types and conditions of people but he remains most at ease when talking to his favourite audiences of teachers, teacher-trainers, and children.

Joseph Lancaster remarked at the end of his life that the teachers of youth need much more cheering on their way than they usually receive. It is in that spirit that the contributors to this volume offer their own peculiar insights into some of the pressing concerns of teacher education today.

V. Alan McClelland   **Ved P. Varma**

TEACHING QUALITY AND THE ACCREDITATION OF INITIAL TEACHER-TRAINING COURSES

Peter H.J.H. Gosden

At a time when the quality of the education and preparation of future teachers has been found to be so seriously amiss that special rules have had to be set down by the Department of Education and Science and a Council for the Accreditation of Teacher Education set up to enforce them, it might be as well to seek to set the present scene in a very slightly longer term perspective.

The fully trained or 'certificated' teacher at the time of the Butler Act had spent two years after leaving school in a training college which typically had about one hundred and twenty students and six or seven staff. In academic terms the level of much of the work undertaken was that of the upper forms of the grammar school rather than of higher education. Within the Board of Education it was admitted that appointment to the staff of a training college was not seen as promotion for a well-established and experienced teacher in a school with the result that the staff of some training colleges contained 'dull and unenterprising lecturers who became more so as they grew older'. The Board was particularly concerned at the narrowness of the experience and outlook of future teachers who went directly from school to be segregated in small single-sex colleges.[1] From the 1920s the Board of Education ceased from setting and marking the final-year examination papers but HM Inspectors of Schools examined the practical teaching of student teachers until the 1940s and were criticized for accepting low standards.

Closer association of teacher-training with the universities was the method chosen to improve quality and the mechanism for achieving this was the area training organization (ATO). The first four of these were set up in 1947 and within five years they were established throughout the country. Essentially the ATOs, or Institutes of Education as they were generally called, had in membership all institutions training teachers in their districts and were governed by delegacies subject to the ultimate control of the university and including representatives of colleges, local education authorities, and the university. Their principal activities centred on their basic function of supervising all aspects of courses for the initial training of teachers and of recommending to the minister for recognition as qualified teachers those students who had successfully completed their courses. Closer contacts with the universities and between the colleges themselves had the effect of both strengthening and broadening the professional and academic aspects of training. Increased confidence in the quality of the work lay behind the decision to have more of it by extending the basic initial training course from two to three years from 1960.

The Robbins Committee began its deliberations in that year and its recommendations on the training colleges would have led to the completion of their movement towards the universities, but most of these were not accepted by the government. Since the main course did not last for the same length of time as most degree courses, the committee had recommended that a degree of Bachelor of Education should be awarded to those who successfully completed an additional, fourth, year of study and preparation for entry to the teaching profession. This recommendation was accepted so that within twenty years of the establishment of the earliest ATOs, the colleges of education (as they were now styled) were able to offer to some of their successful students the prospect of graduation, the traditional hallmark of a higher education. By the early 1980s all those entering the teaching profession were graduates with the exception of a small number in certain specialist areas. They had all had three or four years of higher education and professional training.

This very remarkable transformation and - in a fundamental sense - the raising of the quality of preparation for school teaching had been accomplished through a devolved system of accreditation. Had the detailed and traditional involvement of the central ministry continued after the Second World War, it would have been very difficult for the necessary changes to have been undertaken within the closely regulated and slow-moving system of control.

The achievement was the greater for being accomplished at a time when the demand for teachers was rising rapidly. In 1945 there were slightly fewer than 5 million pupils in elementary and secondary schools; in 1975 there were nearly 9 million primary and secondary school pupils. The general mood of confidence and expansion in these years made it possible to improve quality and to expand greatly the numbers qualifying at the same time.

The training and accreditation of teachers can never be considered for long in isolation from developments in education more generally. The political and educational conflict over the organization of secondary education became intense in the 1960s. Those who favoured the reorganization of secondary schools on comprehensive lines often stressed the social divisiveness of separate grammar and modern schools and felt that a greater equality of opportunity could be achieved through a system of common secondary schools. Opponents feared the loss of the high standards which had come to be associated with many maintained grammar schools and saw in their demise the disappearance of opportunities for many young people. They argued also that the economy was suffering as a result of the lack of rigour or unsuitability of the education being offered in many schools with the wider acceptance of such methods as mixed ability teaching. Public examinations in secondary schools became one of the focal points of controversy, simply because their use and form have immediate and obvious philosophical or political implications. Thus Rhodes Boyson in <u>Black Paper Three</u>[2] wrote that contemporary opposition to examinations was arising more from the pressure for an uncompetitive egalitarian society than from any technical inefficiencies in the examinations themselves. 'If one believes that all men are in all ways equal, then clearly examinations have no point', but for the vast majority of people an egalitarian society was as far removed 'from their desire as it is from reality'.

Teacher-training of itself is never likely to prove of great interest to the public. In any case the training institutions could have little impact on the battles between the political grouping which stood for greater equality, comprehensive schools, less divisiveness, and an end to what came to be called 'elitism' and the other political grouping which opposed the political concepts behind these aims by emphasising the need to maintain standards, to see that the manpower requirements of the economy were fully met, that the ablest were given every opportunity to prepare for the most responsible posts in society. The increasing influence of the latter grouping became evident well before the general election of 1979 but it was after that event that the fruits of ideas associated with it began to become prominent. While the Assessment of Performance Unit was established in 1976 and the Schools Council for the Curriculum and Examinations encountered growing difficulties in the late 1970s, the final abolition of the Council and the transfer of its functions directly to the DES, operating in future only through committees consisting of ministerial nominees, took place in the early 1980s. The new mechanism was intended to enable increasing emphasis to be laid upon standards, these to be enforced through the widespread use of public examinations and testing.

In teacher-training the earliest expression in official policy of the reaction against the direction of post-war developments was the establishment of a small committee with Lord James as chairman to inquire into arrangements for the education, training, and probation of teachers. The committee was the direct outcome of an undertaking given in the course of the general election of 1970 by the Conservatives to set up such an inquiry if they were victorious. Thus Mrs Thatcher appointed this small committee of only seven members under a chairman noted for his critical attitude to much in teacher education. The proposals in their report would have changed drastically the whole pattern by separating personal education from training. The first cycle was to consist of two or three years of academic study for a diploma in higher education or a degree. The second cycle comprised a year of training for teaching in a department or a college followed by a year of induction in a school: this last was to replace the existing probationary year. There was also to be a third cycle consisting of a fully organized system of in-service training with each teacher spending one term in every seven years on this activity. Although there were those inside the Department of Education and Science who favoured the general direction of the Report, it met with strong opposition from the education service generally and from the teacher training sector in particular. In some ways the possible impact of the James Report was overtaken by the fall in the birth-rate after 1964, the decline in the number of pupils likely to enter the schools in due course, and the consequent drop in the demand for newly trained teachers.

The greatly increased number of places in the colleges of education appeared to provide at least part of the answer to the problem of finding additional public sector places in higher education generally and the policy adopted by the DES was to end teacher education as a distinct sector, merging it into further and higher education. In this way college buildings could be used to help in meeting the demand for more places in advanced further education and the call for additional capital expenditure could be greatly reduced. This reduction in numbers played its part in facilitating the construction of a much more centralized system of control over standards and setting up a form of governmental accreditation machinery since it reduced the number of courses and institutions with which the controllers would have to deal.

The changed attitude by officials of the DES and by members of the Inspectorate from the later 1970s to the education system which they had themselves done so much to foster and build up has been commented on before. The draft of the so-called Yellow Book which was prepared during the Callaghan government's period of office asserted the need for the DES to give a firmer lead, that there need be no inhibition that it would not be able to make good use of enhanced opportunity to exercise influence over teaching methods and that the Inspectorate would have a leading role to play here and stood ready 'to fulfil that responsibility'.[3] It was therefore not surprising that less than two years later inspectors found that children in the primary schools were being held back because their teachers did not know enough about their subject, their training having been inadequate.

It was against this developing background that the election of 1979 led to a change of government while the appointment of Sir Keith Joseph, as he then was, to the office of Secretary of State for Education and Science in 1981 hastened the reaction against the post-1945 developments. Increased emphasis came to be laid on obtaining value for the expenditure of public money and this seemed to be measured by how much of particular subjects or skills were taught in the schools while less emphasis came to be placed on the wider pastoral and cultural aspects of education. Teacher-training courses needed to prepare their students to be well informed as instructors rather than to be practitioners of informal and free expression methods.

By way of preparation for the new policies a survey of teachers in their first year of teaching by HM Inspectors of

Schools was issued which commented that it was disturbing to find that in nearly a quarter of the primary school lessons seen teachers showed signs of insecurity in the subject being taught.[4] The insecurity in some cases led to the choice of undemanding or unsuitable materials, unrealistic tasks for pupils in which the teachers could offer little help, and failure to recognize opportunities to extend or deepen children's understanding and skills. On the other hand, among new secondary-school teachers only one in ten apparently 'revealed insecurity in the subject they were teaching' and thus led to teaching approaches which maintained an often slavish adherence to the textbook, reliance on narrow questions often requiring monosyllabic answers, an inability to follow up and extend pupils' answers and an over-prescription method whereby the teacher was able to remain within a constricted pattern of work. In fact, from the small proportion of new teachers having some difficulties, it was clear that the great majority of beginners were suitably trained and were being employed in teaching age groupings and subjects for which they were suitably qualified.

The government accepted that in primary schools teachers would continue to be essentially class teachers but hoped that they would also have training which would enable them to act as the member of the staff who could be a school's expert or consultant able to advise colleagues in one subject area. In the secondary schools an inquiry in 1979 had found that difficulties arose over an insufficient match between teachers' qualifications and the subject they were teaching. This problem was especially marked in physics, English, mathematics, religious education, and metalwork. It was now stated as the opinion of the government that newly appointed teachers taking pupils to GCE Advanced level should have a single or joint honours degree in the relevant subject while those not teaching further than the 16+ examinations should include the subject taught as one of two or three in a BA or BSc degree or as the main subject in a BEd.

It was against this background that inspectors prepared a paper for the Advisory Committee on the Supply and Education of Teachers (ACSET) on the content of initial training courses and in a revised form this was later published.[5] In March 1983 the government proposed further steps to strengthen initial teacher training to try to promote the recruitment to it of academically well-qualified people and to improve the match between training and qualifications and the teaching programmes of individual teachers in the schools. This latter must always be the most difficult to achieve in the context of the very diffuse system of administration of the schools in this country. The criteria which the Secretary of State intended to impose would contain three main requirements. The first was that the higher education and initial training of all qualified teachers should include at least two full years of course time devoted to subject studies at a level appropriate to higher education. The second was that the initial training of all qualified teachers should include adequate attention to teaching method work in the main subjects and that this should also be differentiated by age of intended pupils. All primary courses would need to include a substantial element concerned with language and mathematics development. Finally the initial training of all qualified teachers would have to include studies closely linked with practical experience in school and involving the participation of practising school teachers. Apart from these criteria, the DES also stated that if the final requirement were to be satisfied adequately, the staff of training institutions who were concerned with pedagogy would need to have regular contact with classroom teaching. The selection of students for training also needed to be improved and while there was no indication of how this might be achieved, apart from taking greater care, it was suggested that the participation of suitable practising teachers in the process was desirable.

ACSET was to undertake further work on these points. It was through that body that the criteria were elaborated in 1983 and the machinery for their enforcement was made known. The relationship of any criteria which the DES might demand to the requirements for either a degree which incorporated a teaching qualification or a postgraduate certificate in education was not easy to define. The circular setting out the new arrangements for the approval of courses did indeed say that the two functions were clearly interrelated and could not be carried out in isolation from each other. The area training organizations which were abolished in 1975 had brought the professional and academic aspects of training together. After their disbandment, the Secretary of State received recommendations for the conferment of qualified teacher status directly from institutions and bodies awarding qualifying degrees or certificates were enjoined to establish a committee or delegacy on which members of the teaching profession and their employers were represented to advise on the professional aspects of such courses 'including their duration, standard and academic supervision and the adequacy of the arrangements of the institutions providing them for recommending suitability for the teaching profession.'[6] In 1977 the DES stated that the Secretary of State would rely on the recommendation of professional committees or delegacies in approving new courses.

The ineffectiveness of the local professional committees and even somewhat shadowy nature of their very existence in some places was one of the arguments advanced in support of the case for a central committee to oversee the application of professional criteria. A single body would ensure the achievement of consistency in the assessment of courses. The Council for the Accreditation of Teacher Education was therefore established 'to advise the Secretaries of State for Education and Science and for Wales on the approval of initial teacher training courses in England and Wales'. In the first instance the Council was to undertake a review of all existing approved courses of initial teacher training, and to scrutinize any proposals for new courses for which an allocation of student places had been made. It was stated that the first review would be completed in three to four years after which the future of the Council would be reconsidered, although it was also intended that training courses should be reassessed at regular intervals.

The members of the Council were to be appointed by the Secretary of State 'on a personal basis' and in fact the membership of the Council has been such as to prevent it from appearing or operating as peer review bodies do in other professions such as engineering or medicine. Only a small minority were drawn from among those employed in teacher-training; others to be included were a number of members and officials of local authorities, three from schools, and individuals employed by organizations such as Hewlett Packard, Sainsbury, and the Financial Times. The Council could consider a course for approval only if it had the support of a local committee on which the training institution, the local education authorities in the area, local school teachers, and individuals from outside the education service were all represented. These local committees were to meet regularly, were to discuss all aspects of initial teacher training, and were to play a particularly important role in promoting links between training institutions, schools, and the community. They were not, however, to act in any way as subcommittees of the Council. According to the Circular announcing its creation, when formulating its advice to the Secretary of State the Council was to draw on all relevant information, 'including submissions made by individual institutions, <u>evidence based on any visits made by</u> <u>members of the Council or any working parties it might</u> <u>establish for the purpose, and in all cases the findings of</u> <u>HMI visits.'[7]</u> It is, perhaps, worth noting at this point the emphasis which the circular put here on evidence drawn from sources other than the institutions for it serves to illustrate the lack of trust, indeed suspicion, in which bodies concerned with training teachers were held by the Secretary of State. The responsible deputy secretary was no doubt correctly interpreting the governmental will in the minatory tone imparted to the circular here and elsewhere by the use of underlining and sidelining.

The Council was to advise the Secretary of State on whether a course conformed to the criteria set out in the annex to the circular. But here too the attitude of distrust towards institutions was again emphasized for one of the criteria was then brought into the body of the circular and both underlined and sidelined:

> <u>The Secretaries of State consider that PGCE courses of</u> <u>less than 36 weeks will be incapable of meeting the</u> <u>criteria. Institutions offering such courses will be</u> <u>expected to extend them to a minimum of 36 weeks as</u> <u>soon as is practicable.</u>

No doubt one day when they are open to public access the minutes behind the minimum length of the PGCE course will provide interesting reading. For some time many staff in training institutions had argued that one year was too short a time in which to provide adequate training for graduates intending to teach. Additional costs and the need for more staff and resources had so far made the proposal unacceptable.

But the response of the then Secretary of State was apparently to think that if the courses, which often appeared to last only for the usual thirty weeks of the university undergraduate year, were extended to forty-four weeks, that would go some way to meet the point. Forty-four weeks was seen as a reasonable working year after making allowance for public holidays and annual leave on the scale normal in society generally. The figure of thirty-six weeks eventually emerged after a certain amount of internal discussion and persuasion in the DES.

Although the new arrangements were intended to prepare teachers to teach pupils within specified age ranges and, with secondary courses, one or two specific subjects, the exigencies of staffing made it impossible to insist upon any limitation on the age range and subject actually taught by teachers in the schools. The formal letters of recognition as qualified teachers sent to newly trained teachers by the DES were to draw attention to the phase and subjects for which the course they had taken had been approved. It was claimed in the circular that this 'should act as a guide to employers and schools' in improving the match between the formal qualifications of teachers and the teaching expected of them in the schools. It is difficult to see any practical difference between this and the situation which existed prior to the new policy where the training institutions already made these points clear to future employers of their students on appointment. The only way of ensuring that those teachers not fully trained in a particular subject or age phase are not involved in teaching it is to staff the schools sufficiently generously to avoid teachers who are needed for teaching the subject for which they are qualified for three-quarters of their timetable having then to help out with something else for the other quarter. In any case the Secretary of State made it clear that there would be no additional financial support to carry out the policies set out in the circular. The final paragraph stated specifically that any 'small additional expenditure' in future years was to be met from 'within the provision of those years, including the cost of employing teachers'. It was said to be for local authorities to decide where any necessary savings should be made.

The actual criteria against which the new Council for the Accreditation of Teacher Education was to judge all courses were set out in an annex to Circular 3/84 and it might be noted in passing that of its seventeen paragraphs, the only one sidelined and underlined was that concerned with the supposed shortcomings of staff concerned with teaching pedagogy. In an effort to clarify the requirements which teacher-training courses would have to meet, the Council produced four Notes. The first of these set out the approach the Council intended to follow, but before doing so, it explained the various official controls to which teacher-training courses have now been made subject and their relationship to each other.

Each course now required three different forms or levels of approval. The first of these was administrative course approval which, in the case of a public sector institution, meant the approval of the Secretary of State under the Education (Schools and FE) Regulations by which he or she has power to specify the numbers and categories of students by age phase and subject to be admitted to a course. In universities this control was exercised by the UGC in distributing the total number of places allocated to the university sector by the Secretary of State. The second approval was that given by a university or the CNAA whose award was given to individual students on the successful completion of the course. The Council's Note referred to this somewhat misleadingly as 'academic' approval, but success in professional elements and quite obviously in practical teaching had for many years been required before awards which involve certifying ability to teach were made to students taking courses.

The third and additional layer was Schedule 5 approval or approval of a course by the Secretary of State under Schedule 5 of the Education (Teachers) Regulations 1982 as suitable for the professional preparation of teachers and therefore for the award of qualified teacher status to those completing it successfully. The Note set out the actual procedure that the Council intended to follow in exploring whether the criteria had been properly adhered to. This included a questionnaire on the details concerning a course, a possible meeting between a group of members and persons from the institution, and a possible visit to an institution to help in judging the extent to which certain aspects of a course might meet the DES criteria. It was also made clear that any revision of an approved course, apart from revisions of detail, would require renewed application, consideration and so forth, leading to the need for further Schedule 5 approval by the Secretary of State before any changes could be put into effect. So far the Council's members have rarely visited institutions on whose courses they have pronounced, but the Council is always required to take into account the findings of the inspectors who will have visited an institution before its courses can be considered. The actual arrangements set out in Note 1 made clear the very limited extent of the discretion available to the Council. The criteria which it was to apply were given to it by the Department of Education and Science and it had no power to modify them while it was also required to take into account the findings of the inspectors in each case it considered.

The three other Notes which the Council issued dealt with the way in which it saw some of the other criteria which it was to enforce. The second Note dealt with local committees and while it said a good deal about their membership and structure, it had little to say on their functions. In essence, the committees had to be created because accreditation could not be gained for courses without them, but their terms of reference were for local determination although they were to meet at least three times each year. Their specific function was to undertake regular reviews of the initial teacher-training courses provided by an institution but they were also to facilitate the development and strengthening of links between the institution, schools, and the community generally. One committee could serve more than one institution.

The third Note discussed the issue of subject studies and set out the Council's understanding of what the criteria required. The subject studies should not be pursued in ways narrowly related to their application in the classroom and it was considered that there was a risk of this if the whole of a BEd course was the responsibility of staff whose main concern was the pedagogy. The specialist subject studies of all intending teachers, both primary and secondary, were an essential element of their undergraduate education and were to be at an intellectually demanding level. The equivalent of one-half of a four-year or two-thirds of a three-year undergraduate course was to be devoted to 'subject studies'. So far as intending secondary teachers were concerned, the subject studies might consist of one or two specialist subjects, or one main and one subsidiary specialist subject or a main specialist subject and a related area of the curriculum. The methodology of teaching the subjects was not to count as 'subject studies'. For primary courses, students could take one or two specialist subjects or a wider area of the curriculum. In addition, and outside the 'subject studies' category, students were to spend at least 100 hours in the study, observation, and practice of mathematics teaching, 100 hours on language teaching, and a suitable amount of time on the study, observation, and teaching of other subjects in the school curriculum. Postgraduate courses were to include all the elements shown here as falling outside of subject studies. Moreover the initial degrees taken by postgraduate students were required to be related to the work of primary or secondary schools while their professional preparation was to be focused on the teaching of not more than two subjects in which they had already gained specialist knowledge.

The fourth and at the time of writing final Note was concerned with links between teacher-training institutions and schools. For some years close links with schools had been developed by many training institutions, but these links did not serve to defend those working in such institutions from the accusation of being removed from the realities of the classroom and it was this sentiment from the environment of the Black Paper which lay behind the emphasis placed in Circular 3/84 on the absolute requirement on staff 'to demonstrate their teaching effectiveness in schools' and to maintain 'regular and frequent experience of classroom teaching'. In the eyes of some people it was the absence of this which above all else accounted for the various weaknesses they perceived in the system of teacher education. Undoubtedly there were strong feelings over this particular issue and the Council attempted to take a positive attitude in its Note. In effect all criteria must by definition be prescriptive but in the opening paragraph it was at least said that the contents were 'not intended to be prescriptive'. There were many different ways in which mutually beneficial links could be established between institutions and schools and their development was properly a matter for local determination. The management and assessment of students' teaching practice and school experience, the involvement of school teachers in the selection and training of students, and the provision of opportunities for staff of institutions to teach in schools were all areas in which links might be encouraged.

The many varieties of contact which are involved in students' school experience are perhaps those which arise most naturally in the regular course of business and the Note pointed to various ways in which these could be taken further. Experienced teachers have been able to offer a very welcome additional strength in training institutions for many years. One specific requirement arising from the criteria which was met in some places but not universally was that practising school teachers should be involved in some way in the selection of students, although not necessarily through participating in interviewing applicants. Numerous other ways in which school teachers might be involved were set out. On teaching by lecturers in schools, the Council claimed that of the various possibilities, secondment to classroom teaching was particularly valuable. It went on to add that classroom experience could be 'usefully renewed' through participation in IT/INSET and similar schemes, through consultancy work in schools and through action research, provided that these involved experience of actual teaching. In view of the emphasis which the Council has placed on renewing experience by secondment rather than on a continuous experience on a regular basis, staff experience renewal plans have become essential since clearly it is not practicable for more than a limited number of the staff of an institution to be released on secondment at any one time. Thus rolling plans which could only be implemented over a cycle of some years became necessary. The Note rightly emphasized the need for a collaborative and co-operative effort on the part of schools and school teachers if institutions were to achieve what was required of them by these criteria. While criteria covering such matters as length or content of a course are matters on which it is within the power of institutions to conform, clearly they can meet the criteria set out in the fourth Note only if they have the co-operation and assistance of willing schools and school teachers. The dispersed nature of the administrative system has meant that some local authorities, with no additional resources to meet additional costs, have been unwilling or unable to make official provision. The fulfilment of those criteria has therefore been heavily dependent on the goodwill of individual head and assistant teachers.

The emphasis which Circular 3/84 placed upon the role of the inspectorate in operating the accreditation process was very marked. While the Council could not modify the criteria, only enforce them, members of the inspectorate had been closely involved in their formulation and in steering them through ACSET. The Council was not permitted to consider accreditation of a course until it had a full report on the training institution from the inspectorate. Since members of the Council have not themselves normally undertaken visitations of the institutions, they have been more likely to attach additional weight to the opinions of those who have done so, the inspectors. Finally, as the circular pointed out, when the

Council is at work 'HMI knowledge of teacher training institutions will be available to the Council through its HMI assessors' who, as one member put it in the early days, 'nanny us'. The whole accreditation process could, presumably, have been operated directly by the DES through the agency of its inspectorate. The argument against doing so must have rested heavily upon the need to achieve some positive response from the institutions - which meant in effect from their staffs - and experience showed that this was much more likely to be achieved with a Council than without one. A Council mechanism was also likely to facilitate the introduction of a Schedule 5 accreditation for those courses based in universities. It was argued that universities had long accepted review groups and judgements on their courses in medicine, dentistry, and some other subjects. Although the proposed body would not be strictly comparable since it would not be a professional body but a body of ministerial appointees, yet there would be enough similarity to help overcome problems of acceptance.

Teacher-training courses in universities had not been inspected for very many years and the extension of inspection to university departments or schools of education raised issues which had to be cleared with the universities themselves. Because of their independent, chartered existence, inspectors could undertake inspections of university departments only by invitation. The rules required that the Council for the Accreditation of Teacher Education (CATE) could consider a course only when it had the report of an inspection. In the phraseology of the CVCP letter to vice-chancellors in the autumn of 1984, 'universities which have not yet issued invitations to the Inspectorate may now wish to consider doing so'.[8] Since the inspections have been carried out by invitation, it has followed that every university has had discretion over whether to publish the subsequent report, although this has, of course, gone to the CATE and the University Grants Committee (UGC) as well as to the Secretary of State. Institutions are free to send their own comments on any matters referred to in a report and the Universities Council for the Education of Teachers advised all heads of university departments of education to send their responses direct to the Secretary of State, to the CATE (twenty copies) and to the UGC (twenty copies) so that when the inspectors' views were read by members of the CATE (or by the UGC education subcommittee) the institution's views would also be available.

15

It is much too soon to attempt any appraisal of the effect of Schedule 5 accreditation in achieving the aim of improving the quality of teaching in schools or even on the quality of work in the training institutions. At the close of 1987 the Council was perhaps half-way through the total number of courses with which it had to deal. The initial three-year period of appointment has had to be extended to five years. The most radical and far-reaching of the changes which the criteria have required has been the increased emphasis on subject studies in undergraduate teacher-training courses. The requirement for the equivalent of two years of study in this area at the normal higher education level has caused a widespread revision of courses and has also provoked a good deal of dispute.

There has been strong opposition from lecturers who believe that far more emphasis should have been placed on developmental studies, on the study of the child and on the issues involved in actually teaching children of primary school age. The value to the good generalist class teacher of young children of two years of subject study has seemed very limited and this requirement has been viewed as putting primary BEds back twenty years. This issue was taken up by the Undergraduate Primary Teacher Education Conference and in a report in 1986 a Select Committee of the Commons was so disturbed by this that it wrote of a serious and potentially damaging breakdown in understanding between the Secretary of State, the inspectorate, and the CATE on the one side and the training institutions on the other. The Select Committee proposed that the CATE should be abolished and that the Council for National Academic Awards (CNAA) and universities should handle the approval of courses. The CATE can enforce and interpret the criteria, but it cannot change them and in that sense universities and the CNAA have a much wider remit for they are not obliged to accept criteria handed down by the DES. It was not surprising that the Select Committee's proposals were not accepted.

The question has arisen of the extent to which smaller monotechnic institutions have the resources to offer all that is sought by way of subject studies. This is being overcome by arranging for students in these institutions to attend associated universities or polytechnics for a year of their course concentrating them on subject studies. Other institutions have been able to meet the requirements by internal reorganization.

To a large extent the whole of this exercise in teacher-training is part of the wider reaction against the direction in which ministers and officials of the DES and the inspectorate led the education system of this country for a quarter of a century following the Butler Act. At the end of its first Note, the CATE having sought to explain and define the various forms of approval control which now exist, stated that:

> The improvement of teacher education, to which the Council and the staff and authorities of institutions are together committed, can only be assured by cooperation among those concerned with all stages and aspects of the professional preparation and development of teachers. The Council wishes to ensure that its procedures and practices are consistent with that commitment.

It may well be that in retrospect the whole machinery of accreditation and closer control will be seen as a way in which the considerable hostility of some politicians was adapted to positive rather than negative purposes by the advice and persuasion of officials and the inspectorate. In other words the exercise has been a way of averting more serious damage.

Apart from the usefulness and value of the present criteria in improving - or, as some claim, harming - the future quality of education in the maintained schools, the more lasting and potentially damaging consequences may lie in the degree of government control established. The actual layers of approval now needed - for numbers, subject, phase, from the Secretary of State, the UGC, or NAB, then the normal process of validation, then the additional layer of Schedule 5 accreditation - will have an inhibiting and ossifying effect on teacher education. The sheer bureaucratic tedium of seeking so much approval will surely deter many institutions from ever attempting any significant modification or reform of their courses. In this sense it will lead to stasis rather than adaptability and development.

NOTES AND REFERENCES

1   S.H. Wood, 'The recruitment and training of teachers', PRO, ED 46/155, January 1941, para 21(e).
2   Rhodes Boyson, 'In defence of examinations: the

unanswered case', in Black Paper Three, C.B. Cox and A.E. Dyson (eds), London, n.d., 1970, p.100.

3   'Edited extracts from the Yellow Book, the DES memorandum to the Prime Minister', Times Educational Supplement, 15 October 1976.

4   HMI, The New Teacher in School, HMI Series: Matters for Discussion 15, London, HMSO, 1982.

5   DES, Teaching in Schools: The Content of Initial Training, HMI Discussion paper, London, DES, 1983.

6   DES, The Further Education Regulations 1975, Circular 5/75, London, DES, 1975.

7   DES, Initial Teacher Training: Approval of Courses, Circular 3/84, London, HMSO, 1984.

8   CVCP, Secretary General to Vice-Chancellors, 31 October 1984.

2

REFLECTIONS ON A CHANGING CONCEPT
OF TEACHER EDUCATION

V. Alan McClelland

Definitions of schools and schooling are legion but one that seems to bear a fundamental significance today as we contemplate the effects upon children and teachers of the Education Reform Act is that issued in Rome in 1977 by the Sacred Congregation for Catholic Education in the wake of the Second Vatican Council. A school is declared to be 'a place of integral formation by means of a systematic and critical assimilation of culture'. It is designated as a privileged institution 'in which, through a living encounter with a cultural inheritance, integral formation occurs'.[1] The key phrase in both parts of the definition is 'integral formation' or what, in another context, I have referred to as a commitment to 'oneness and totality' that leads to 'self-integration' in the process of human formation and development.[2] Others have described it differently: Rosemary Haughton as the creating of a sense of harmony between a child and his environment, 'both human and non-human';[3] Philip May as the quest for 'maturity'.[4]

Roy Stevens in Education and the Death of Love has identified ways in which schools have been tempted by various blandishments to over-emphasize and over-value the training of intellect at the expense of a concern for humane wholeness.[5] Writing shortly after Stevens in 1981, Professor Brian Cox, however, rejected such an analysis which he regarded as subversive.[6] To him the malaise in education in the late 1970s was to be accounted for by a 'move away from a capitalist bourgeois ethos based on achievement and discipline and excellence' to an 'egalitarian system of values' in schools. Cox scorned 'the dream of an open society in which people will work generously without the motivation of reward', dubbing it 'destructive and utopian'. Hooliganism and violence among the young were the progeny of such thinking, he contended, whereas competitive examinations, testing, and the work-ethic upon which they were supposedly based seemed to be the only forces capable of holding in check what he described as 'the worst excesses of the new consciousness, the new hegemony'.

With the gift of hindsight we now know that the Thatcherite democracy of the 1980s has endorsed Cox's analysis and rejected the Stevens panacea. Cox's views, regarded as eccentric when first propounded even in Conservative Party circles, became stridently propagated with the formation of the right-wing Hillgate Group, a pressure caucus of singular influence within the higher echelons of the Conservative Party and a body pledged to root out the remaining vestiges of what it sees as 'egalitarianism' within the school system.[7] Part of its task has been achieved, of course, by the Education Reform Act, 1988, with its prescription for a national curriculum based upon the philosophy that work, achievement, productivity, and monetary reward are the cornerstones of democratic education in a free society, with its disarming provisions governing parental choice and open enrolment which will inevitably be operated solely upon the basis of a sharp competitiveness grounded on published examination results and, perhaps more significantly, in its provisions for schools to be facilitated to 'opt out' of local education authority control regardless of the effect such a decision could have upon the network of overall school provision in a particular locality. The appeal to self-interest and materialism that this packet of measures represents is an unmistakeable delineation of the Coxian blueprint of seven years ago. There remains one further task to be tackled, the 'problem' of teacher education, the Hillgate Group being vociferously suspicious that teacher educators remain a force likely to endorse an 'egalitarian ideal' for education or at least a body which will give wide currency to old liberal shibboleths. Recently it has found an unexpected ally in the philosopher Mary Warnock, who has spent much of her energy in attacking existing arrangements for teacher education.[8] The process of the reorientation of teacher-training courses, commenced some four years ago, has now been carried a stage further in 1988 by a proposal to admit a traunch of untrained teachers in shortage subject areas directly into the schools to learn 'the craft' of teaching while, for the most part, 'sitting by Nellie'.

If one examines DES Circular 3/84 (Circular 21/84 of

the Welsh Office), which laid down the criteria to be applied in the process of considering initial teacher-training courses for approval by the Council for the Accreditation of Teacher Education (CATE) established by the government for the purpose in 1984, a Coxian scenario is easily recognizable. Criteria are laid down for the on-going involvement and support of local committees, for the establishing of improved links between training institutions and schools, for the professional updating of the staff employed in pedagogical work, and for the better organization of periods of school experience and teaching practice for students. All these are important matters and are to be welcomed for the greater effectiveness of existing teacher-training programmes, as are prescriptions relating to the apportionment of time to be allocated between subject studies and subject methods and those concerning the nature of studies seen to be germane to the task of teaching in the contemporary situation. Also to be welcomed are regulations governing better selection and admission procedures. But there is a fundamental flaw - and it cannot be fortuitous! Apart from a vague and nebulous reference to the fact that 'students should be made aware of the wide range of relationships - with parents and others - which teachers can expect to develop in a diverse society, and of the role of the school within a community'[9] there is no presentation of a clearly worked out philosophy of teacher formation and there is no concern with matters which cannot be designated as 'the nuts and bolts' of the training exercise. It is as though the formation of teachers can be viewed as simply a mechanical process divorced from reference to an overall conception of the meaning and purpose of the life-long process in which they will be involved and which should act as the touchstone of their professional life.

A similar myopia is evident in the digest of the criteria published by the CATE in June 1985, although in the Council's excuse it can be argued that in producing such a list it was not empowered to go beyond the criteria as laid down in Circular 3/84, itself based upon the limited nature of recommendation 119(b) of the White Paper Teaching Quality of March 1983.[10] Acknowledging this fact, however, there is no concern in the documentation with the matter of the formation of a teacher in his totality, no consideration of concepts of wholeness, integration, or community awareness, no attempt to view the educative process in connection with which the teacher is being prepared on a continuum of formative influences made up of family, church (where applicable), school, and other socializing agencies. The process of continuity in education, reaching into adulthood and not ending with physical maturity, is ignored for the doubtful benefit of an increased emphasis upon skill acquisition and methodological processes. Important as these aspects of teacher-training may be, they lack context and represent a vision of schooling amenable to the overweening concern in government policy with skill-acquisition, competitiveness, testing, examinations, and meeting the needs of the economy: what Professor Brian Cox and his associates would term 'the giving of value for money'. It constitutes a soulless prescription, concerned with processes rather than purposes, with quantity rather than quality, with earning a living rather than making a life, with ephemera rather than with the cultivation of attitudes and values that will act as permanent guides throughout one's working life. Furthermore, its productivity aspects are likely to be a chimera. John Passmore has stated the issue succinctly when he writes:

> there is no question of anyone ever 'mastering' teaching, discovering a 'secret' which will rule out the possibility of his ever failing to teach a child successfully. There is no such thing as having nothing further to learn about teaching, or of the teacher reaching a point at which he has rules for dealing with every situation which can possibly arise. So it is no objection to a course of training that at the end of it a potential teacher has not completely mastered the art of teaching, any more than it is an objection to a tennis-coaching course that at the end of it the pupils have not mastered tennis.[11]

Rather, teaching is an open capacity exercise and its effectiveness will ultimately rest, not solely upon the methodological skills a teacher has acquired, but upon his or her personal formation as a thinking, reflective, and compassionate professional. Thus the criteria of 1984 (a significant date!) have nothing of permanence to contribute to the true process of teacher formation.

It cannot be maintained that HMI visits to training institutions in connection with the CATE accreditation process redressed the balance. Rarely was comment made upon the overall philosophy or thrust of a course. Such visits were also constrained in fact, if not in theory, by the nature of the criteria to be applied by the Council and by the need to observe whether or not training institutions were measuring up to them. HMI had little to say as to how a course was designed to prepare teachers for dealing with the wider non-vocational, 'non-academic' concerns of pupils, or with how to build up a rapport with parents, or with how to deal with the great inevitables of every child's future, adolescence, marriage, employment and unemployment, leisure, health, and death. Such matters were too often seen as peripheral to the training process and were thought to be better left to the attention of religious and moral education specialists or, worse, to 'pastoral care' experts. And yet young teachers entering the education service today are not worth employing unless they show in practice that their course of formation has trained them to cope with such matters of major concern to children and to families. They must be able to talk with parents and communicate effectively with them and they must be aware of the range of community support systems and their relevance for teachers' work. Evidence should be sought of these qualities while students are on teaching practice and the decision as to their suitability for the profession should be influenced by this wider view of a teacher's future responsibilities, as well as by their willingness to build up relationships with children in out-of-school activities.

Halsey's research indicated that major determinants of the quality of learning achieved by children in school lay in the nature of the support they received outside of the classroom, in the family, in the church, in the wider social communities of which they were members and in the propensity of such groups to resolve worries and fears which were assuming an exaggerated importance in their lives. The quality of classroom learning is profoundly affected by the nature of the caring relationship teachers are able to forge with all their pupils and their families and by the contribution they are able to make in ensuring that their school - and their classroom in particular - bears the marks of a supportive community. The ability to do this well does not come naturally to many teachers, as the forging of relationships do not feature strongly in some other people's lives, yet, for a teacher, it is as important as the capacity to teach well an academic discipline or age cohort and careful induction is needed to facilitate the process.

Opportunities to assess student progress in schools in this regard should be part and parcel of the teacher formation programme. There is, however, some justice in the criticism by teacher-trainers that the CATE, by rigidly adhering to its formulae, has frustrated professional innovation in this regard and has introduced an unacceptable compartmentalization of knowledge, skills, and professional requirements into the teacher-training system which allows little room for the concept of 'wholeness' in the formation of a teacher. In the long term, if the criteria remain unchallenged and unchanged, they will prove detrimental to the producing of a fully rounded, competent, socially and spiritually aware professional who recognizes the interdependence of children, families, friends, and teachers in the educative process and, more importantly, who is prepared to exercise his or her trust in that light. As C.H. Spurgeon once observed: 'Not all change is progress as the pigeon said when it got out of the net into the pie'.

The two key concepts that should constantly be before any teacher-educator are those of 'wholeness' and 'community'. Let us consider the second of these because its successful organization in a school quite often subsumes the first and because there is little doubt that even a young child finds it relatively easy to understand the idea of being a member of a community. Student teachers find it less simple to understand the importance of the concept of community because their adult-educational system has already conditioned them to protect fiercely their individuality and to seek self-interest on the single-minded road to academic achievement. As potential teachers they have now to rethink that philosophy in the interests of their professional success in the classroom. To the Christian, of course, the concept bears few traumas, for as Rosemary Haughton puts it, 'we are redeemed not as individuals but as members of a community and it is as members of a community, related essentially to our fellow men, that we must work out our salvation'.[12]

From the earliest years children are conscious of the interconnection between their needs and desires on the one hand and those responses of the adults who meet and satisfy them in a spirit of love and devotion. Gradually they learn that there are other communities outside of the family of which they are an intimate part, and of a different nature from the community formed by their friends or more distant relatives. There is the street in which they live and its inhabitants, for instance, there is the playgroup they attend, there is the church community of which they are members if their parents give them the opportunity to participate in it. In such contacts the child has grown accustomed to realizing that each community is different, has its own customs and needs, its own duties and dependencies, its own sense of what is proper and acceptable behaviour and what is not. Furthermore, this sense of community is acquired to some considerable extent before children enter upon formal schooling. Even if they have already experienced the effects of, say, marital breakdown or of being a child in a one-parent family, the sense of community is not entirely absent, although it may be impaired. On entering school, therefore, children are ready to experience a further extension of their understanding of community but this time, by encountering one that operates consciously within an interactive teaching and learning environment and in which their associates and companions will soon be striving to attain common community goals while enjoying similar experiences and stimuli. Indeed Plato considered such a community-drive, which brings the whole environmental forces to work upon a child, as the greatest of educational forces.

As we have acknowledged, the teacher's sense of community does not come as naturally or as easily as that of the child and yet it rests upon the teacher to create the atmosphere and conditions within which it can flourish. In the task teachers may sometimes have to work alone but, in doing so, their greatest asset is the knowledge that they have a considerable human resource at their disposal which is instinctively aware of how a community operates. Community formation is not an end in itself, of course, but it is the most significant factor in developing the sharing, loving, and openness to truth that constitute the most valuable asset in the forming of persons. By nurturing the sense of community, by fostering a school atmosphere in which that sense can flourish, deepen, and grow, teachers can convey the most important knowledge of all, that they value children - their children in a very real sense - for what they are, warts and all, and not simply because they are potential adults capable of being developed. By responding to children as they are, teachers ensure their classroom, and also in time their school, is a happy community within which the unfolding of values for living are of as prime importance to the teachers as the legitimate aims of learning and scholarship which the children are daily pursuing. Provided the school community is a loving, caring, valuing family, united in the happy pursuit of a common endeavour, and that the teachers are themselves an integral part of that community (and not seen somehow as being outside of it, or manipulating it, or seeking special privileges within it), the problems experienced by some children in coming to terms with new skills and unaccustomed modes of thinking and acting will not result in loss of confidence in the power to achieve, nor in feelings of inferiority where achievement is less than anticipated. Brian Cox may detect the stench of 'egalitarianism' in such a classroom polity but a school which tries not to exacerbate differences but encourages community co-operation among its pupils, in cultivating a sense of shared purpose and energy, is creating a stimulus to achievement that periodic bouts of testing can by no means provide. In such a way the school transmits a feeling for what John Westerhoff has identified as the interdependent and interactive processes of the acquisition of knowledge and attitudes, the growth of values and appropriate behaviour patterns, and the openness to the sensibilities and concern of others: a recipe, in fact, for complete living.[13] The prime educational force of any school thus becomes one arising naturally out of living in the school environment. By means of exercising community duties and developing community relationships, children begin to understand the nature of their own autonomy, the importance of their own uniqueness, the value of their own independence. More importantly, they learn how to subject their individuality to the needs of the community when it requires it and to do so with a conscious realization of the ensuing benefit and good of the whole. The ability to be self-confident, the power to take the initiative and the willingness to accept responsibility for one's own actions are the indicators that the school community of which the children are members is providing an appropriately loving and caring 'métier'. E.B. Castle stated it thus:

> When we have a clear vision of other people's rights, when we feel these rights operating on us and willingly recognize their validity, there exist conditions for developing the inner compulsions of self-discipline which flourish when there is socially enforced appreciation of social requirements.[14]

This is the form of 'egalitarianism' a teacher-formation

course would wish its students to possess. Without this commitment to the development of persons teachers will never raise themselves beyond the level of competent instructors to that of professional educators.

In the matter of the development of a spirit of community, of course, teachers who take up their first teaching assignments in denominational schools do perhaps have an added advantage over those who enter the non-denominational sector. And those who work in confessional schools (Roman Catholic, Jewish, Muslim) have a further advantage over those who work in a Church of England school which, as part of its Christian heritage, exists to serve the general needs of the people at large and, as a consequence, is more likely to reflect divergencies of religious commitment. In the document 'Gravissimum educationis' of the Second Vatican Council we are told that 'what makes the Catholic school distinctive is its attempt to generate a community climate in the school that is permeated by the Gospel spirit of freedom and love', a desirable aim that would be acceptable to the schools of other forms of the Christian tradition.[15] The teacher in the secular school system, on the other hand, has to find other ways than the sharing of a common religious faith to show the importance and reasonableness of behaving justly and lovingly with one's fellow creatures, for the forging of true community relationship cannot be achieved without such effort. It is a more difficult task, however, when religion cannot act as the unifying element in the curriculum, as it does in the denominational school, pervading its ethos as freely as the air which circulates therein. John Wolfenden puts it this way:

> It may be enough to say that the cardinal point of the Incarnation to a Christian is that, in that historical event, when the divine and the human were fused in one Person, we were given a demonstration and guarantee that the two orders were in real historical fact, then, now and for ever inseparable.[16]

It is on such a basis that the Christian school is constructed and its peculiar spirit of community presented. It loses its purpose, in fact, 'without constant reference to the Gospel and a frequent encounter with Christ' in His sacraments,[17] for in this way it involves ... believing, and acting on the belief, that the events of our own lives, the events of past history, the discoveries of the scientist, and our relationship with our fellow-men, all have a reference and a meaning beyond the particular moments in space and time where they occur.[18]

A school in which this philosophy is operative has its community and its sense of community already formed; teachers, assuming they are in sympathy with the aims and spirit of the school, need but to immerse themselves in the prevailing atmosphere. Within such a 'métier' learning, enjoying, contributing, and participating all become means leading to the one supreme end of supernatural union with God, a union which cannot be attained unless such processes are accompanied by a right ordering of relationships with one's fellow-humans. For to treat others as ends and never as means is not simply a matter of 'social justice' in a Christian school but 'a recognition of the divinity which resides in man qua man'.[19] This is what is meant by the concept of 'wholeness' because the question 'what am I as a being?' cannot be dissociated from its corollary 'How must I conduct myself in such a way that my actions are in harmony with the purpose for which I exist?'[20] Recently this point has been put most felicitously by Bishop Patrick Kelly of Salford in an address on Catholic schools delivered to priests of his diocese:

we are convinced that our discipleship is not something which is alongside the rest of life; it is the beginning, the context and the goal of all our living. We therefore do not see the various elements which are part of a young person's formation as fragmented and unrelated. ... For us it would be false to the whole truth to say that subjects can be taught in some neutral fashion with formal religious education offered alongside them. For us neutral education is a loss of the wholeness offered to us in our Lord. And therefore our service to the whole educational enterprise is not accomplished by becoming part of a 'series ...' system where the various elements are offered in isolation from an overall vision. Our contribution must be education seen as a wholesome endeavour, related to a community's vision and way of life ... Our service of all schooling is the testimony of schools rooted in a community with a shared vision and whose schooling is therefore integrated and wholesome.[21]

Other Christian denominations and other types of confessional school would endorse the subscription to 'wholeness' and 'integration' as delineated in this statement. Religion is met experientially in every facet of human endeavour and, to the one nurtured in a religious ambience, it has profound implications for the form and nature of community operating in a school. Archbishop Coggan in his address to the Farmington Institute in 1978 emphasized the point when he described education as a process of 'nurturing' which 'requires interaction with people' and engages the emotions and will in a life-long process of understanding and growth.[22] Here 'community' and 'wholeness' blend together in an inextricable way.

The great majority of teachers, of course, are not destined to teach in schools possessing a clear credal commitment and it is all the more necessary, therefore, to alert them to ways in which forms of 'wholeness' and 'integration' can be achieved within schools not committed to any one religious faith. Fundamentally we return to the concept of community and the ability to ensure that the school and the classroom constitute receptive environments within which quality of relationship becomes paramount and where learning can be pursued unhindered by feelings of injustice or hurt, a place where the education of 'the whole person' - not only intellect, but also heart, will, and character - can take place within the context of the common good. How this can best be achieved is a task in which to involve the parents of the children in free and frank collaboration. It is vitally important to assure them that the school seeks dialogue, that it is not interested solely in training their children to pass examinations successfully or in preparing them for suitable careers in business or workshop, important as these functions may be. It is more profoundly concerned with encouraging their children to become responsible members of a community characterized by humane values and honest endeavour. The initiation of such a dialogue has implications too for cross-cultural understanding and a knowledge of the varying concepts of the good life to be found therein. Indeed, such interaction can lead to a clearer affirmation of what Professor Peter Gordon has described as 'the perennial values of civilised society'.[23] Out of such a dialogue with parents there may emerge a school philosophy that possesses clear signs of coherence, one 'that respects all its members equally, that forms a community based partly upon rationality, partly upon the valuing of what is human'.[24] The essence of such wider involvement in the life of the school will not lie so much in the insights the teachers can provide but in what they can share with the parents and with each other. Parental dialogue can become the essential catalytic force that will generate the 'wholeness' and 'integration' that is sought. In this way the school can become a centre in which the community of its immediate members and those of its extended family can recognize an operative educational philosophy, one that is meaningful to them and which provides for a truly caring environment.

The process of consultation and co-operation envisaged here gains added importance in the light of recent HMI references in the context of evaluation and appraisal. In a document issued in 1985 on this subject, the inspectorate declared that:

> greater recognition could also be given to the function of groups external to the school in the process of evaluation. Parents, governors, employers and the wider community have expectations of schools and of individual pupils. These need to be clearly articulated and schools might do more to seek and consider these views.[25]

This suggestion is surely to be welcomed and encouraged as a positive step in the enhancement of the concept of community, provided that it takes cognizance of the overall philosophy of the school as a vibrant and socially active institution and does not copperfasten itself to the curricular, pastoral, and vocational issues outlined earlier in the document.[26]

Professor Hugh Sockett, in an inaugural lecture at the University of East Anglia in 1984, declared that one of the matters giving him cause for concern in relation to the criteria being operated by the Council for the Accreditation of Teacher Education was that they contained 'no cogent, implicit or explicit view of teacher education',[27] and he attacked Circular 3/84 for offering little else than 'a rag-bag of content-objectives culled from contemporary pressures' and criteria which constituted 'a second-rate, second-hand list of banalities'.[28] I would place the emphasis differently. By treating teacher formation as little more than the sum of its parts, Circular 3/84 has propagated the dangerous myth that teacher-education ought to concern itself primarily, if not exclusively, with a training in performance, 'as though student-teachers were superior rats, cats or dogs',[29] as Louis Arnaud Reid would have put it. On the contrary, teacher formation is a very special kind of education in which are subtly blended theory and practice, aims and motivation, intelligence and technique, foresight and personality, for a teacher's work with children is more akin to that of a catalyst than that of an instructor. The process of making persons is an art-form not a mechanical operation and the 'modus operandi' involves 'knowing that and to what end' as well as 'knowing how', as R.S. Peters might have expressed it. Michael Hollings and Etta Gullick have an evocative prayer, which they print in an anthology entitled It's Me, O Lord.[30] In a way it has profound significance, as a 'cri de coeur', for the nature of the task of teacher formation in an age when the concept of the value of persons is being given so little attention:

I went through the power plant today, Lord. It was frightening, so few men about, Lord, just metal and steam and valves and pipes. Are men on the way out? Is it all to be computers and machines? Where are we going, Lord?

NOTES AND REFERENCES

1 A. Flannery, Vatican Council II: More Post-Conciliar Documents, Leominster, Fowler Wright, 1982, p. 612.
2 V.A. McClelland (ed.) Christian Education in a Pluralist Society, London, Routledge, 1988, pp. 20 et seq.
3 Rosemary Haughton in B. Tucker (ed.) Catholic Education in a Secular Society, London, Sheed & Ward, 1968, p. 204.
4 P. May, Which Way to School?, Tring, Herts, Lion Publishing, 1972, p. 25.
5 R. Stevens, Education and the Death of Love, London, Epworth Press, 1978. See my development of this argument printed in P. Gordon (ed.) The Study of Education, Vol. 3: The Changing Scene, London, Woburn Press, 1988, p. 40.
6 C.B. Cox, Education: The Next Decade, London,

Conservative Political Centre, 1981, pp. 5 et seq.

7 For its philosophy, see The Reform of British Education: From Principle to Practice, London, Hillgate Group, 1987.

8 See especially her recent book, M. Warnock, A Common Policy for Education, Oxford University Press, 1988.

9 Similar criticism is encapsulated in a recent report of the standing Conference of Principals and the Polytechnic Council for the Education of Teachers when they reviewed the CATE and Circular 3/84. It speaks of the 'unhelpful and specious separation between the pedagogy of subject studies' and the overall development of professional skills which were 'inseparable' in the teaching process. It drew attention to the 'interrelated character' of the teacher's knowledge, skills, and professional requirements.

10 This recommended that 'the criteria should relate to the initial selection of students, the level and amount of subject content of courses, professional content, and links between training institutions and schools and should reflect the complexities of the educational system'. (Summary of Recommendations, based upon paragraphs 107-13 of Teaching Quality, London, HMSO, 1983, p. 35).

11 J. Passmore, The Philosophy of Teaching, London, Duckworth, 1980, p. 50.

12 Haughton, op. cit., p. 131.

13 J.H. Westerhoff III, Will Our Children Have Faith?, New York, Seabury Press, 1976, p. 17.

14 E.B. Castle, 'Ends and means in education', Hibbert Journal, April 1955, pp. 262-72.

15 Declaration on Christian Education, 28 October 1965.

16 Sir John Wolfenden, The Educated Man Today and Tomorrow, London, SCM Press, 1959, p. 21.

17 Flannery, op. cit., p. 618.

18 Wolfenden, op. cit., p. 22.

19 Ibid., p. 23.

20 McClelland, op. cit., p. 22.

21 P. Kelly, Catholic Schools: A Briefing for Priests, especially those who are Governors of Schools: 9 December 1987.

22 Speech reported in full in The Tablet-Educational Supplement, 5 August 1978, p. 749.

23 Gordon, op. cit., p. 291.

24 D. Plunkett, Deciding Educational Values: End of the

Phoney War?, Occasional Papers, Oxford, Farmington Institute for Christian Studies, no. 25, 1988, p. 2.

25 DES, Quality in Schools: Evaluation and Appraisal, London, HMSO, 1985, p. 147.

26 Ibid., p. 137.

27 What is a School of Education?, printed in Gordon, op. cit., pp. 300-18. The quotation is from p. 308.

28 Ibid., p. 309.

29 L.A. Reid, Philosophy and the Theory and Practice of Education, a valedictory lecture, 14 June 1962, London, Evans 1965, pp. 32-3.

30 M. Hollings and E. Gullick, Its Me, O Lord, London, Hodder & Stoughton, 1972.

3

PRIMARY TEACHER-TRAINING:
A PRACTICE IN SEARCH OF PEDAGOGY

Maurice Galton

Consider the following incidents which took place in the same primary school where two student teachers were in the last week of their final practice of a PGCE course.

Student A, a 25-year-old male with a good Honours Degree in Biology has organized the class of twenty-five 9-year-olds in four mixed-ability groups. Laid out on the tables prior to the childrens' entry are a series of varying tasks, ranging from a mathematical crossword to an experiment to wire up a set of traffic lights, using torch bulbs, batteries, and paperclips as switches. Round the wall there is evidence in the display that during the practice a number of interesting curriculum initiatives have been tried.

The children come in from assembly, laughing and in some cases shouting. Mr A tries to calm them by calling for quiet in a mild-mannered voice. Eventually they sit down on the carpeted area and Mr A calls the register. He continually has to break off in the process to ask children to be quiet or to sit still or not to interfere with a neighbour. He begins to tell the pupils what to do and having instructed the first group they get up and go to their table which is at the far end of the room out of the direct line of Mr A's sight. They immediately begin to cause a disturbance, failing to read the instructions on the card and snatching pieces of equipment from one another. Mr A has to get up from his place and go and settle them, whereupon children who remain seated on the carpet begin to push one another and generally misbehave. Mr A returns to these children and after repeated interruptions to reprimand children or to request silence he finishes telling them what they are going to do. Eventually, half an hour after the lesson started, all pupils are seated at their tables. Disruption, however, continues. Children get up from their places and wander about the classroom at will.

This episode is, apparently, fairly typical of Mr A's lessons. The class teacher says that while the work on display is imaginative and of genuine quality it has largely been achieved while she has been present in the classroom. She tells the college tutor that she has repeatedly told Mr A to take a stand, and to raise his voice, if necessary, so that the children are 'clearly aware of who is in charge'. Mr A, however, tells the tutor that he cannot bring himself to do this because 'I am not that kind of person' and because 'I don't think my relationship with the children should be based upon their fear of me'.

Down the corridor Miss B is teaching the top infant class. They have visited a wildlife park and are now busy making a display to commemorate their visit. Miss B has brought in cardboard templates of the various animals that they have seen. One group of children are busily cutting out paper replicas of the animals while another group is busy painting these figures. Yet another group of children is copying out a few lines of information about the animals from a set of work cards which have been prepared by Miss B. The atmosphere is very efficient and business-like and reminiscent of a factory production line. Occasionally the noise rises to an unacceptable level and Miss B will then either tell the children to 'Listen', or, if this fails to quieten them, she shouts out 'Hands'. The children then all wave their hands in the air. She then instructs the children to put their 'Hands on head' and then their 'Finger on lips'. There is immediate silence and Miss B then praises the children and tells them to continue their work quietly. On one such occasion the following exchange takes place with a pupil called Mary:

Miss B: 'Children listen. Mary! Listen carefully Mary!' (Mary is talking to her friend.) 'I said listen. What do I mean when I say listen?'

Mary: 'Fold my arms and look at you, Miss.'

35

Miss B passed the teaching practice, Mr A did not. We do not know what advice the tutor gave Mr A after this particular lesson nor whether had Mr A's practice taken place in a different school he might have emerged from his ordeal more successfully. Every year across the country hundreds of students undergo experiences of this kind. Success or failure, in part, depends on the climate of the school and the extent of the support given by the class teacher and the tutor. These are the expected uncertainties, given the variability of human nature. What is questionable, however, is the degree of variation that is likely to exist between different tutors concerning the criteria used to judge the success or failure of a lesson and the advice and methods used to bring about an improvement in the student's teaching. While there may be general agreement over the categories to be used when judging teaching performance, phrases such as 'establishing good relationships with the class', or 'providing meaningful opportunities for learning' are capable of so many different interpretations that they inevitably lead to the same kind of 'laissez-faire' practice which according to Richards characterizes so much primary teaching in schools.[1] An examination of course handbooks or submissions to the Council for Accreditation of Teacher Education (CATE) or the CNAA provides no obvious examples where a theory of pedagogy has been used to provide a rationale for the training programme, thereby creating the framework in which the deficiencies of students such as Mr A can be dealt with fairly and consistently.

Most primary tutors, especially those who were themselves once primary teachers, seek to incorporate the best aspects of school practice into their courses. Tutors are, for the most part, hard-working and dedicated. They attach a great deal of importance to individual needs and individual relationships and will go to great lengths in supporting and defending students with genuine personal or professional problems. Nevertheless in spite of this emphasis, training programmes, however constituted, can usually be found to share the following four common characteristics. First, they will be inefficient and ineffective in their execution. Second, they will be atheoretical in their conception. Third, their ideology will be largely anti-intellectual with time spent in the classroom, albeit in many cases time spent over a decade ago, as the only valid criterion for doing the job successfully. Fourth, any training programme will be pragmatic in its application, giving rise to large inconsistencies in the treatment of students.

Primary teacher-training is a highly inefficient process; it also appears to be ineffective. Recent international studies of primary teaching show very limited variation in teaching styles across countries,[2] although it is known that there are great variations in training methods, including both the duration of training and school experience and the mode of induction (large lecture presentations versus small group seminars). Research has frequently shown that the most important determinant of the student teacher's developing style is the model provided by the supervising teacher in the practice school.[3] There has in recent years, however, been considerable investment in INSET designed to change the practices of experienced primary teachers. This re-examination of primary practice is largely a result of various surveys and researches,[4] which according to Robin Alexander have demonstrated that there is an over-emphasis on the so-called basic skills which are largely taught competently but uninspiringly.[5]

Descriptions by HM Inspectors of new teachers in school bear a remarkable similarity to the practices of more experienced teachers, as chronicled in these and other research studies of primary teaching.[6] Consequently we have a system of initial training whereby student teachers largely model their practice on that of their experienced colleagues while at the same time local authority advisers are seeking our help in changing the practices of these same colleagues on in-service courses. While many teacher-trainers are aware of this dilemma, few have found the answer to the admission of many students that they teach two kinds of lessons, one for the tutor and one for the class teacher.[7]

Primary training is largely atheoretical in its approach. The debate on theory and practice has a long history and has been chronicled by Robin Alexander in great detail.[8] In the 1970s there were moves away from attempts to apply concepts, derived from the educational disciplines, to the solution of everyday professional tasks, to integration of these concepts around key themes. The debate has now gone on to consider whether by observation and analysis of teachers' 'professional discourse' it is possible 'to codify the craft knowledge' of serving teachers in order to use it as a basis for initial training, so that it becomes more than simply a set of familiar tips to be obtained while 'sitting at the feet of Nelly'.[9]

More recently the notion of a 'reflective' teacher has begun to dominate thinking,[10] whereby the craft knowledge of practising teachers is allied to the findings of empirical research,[11] so that according to Alexander:

> The student teacher, not as a recipient of recipe theory but as the active agent in the construction of his or her own professional theory, complements the teacher as researcher and school based INSET principles invoked by Stenhouse (1975) and others as an alternative basis for subsequent professional development to going on a course.[12]

However, Alexander points out:

> the position and mutual challenging of different sorts of theory/theorising in this 'reflective' model needs emphasising because otherwise it can easily be used to justify regression to an apprenticeship model of professional development in which only the everyday knowledge of the serving teacher has validity.[13]

Primary teacher-training is therefore largely dominated by the anti-intellectual stance taken by many of its practitioners which is reflected by the teaching profession in general. Writing towards the end of the 1960s William Taylor, in whose honour this book is published, described the world of teacher-training as one of:

> Social and literary romanticism [in which there was] suspicion of the intellect and the intellectual: a lack of interest in political and structural change: a stress upon intuitive and the intangible, upon spontaneity and creativity ... and a flight from rationality.[14]

Quoting these remarks Alexander comments, 'Taylor was writing about a 1950's/1960's college: he could equally be writing about the 1980's primary school'.[15]

In this country quite the largest volume of research into teaching and learning has been carried out at primary level. Very few contributions to this knowledge base have been made by those involved in the practical training of teachers. In this country there are few published observational studies which attempt to portray and analyse the experiences of student teachers as seen through the eyes of the tutor. There are no analyses of the discussions which take place after a lesson on which a tutor has sat in: such material would provide a rich source of data and could be used to develop a more coherent theory of training. In terms of the vignettes presented at the beginning of this chapter, it could have been most valuable to build up a case study describing the 'negotiations' which took place between the two students, the supervising tutors, and the teachers, and the manner in which the decisions to pass or fail the students were reached.

In the minds of many tutors, previous experience of primary teaching remains perhaps the sole criterion of competence, even though this experience may have occurred under a very different schooling system a decade or so earlier. There are cases, for example, where teachers with considerable experience of primary research, although secondary trained, have been rejected by colleagues even though they agreed to do a 'refresher course' at primary level. Current notions of 'reflective' teaching do not seem to place a high priority on the tutors' demonstrated capacity for reflection at the personal level. Interviewing PGCE students as an external examiner can be particularly illuminating. They often appear to have been made to feel that their subject knowledge is irrelevant in the context of teaching young children. I once had an interesting experience in one institution of being asked to give a lecture to students on the ORACLE (Observation Research and Classroom Learning Evaluation) research, not because it was relevant to what the students were doing but 'because they keep getting asked about it when they go on interview'.

The atheoretical nature of primary teacher-training, coupled with the anti-intellectual stance of many trainers, is bound to give rise to a largely pragmatic approach and to lead to inconsistencies in practice between tutors. Given the powerful position which tutors hold in relation to the group whom they induct and assess, this pragmatism opens up the possibility of grave injustices being done to students. Sharp and Green, for example, remark on the way in which tutors at certain 'progressive' colleges forced particular views on their students, although the underlying principle behind the philosophy of progressivism is the use of differentiated teaching methods to match individual needs.[16] While similar charges might be levelled at secondary training, especially in the social sciences and humanities, by and large secondary tutors can be characterized by a more critical approach. This is partly because secondary training is largely preoccupied with the subject's discipline and different perspectives on the approach to the content demand a different emphasis in teaching. Science students, for example, will examine the implications for teaching concepts using both Piagetian and metacognitive approaches. English students will discuss post-structuralist and classical approaches to their subject.

In primary teacher-training, however, the subject matter is secondary to the pedagogy and there are no well-developed theories of pedagogy to inform the discussion. Lacking this framework it is little wonder that primary tutors fall back on the twin precepts of 'virtue and industry' which were the characteristics of the early elementary tradition when teacher-training was largely the province of the religious societies.[17] Business (keeping files up to date), punctuality (handing in work on time), reliability (turning up to tutorials), all are important criteria by which a good student is often identified. The tutors themselves set the example. They work hard, devote large amounts of time to their students, offering support in ways that are sometimes reminiscent of a 'mother hen'. Students soon learn that they can depend on their tutor whenever needed; this dependency, in turn, is often transmitted by the students to their pupils when they enter the classroom, thus completing the cycle which is the root cause of so much routine, undemanding practice in the primary school.[18]

The question of why English education, and English primary education in particular, should be characterized by lack of serious concern for pedagogy has been explored by Brian Simon.[19] He argues forcibly that the omission arises largely because of the elitest system of education which operates in this country, as represented by the dominant influence of the public schools and the Universities of Oxford and Cambridge upon educational policy and provision.

Simon defines pedagogy as the 'science of teaching' and he contrasts the situation in Britain, where 'the term is generally shunned' with the implication that 'such a science is either undesirable or impossible of achievement', with other European countries both in the west and east where the term 'pedagogy' has an honoured place. Simon argues that 'the most striking aspect of the current thinking and discussion about education [in England] is its eclectic character, reflecting deep confusing of thought and aims and purposes, relating to learning and teaching: to pedagogy'.[20] By way of example, he cites the work of the Schools Council from its establishment in 1962 to its demise at the beginning of the 1980s. According to Simon, the key feature of the Council's attempts to reform the curriculum has been:

> the theoretical pragmatic approach adopted, ... the overall approach has not been informed by any generally accepted (or publicly formulated) ideas or theories about the nature of the child or the learning/teaching process - by any science of teaching or pedagogy. In particular, there has been an almost total failure to provide psychological underpinning for the new programmes proposed. In general, the Schools Council approach has reflected a pluralism run wild - a mass of disparate projects.[21]

The above criticism almost parallels those which have been made earlier about teacher-training. Simon absolves the Schools Council from blame because:

> the concept of pedagogy - of a science of teaching embodying both curriculum and methodology - is alien to our experience and the way of thinking. There are, no doubt, many reasons why this is so; among them wide acceptance of unresolved dichotomies between 'progressive' and 'traditional' approaches, between 'child-centred' and 'subject-centred' approaches or more generally, between the 'informal' and 'formal'. Such crude, generalized categories are basically meaningless but expressed in this form deflect attention from the real problems of teaching and learning. Indeed so disparate are the views expressed that to resuscitate the concept of a science of teaching which underlines that of 'pedagogy' may seem to be crying for the moon.[22]

Simon's argument is that essentially any serious study of teaching in this country ended with the demise of the elementary tradition and its ideal of universal education. Within the period when the elementary school system flourished, the training manuals written for students all tended to stress the need for teachers to examine their own behaviour when seeking a cause for a child's failure to develop his or her abilities to the full. Only rarely was school failure attributed to 'the disabilities in the child', such as lack of intelligence.

The growth of the separate secondary school system, in parallel but quite separate from the elementary system during the early years of the present century, changed this situation:

> The old belief in 'a positive pedagogy based on scientific procedures and understanding and relevant for all' was no longer seen as appropriate or required ... the social-disciplinary 'containment' function of elementary education was now especially emphasised.[23]

The requirements of this new secondary system, together with the development of psychometric theories where inherited ability, rather than teaching, was seen as the major determinant of attainment, put an end to the search for an effective pedagogy. Even prominent exponents of 'progressivism', such as Susan Isaacs, accepted as axiomatic the concepts of intelligence and supported streaming. The teacher's task was to provide a stimulating environment that enabled the children to perform to their maximum potential. Just as different plants needed different conditions for growth so too children of different abilities required different environments. For the teacher to be able to detect the child was 'ready' to engage in a particular activity, to create the necessary environment which would then 'spark off' the child in a spontaneous way, was a task more akin to an art than to a science.

This romantic view of teaching as an art, coupled with the emphasis on the psychology of child development, gathered strength throughout the Second World War and continued into the Plowden era. College students of that period could always rely on the examination question, 'Is teaching an art or a science?', and knew where their tutor's sympathies lay. Gilbert Highet's book, The Art of Teaching, first published in 1951 and reprinted seven times in the next fifteen years, was a standard work on most college book lists.[24] Educational psychology books of the period might be perused, in vain, for any reference to teaching. In Highet's work students were recommended to model themselves on three great educators: Plato, Aristotle, and Jesus Christ.

The art-science dichotomy has inevitably been

reflected in the broad polarization in styles of teacher-training which, to a large extent, have continued into the present day. The 1970s saw the publication of The First Handbook of Research on Teaching,[25] with its theory that there was at least some science to the 'art'.[26] Skills-based training approaches, particularly micro-teaching, became established.[27] In its less enlightened form, as practised in many training institutions, attempts to induct students into the 'essential skills' were less systematic, becoming in effect little more than 'tips for teaching' often derived from the tutor's own experience rather than from any serious study of the literature. Students would be inundated with advice, some of it excellent, about ways of improving their teaching. 'Keep your introduction simple.' 'Don't dismiss the children all at once, let them go by table.' 'Don't smile during the first few weeks. The children will think you're soft and take advantage.' Such interventions characterize what might be termed 'a golf training model' where the coach analyses the task of propelling the golf-ball from the tee to the fairway into a series of discrete tasks and then works steadily on the weakest part of the player's game. In an analogous manner new teachers are coached in such procedures as starting the lesson, dealing with individual children, questioning, finishing, clearing up, and other topics.

The trouble with the model, however, is that teaching teachers is not like coaching golfers. In golf, if the player misses the ball or hits it badly, the coach simply puts another one in the same place and asks the player to try again. In the classroom, however, one incident in teaching is never quite like another; what works one day may not work the next because of events or happenings outside the teacher's control. What is worse, what often appears to be sound advice turns out to be highly problematic when attempts are made to put it into practice. A tutor may suggest to a student, for example, that the reason why pupils were restless while sitting on the mat was because they were in a cramped environment for too long and became bored. The solution may be to make the introduction to the lesson simpler and shorter. The student will, therefore, try to simplify the introduction but perhaps to no avail because, as many experienced teachers will testify, the time one generally finds out that one's instructions are not simply enough is after the lesson has begun. Students do not, therefore, need tips on how to avoid trouble so much as sets of 'exiting strategies' which allow them to escape from difficult situations without losing face.

At the other extreme, tutors who regard teaching as an art form are likely to adopt an experiential approach to training using what might be termed the 'bicycle training model'. Learner riders will be given the minimum instruction and then sent off to a safe environment to practice. Whenever they fall off the trainer is there, as counsellor, to offer support and to listen to the riders' explanations for their failure. Eventually, through talking with the trainer, and perhaps others, learners gradually begin to make sense of the experience and get the 'feel' of what it is like to ride their machines. They are then ready to be launched into the more dangerous environment of the public highway. In a similar manner student teachers may be sent to the classroom initially to teach one child, before graduating to groups and then to the whole class. The course will place great emphasis on sharing one's experiences and learning from each other. Initially students are not challenged with complex ideas about practice or with research findings because, it is argued, they should first be allowed to build up their confidence. This process continues until they are unrecognizable in their attitudes and their practice from more experienced teachers, by which time they are so confident that they no longer feel the need for the theory.

To enable primary teacher-training to break out of this mould requires a detailed critical analysis of the current ideology of primary practice, using research evidence to question assumptions and expose the rhetoric. For Simon,[28] this re-evaluation should begin with the Plowden Report.[29] Simon argues that the very philosophy of the report with its emphasis on the individualization of the teaching and learning process has 'created a situation from which it is impossible to derive an effective pedagogy' since:

> if each child is unique, and each requires a specific pedagogical approach appropriate to him or her and to no other, the construction of an all-embracing pedagogy, or general principles of teaching becomes an impossibility. ...
>
> To develop effective pedagogy involves starting from the opposite standpoint, from what the children have in common as members of the human species: to establish the general principles of teaching and, in the light of these, to determine what modifications of

practice are needed to meet specific individual needs.[30]

If this analysis is correct then it suggests that the starting-point for any new approach to pedagogical theory should come from our study of learning as a social rather than as a cognitive process, since the latter is concerned to emphasize the differences between individual children and between children and adults, while the former emphasizes those aspects of learning that are common to the human species at every age. For example, non-participation in group discussion and negotiating for easy tasks to guarantee success, are strategies which can be related to risk-taking and risk-avoidance in adult as well as pupil settings.

There is now a considerable body of work in Britain which describes the behaviour of pupils in various learning settings.[31] Many of the observations recorded by researchers fit in well with the explanations of social psychologists, particularly in their analysis of one of the central activities in the classroom, task-setting by the teacher and task-accomplishment by the pupils.[32] From the standpoint of these theories, the failure of teachers to implement the Plowden prescriptions; unsatisfactory matching of tasks to pupils' needs and abilities; the predominance of low-level practice tasks designed to maintain busyness;[33] and the emphasis on didactic expository teaching[34] are not so much, as Simon suggests, due to the impossibility of a teacher coping with the individual needs of thirty pupils, but more the result of the classroom climate where the pupils are reluctant to engage in any form of unsupervised challenging learning activity as called for by Plowden. Pupils appear to retain a dependence on the teacher, reminiscent of the traditional forms of instruction, and engage in increasingly disruptive behaviour whenever more complex tasks are set. Or they employ task-avoidance strategies, such as working intermittently, or working as slowly as possible, without attracting the teacher's attention.[35] These and other research findings can all be used to develop a powerful framework in which beginning teachers can analyse the consequence of their actions for their pupils. Most importantly, they fulfil Simon's criterion for establishing the new pedagogy by switching the discussion away from consideration of learning failure as the child's problem, concentrating instead on the teacher's actions and the interpretation of the teacher's behaviour, as seen from the child's point of view.

In developing theories of effective classroom practice, there is a need also, as Alexander argues, to take into account teachers' own explanations for their behaviour.[36] There is, however, a danger that, as embodied in schemes such as IT-INSET,[37] and other attempts at reflective teaching, that teacher explanations of classroom events will be given primacy over those offered by pupils, simply because they are easier to obtain. Such explanations are bound to be of limited value because the lack of any pedagogical tradition in this country has impoverished teachers' thinking on such matters so that they mostly interpret events in the classroom either in terms of individual pupil learning difficulties or in terms of organization or resource problems.

Alexander himself appears to over-emphasize the importance of teacher explanations in developing theories of classroom practice,[38] when he criticizes the tendency of advisers to use the results of the ORACLE research,[39] particularly the recommendation to increase the use of collaborative group work, as an alternative to individualization. Alexander reports the results of discussions with teachers in which they offer explanations for using other forms of grouping which allow children to work individually. He quotes, with approval, the strategy of one teacher who sends children off to do tasks which do not require much supervision (painting a picture, using a worksheet, or collective problem-solving) while she concentrates on more complex activities in which the children need her help. This, according to Alexander, seems an appropriate means of managing her time and superior to the strategy of putting children into collaborative groups, which may be less suited to meeting the needs of individual pupils.

Seen from the teacher's viewpoint, Alexander's case seems unanswerable. However, once we begin to examine the teacher's strategy through the pupil's eyes, a different perspective emerges. Given the extent of pupil dependency on teachers, evident in many primary classrooms, children are likely to obtain an impression of the relative importance of each task by evaluating the time that the teacher spends on it. Recent research shows that in many primary classrooms teachers tend to concentrate their attention on the core subjects, leaving children to work by themselves on play and aesthetic activities.[40] This may well afford the explanation of the commonly reported remark by children that if they have done no writing they have done no 'real' work. Indeed, in one case study carried out as part of the follow-up project to ORACLE, <u>Effective Group Work in the Primary Classroom</u>, the teacher employed the 'low investment' problem-solving strategy described by Alexander, by sending a group of top infants out into the playground to build a tower while concentrating her attention on individuals in small groups inside the classroom who were either reading or doing mathematics and English.[41] The children built an excellent tower of bricks in the wind, collaborating freely and sharing ideas, being on-task for about 90 per cent of the time. This was done, however, during playtime. In the previous hour, in which the same activity had been the legitimate learning task, the children concentrated on building the tower intermittently. For over half the time, they fooled around, went to play in the sand and were generally unwilling to work together. Afterwards, the teacher's explanation for the relative lack of success largely concentrated on factors relating to organization:

> there were probably too many children in the group. One or two of them are inclined to be a bit silly and they set the others off. In retrospect, I don't think it was the best place to set up the task as they were able to wander off too easily without my seeing them.

The children, however, seem to have a different view of the incident, one that stressed their relative isolation from the other pupils in the class and which appeared to put a very low value on working independently of the teacher. Asked why they had fooled around during class time but then became fully involved in the task during the morning break, they replied:

> well it was play, wasn't it? It's not real work. ... real work, that's what you do with the teacher. Maths, writing, things like that. ... That's what the others were doing while we were stuck out here without anyone else.

Conversations with children, as part of the follow-up project to ORACLE, <u>Effective Group Work in the Primary Classroom</u>, produced a number of instances where the pupils' interpretation of the situation was at variance with the teacher's intention.[42] From the child's point of view the

47

classroom is a place of considerable ambiguity - discovering things for yourself without being certain whether you are discovering what the teacher really wants you to find out, not knowing whether you have been asked a question to see if you are paying attention or because the teacher is genuinely interested in your 'inspired' guess, trying to distinguish between redrafting your story and correcting your mistakes - these and many other situations call upon pupils repeatedly to put themselves at risk by exposing themselves to the possibility of failure and loss of 'public' face.

To transform this kind of classroom climate, whereby children's 'fear of failure' drives them towards the use of what Measor and Woods describe as 'knife-edging' strategies,[43] requires that these and other aspects of the 'hidden' curriculum be exposed and debated. Although emphasis has been placed on the social conditions of learning, we also need to take account of the cognitive aspects. Research shows that learners need to have sensible reasons in order to build up clear conceptions about what they are doing and why they are doing it if they are to reproduce what has been learned. A teacher's intentions will be translated into an effective action only if the pupils' beliefs, attitudes, self-efficacy, and sense of purpose are congruent with the learning task. It is important not to lose sight of the fact that 'students think about what they do and what we want them to do, and those thoughts affect what students do'.[44]

A central principle behind this approach is a redefinition of progressivism in terms of negotiated learning between the teacher and pupils.[45] Seen in this light, progressivism loses some of its terrors for the beginning teacher in that it no longer appears to hand power, or try to manipulate a situation so that it appears to hand power, to the children. Within this negotiated framework, children learn not only to think but also to behave. The issue is not whether there should be structure in the classroom but how the decisions about the form the structure should take are arrived at. Progressivism is fully compatible with the kinds of classrooms in which both teachers and pupils make public that they have certain rights and certain needs and where neither party attempts to impose their demands upon the other.

Gordon describes this approach as the 'no-lose' method of resolving conflicts. One purpose of which is to lower the dependency of the children upon the teacher.[46] He contrasts this approach with the more typical situation where either the teacher wins (e.g. 'Mary! I said listen. What do I mean when I say listen?') or like Mr A, the teacher loses by allowing the pupils to get their own way in the hope that by giving in he will avoid a confrontation. Gordon points out that both these solutions inevitably produce resentment and hostility in the loser towards the winner. Teachers who frequently 'give in' to students often develop a dislike for them and eventually for teaching. Mr A subsequently decided not to repeat his practice. Those who argue that it is necessary to be firm because 'students really want limits on their behaviour' need to understand, according to Gordon, that it is one thing for students 'to want to know the limits of the teacher's acceptance' and an entirely different thing to believe that they want or need 'the teacher to set those limits unilaterally, arbitrarily, without the students' inputs and participation'.[47]

Other arguments in favour of firmness often centre around the proposition that power is necessary with certain children and that children respect consistency and fairness. Here again, both arguments need to be seen within the context of a debate which sees the only alternative to authoritarianism as permissiveness. Granted, if the teachers are to use their power and authority to control children, then children would much prefer their teachers to be fair and consistent in the exercise of this power. But while pupils do not respect 'weak' teachers who allow pupils 'to get away with it', increasing external controls on badly behaved pupils either causes them to react even more aggressively or, what is sometimes worse, to employ the same coping mechanisms covertly so that the behaviour is even more difficult to deal with.

An important part of Gordon's teacher-training programme is the distinction between giving orders, directions, and commands and using the same procedures to resolve conflicts in the classroom. A firm statement, 'Sit still' becomes a problem only if the pupils resist. If teachers then use their authority to overcome this resistance, the situation degenerates into one where the pupils lose. It is important to understand, also, that since teachers are human, they will, at times, when under stress, use their authority to resolve conflicts. Gordon argues that in such cases the damage can be limited if teachers first explain to the pupils why they acted as they did, second apologize, third actively listen to the pupils' feelings, and fourth discuss with the pupils how to avoid a similar situation in the future.[48] Under this system the occasional use of teachers' authority to exert control does not seem to damage the relationships with pupils whereby the 'nobody loses' method can be used.[49]

For the 'nobody-loses' method to work the teacher must somehow communicate to the pupils an attitude whereby, together, they try an approach which finds a solution that will meet both the pupils' needs and the teacher's. This involves what Gordon calls 'active listening', that is being able to discern what meanings lie behind the pupils' remarks. This enables problems to be defined in terms of what John Dewey called 'conflicts of needs' rather than 'competing solutions'. The approach also requires teachers to give pupils what Gordon terms 'I' messages. These types of messages express the teachers' real feelings about a situation. They are in contrast to the usual 'you' messages ('You stop that, you ought to know better!') in that they leave the responsibility for the pupils' behaviour with the pupil. Gordon reports the experience of one teacher who experimented for the first time with 'I' messages:

> I was reluctant to try an 'I' message with the kids I have. They are so hard to manage. Finally I screwed up my courage and sent a strong 'I' message to a group of children who were making a mess with water paints in the back of the room by the sink. I said 'When you mix paints and spill them all over the sink and table I have to scrub them up later or get yelled at by the custodian. I am sick of cleaning up after you and I feel helpless to prevent it from happening.' I just stopped then and waited to see what they would do. I really expected them to laugh at me and take that 'I don't care' attitude that they had had all year but they didn't! They stood there looking at me for a minute like they were amazed to find out I was upset and then one of them said, 'Come on, let's clean up.' I was floored. You know, they haven't turned into models of perfection, but they now clean up the sink and tables every day whether they have spilled paint on them or not.[50]

There are, of course, classrooms in many primary schools where teachers are attempting to put these principles into practice. In many instances these teachers are supported by staff from colleges and university departments of education who act as consultants as part of 'action-research' programmes of professional development. But there is as yet in Britain no systematic approach of this kind as there is, for example, in the Netherlands. There, in regional centres (and it is significant that these centres are called Pedagogic Institutes and not Teachers' Centres) attempts are being made to bring about significant changes in practice.

In the late 1970s the Dutch government instituted a programme of primary school reform. Inspectors spent some time looking at the operation of informal methods in the English primary school, at the same time taking account of the HMI survey and other research findings. In planning the reform programme the Dutch authorities sought to provide a coherent philosophy which would eliminate the wide variations in practice observed in the English schools and would help to eliminate the pressure on teachers due to the dependency shown by many pupils. They chose a particular programme developed from social learning theory by Thomas Gordon entitled Teacher Effectiveness Training (TET). Gordon visited the Netherlands and the Pedagogic Institutes have now set up action-research projects based upon his methods.

One account of this programme is presented by Kopmels, who described how teachers reorganized their school so that the more routine basic activities which dominate so much of the English curriculum were largely placed under the control of the children, leaving the teacher free to work with the children on the more challenging problem-solving activity.[51] Spelling, punctuation checks, and computation exercises were placed on to the computer with every child having his or her secret password. The programme, written by one of the parents who worked for a software company, allowed every child to present an up-to-date profile to the teacher on request. This is the reverse of the 'match' strategy proposed by Bennett and Desforges where the teacher engages in clinical diagnosis of individual children's learning difficulties, an immense task with a class of thirty pupils.[52] In the Dutch school the pupils, with the help of their computer profiles, diagnosed their own problems and brought them to the teacher.

But to return to the two students and the descriptions of their lessons. Mr A typifies an all-too-frequent situation where the beginning teacher is in a 'no-win' situation. If he sets out on his own initiative, perhaps with the encouragement of the tutor, to try to modify the class teacher's practice, because it does not suit his personality, then the children will begin to 'test him out' to discover 'just how far they can go'. If, on the other hand, the student falls in with the existing practice and shouts in the same way as the class teacher, he may find, as in Mr A's case, that his high-pitched voice sounds so comical that the children increase the levels of disruption for the amusement it affords them. One possible solution in terms of Gordon's approach would be for the class teacher in the first instance to do as the visiting examiner did after the class had all but reached the level of anarchy. Asking Mr A to leave, it was then possible to confront the children with their action and to ask them the question why? Further questions followed. Did the children know why Mr A was there? How would they feel if they were Mr A? (This produced a stunned silence.) How could we make it fair for Mr A so that he could find out if he liked being a teacher?

The children also had some points to raise. They did not understand some of the work that Mr A set. They reported that, 'sometimes he gets you very mixed up'. In this way bargains were struck, whereby in exchange for talking to Mr A about the work, the children provided the kind of classroom atmosphere which allowed Mr A to learn to teach. The intervention, however, came too late to save the practice, too late to allow Mr A to learn from the experience and to come to terms with the fact that he needed to work considerably harder and to provide a much wider range of learning experiences.

There is also, of course, Miss B. The fact that she and many others enter the teaching profession, making use of 'busy work' techniques and strategies of dependency and control which would be more suitable for dogs rather than children, must be a serious cause of concern. Even if the tutor had persuaded Miss B to move away from what was effectively respondent conditioning of the classical kind, towards more reflective forms of Applied Behaviour Analysis, advocated by Wheldall,[53] Miss B needs to face the logic of this position and perhaps, as Wheldall advocates, to move the desks back into rows and to cease employing the rhetoric about the need for children to learn to think independently.

For this really is the stark choice facing those who train the next generation of teachers. In the past we have tried to convince ourselves that a 'softly, softly' approach is adequate, persuading ourselves that once the students have settled down in their first posts they will gain confidence and begin to experiment in their choice of teaching methods. But the research evidence, including the latest study of ILEA children, denies this fact.[54] Practice has remained relatively unchanged since the first large-scale observation studies during the mid-1970s. At that time many tutors reacted to the poor showing of informal classrooms by arguing that the practice described in these studies was not in any real sense compatible with the theories of progressivism. Progressivism had not failed but had not been fully tested. What seems clear is that if we are to attempt to train the best of our students to meet these high standards, we are going to have to reach a greater level of consensus about the methods used to train such teachers. This consensus needs to be based on a clearly thought out theory of pedagogy designed to reduce pupil dependency on the teacher in order to bring about effective learning in the informal classroom.

Given the traditions of teacher-training described earlier there will be many who question whether these standards are not impossibly high. Certainly the evidence from the evaluation of IT-INSET would suggest that there is much to be done before these aims can be translated into practice. The IT-INSET programme calls for co-operation between student, class teacher, and tutor, during which the practical theorizing which takes place in the classroom is tested against 'research-based' theory mostly, it must be assumed, provided by the tutors. The evaluation reports by a group of teachers experienced in the IT-INSET programme concluded, however, that the least effective examples occurred when the tutor did not understand the IT-INSET concept and did not therefore provide an adequate research base.[55]

Perhaps, as a beginning, we need to try to make more sense of the present pragmatic approach. Anyone who has acted as an external examiner across a number of institutions will acknowledge the richness of the research material contained in the notes which tutors write to students on their assessments. There is a need for research which carries out in-depth case studies of training procedures across a variety of institutions as an alternative to carrying out surveys of tutor and student opinion. More importantly, tutors themselves can contribute to the debate by collating and sharing their materials so that the study of their own pedagogy is recognized as a serious intellectual activity and a necessary part of their responsibilities. Indeed, those who are charged with the management of training institutions, and who shortly will be required to introduce formal appraisal systems, will be in a position to bring such a change about.

Of equal importance, there is a need to emphasize the role of the university departments of education as centres for the development of the new pedagogy and for its dissemination within other institutions of higher education and teacher-training. In the late 1960s and 1970s many college lecturers obtained their posts by virtue of a master's course in some aspect of the educational disciplines. This is one of the main reasons why the disciplines have continued to dominate the BEd programme in one form or another until the intervention by CATE. With the decline in the status of the disciplines, however, the demand for these master's courses ceased. College lecturers with a lengthy sabbatical are more likely now to return to the classroom rather than seek a year of serious reflection and academic study. In some quarters there seems to be a feeling that universities have little to offer by way of academic courses that is now relevant to present thinking about 'theory and practice'.

Universities are, however, changing to meet these post-CATE demands. There now exists sufficient knowledge to provide a totally new style of course which would confront tutors with the implications of their current training programmes and at least attempt to offer a theoretical framework within which some of the problems might be addressed. But if such courses are to flourish over the next decade and to be effective, then they will need to take seriously, perhaps for the first time in over one hundred years, the academic study of pedagogy.

NOTES AND REFERENCES

1   C. Richards, 'Primary education 1974-80', in C. Richards (ed.) New Directions in Primary Education, Sussex, Falmer Press, 1982.
2   L.W. Anderson, 'The classroom environment study: teaching for learning', Comparative Education Review 1987, 31, 1: 69-87.
3   D. Manning, 'The influence of key individuals on student

teachers in urban and suburban settings', <u>Teaching and Teacher Education</u> 1977, 13, 2: 2-8.

4   HMI, <u>Primary Education in Schools: A Survey of HM Inspectors of Schools</u>, DES, London, HMSO, 1978; N. Bennett, <u>Teaching Styles and Pupil Progress</u>, London, Open Books, 1976; M. Galton, B. Simon, and P. Croll, <u>Inside the Primary Classroom</u>, London, Routledge & Kegan Paul, 1980.

5   R. Alexander, <u>Primary Teaching</u>, London, Holt, Rinehart, & Winston, 1984a.

6   HMI, <u>The New Teacher in School</u>, HMI Series: Matters for Discussion 15, London, HMSO, 1982.

7   G. Bernbaum, H. Patrick, and K. Reid, <u>The Structure and Process of Initial Teacher Education within Universities in England and Wales</u>, University of Leicester School of Education, mimeo, 1982.

8   R. Alexander, 'Innovation and continuity in the initial teacher education curriculum', in R. Alexander, M. Craft, and J. Lynch (eds) <u>Change in Teacher Education</u>, London, Holt, Rinehart, & Winston, 1984b.

9   Ibid., pp. 145-6.

10   A. Pollard and S. Tann, <u>Reflective Teaching in the Primary School</u>, London, Cassell, 1987.

11   D. McIntyre, 'The contribution of research to quality in teacher education', in E. Hoyle and J. McGarry (eds) <u>World Year Book of Education: Professional Development of Teachers</u>, London, Kogan Page, 1980.

12   Alexander 1984b, op. cit., p. 146. In the extract Alexander cites L. Stenhouse, <u>An Introduction to Curriculum Research and Development</u>, Heinemann Educational, 1975.

13   Alexander 1984b, op. cit., p. 146.

14   W. Taylor, <u>Society and the Education of Teachers</u>, London, Faber, 1969.

15   Alexander 1984b, op. cit., p. 153.

16   R. Sharp and A. Green, <u>Education and Social Control: A Study in Progressive Primary Education</u>, London, Routledge & Kegan Paul, 1975.

17   G. Bernbaum, <u>Education: The Desert of the Mind</u>, an inaugural lecture, University of Leicester, mimeo, 1976.

18   M. Galton, 'Change and continuity in the primary school: the research evidence', <u>Oxford Review of Education</u> 1987a, 13, 1: 81-94.

19   B. Simon, 'Why no pedagogy in England?', in B. Simon

and W. Taylor (eds) Education in the Eighties, London, Batsford Educational, 1981.
20 Ibid, p. 124.
21 Ibid., p. 125.
22 Ibid., p. 125.
23 Ibid., p. 132.
24 G. Highet, The Art of Teaching, London, Methuen, 1963.
25 N. Gage (ed.) The First Handbook of Research on Teaching, Chicago, Ill., Rand McNally, 1963.
26 N. Gage, The Scientific Basis for the Art of Teaching, New York, Teachers' College Press, University of Columbia, 1978.
27 G.A. Brown, 'Some case studies of teacher preparation', British Journal of Teacher Education 1975, 1: 71-85; E. Wragg, Teaching Teaching, London, David & Charles, 1974.
28 Simon, op. cit.
29 DES, Children and their Primary Schools, 2 vols, Plowden Report, Central Advisory Council for Education in England, London, HMSO, 1967.
30 Simon, op. cit., p. 141.
31 A. Pollard, The Social World of the Primary School, London, Holt, Rinehart, & Winston, 1985; P. Woods, Pupil Strategies, London, Croom Helm, 1980.
32 W. Doyle, 'Classroom tasks and student abilities', in P. Peterson and H.J. Walberg (eds) Research on Teaching: Concepts, Findings and Implications, Berkeley, Calif., McCutchan, 1979; W. Doyle, 'Classroom organisation and management', in M. Wittrock (ed.) The Third Handbook of Research on Teaching, New York, Macmillan, 1986.
33 N. Bennett, C. Desforges, A. Cockburn, and B. Wilkinson, The Quality of Pupil Learning Experiences, London, Lawrence Erlbaum Associates, 1984.
34 M. Galton and B. Simon (eds), Progress and Performance in the Primary Classroom, London, Routledge & Kegan Paul, 1980.
35 M. Galton, 'An ORACLE chronicle: a decade of classroom research' Teaching and Teacher Education 1987b, 3, 4: 299-314.
36 R. Alexander, 'Garden or jungle: teacher's development and informal primary education', in W. Blyth (ed.) Informal Primary Education Today: Essays and Studies, Sussex, Falmer Press, 1988.

37   P. Ashton and A. Peacock, Final Report, University of
      Leicester Centre for Evaluation and Development in
      Teacher Education, mimeo, 1988.
38   Alexander, 1988, op. cit.
39   Galton and Simon, op. cit.
40   M. Galton, H. Patrick, R. Appleyard, L. Hargreaves,
      and G. Bernbaum, 'Curriculum provision in small
      schools: the PRISMS project', Final Report, University
      of Leicester, mimeo, 1987.
41   Effective Group Work in the Primary Classroom,
      sponsored by the Economic and Social Science Research
      Council (formerly the Social Science Research Council:
      SSRC), University of Leicester (1980-3).
42   Galton 1987b, op. cit.
43   L. Measor and P. Woods, Changing Schools: Pupil
      Perspectives on Transfer to a Comprehensive, Milton
      Keynes, Open University Press, 1984.
44   N. Gage and D. Berliner, Educational Psychology,
      Boston, Mass., Houghton Mifflin, 1988, p. 271.
45   Galton, 1987a, op. cit.
46   T. Gordon, T.E.T. Teacher Effectiveness Training, New
      York, Peter Wyden, 1974.
47   Ibid., p. 214.
48   Ibid., p. 281.
49   Galton, 1987b, op. cit.
50   Gordon, op. cit., p. 140.
51   D. Kopmels, Project No 8: Innovation in Primary
      Education. The Contact School Plan: Progress Report,
      submitted by the K.K. Van Duyvenvoordeschool,
      Netherlands, DECS/EGT (86) 50, CDCC Strasbourg,
      mimeo, 1986.
52   Bennett and Desforges, op. cit.
53   K. Wheldall (ed.) 'Behavioural pedagogy or behavioural
      overkill', in 'Behavioural pedagogy: towards a
      behavioural science of teaching', Educational
      Psychology 1982, 2, 3-4: 181-4.
54   P. Mortimore, P. Sammons, L. Stoll, D. Lewis, and R.
      Ecob, The Junior School Project, London, ILEA
      Research and Statistics Branch, mimeo, 1987.
55   Ashton and Peacock, op. cit.

4

THE FORMATION OF SECONDARY TEACHERS

Ron Arnold

There is almost a compulsion to begin a chapter of this kind with a profile of the ideal secondary teacher, for there is a reassuring feel about listing all those qualities of personality, knowledge, and competence that together make up such a teacher. By that means we can match them against the itemized needs of the school, and then draw up a blueprint for delivery. But this is a risky way to start, for it gets progressively more difficult to make a clear and confident statement about how a secondary teacher should be trained. The job never stands still, and as time goes by the demands appear to multiply. Just over ten years ago, HMI completed their substantial survey of secondary schools, and the results were published in Aspects of Secondary Education in England.[1] The picture of schools that emerged was summarized in a subsequent HMI document Teacher Training and the Secondary School, which began by supplying a context for the observations made in the report.[2] In the years in which comprehensive education had been taking shape, schools had encountered the coincidence of many different pressures, some of them in conflict with one another. Most schools had been faced with the simultaneous demands of expansion and internal change, and some had had to meet them with a high proportion of inexperienced teachers. A recognizable system of secondary education for all had emerged, but it was one where the curriculum and the style of teaching had in general failed to change in line with changing expectations and circumstances. If that was true then, what must the situation be today? The pace of change has accelerated, the demands have increased, the framework is being altered by statute. What does all this signify, for the kinds of secondary teachers we now need, and for the ways in which they should be educated and trained?

There is no way of even addressing this question without first attempting to provide the answers to a number of others. The answers to these questions are not the ones we might have given even a decade ago, nor will they be sufficient a decade ahead, but neither time nor circumstance are ever likely to change the questions themselves: What kinds of teachers do we want? What kind of teaching is going on in the schools? What needs changing or strengthening there? What do the teachers themselves think to be their needs? What kinds of young teachers are we actually acquiring? What can be achieved in initial and in-service training to bring this about?

The list of qualities, skills, and attributes that a good secondary teacher is held to need is exhaustive. One after another publication has added to them, or at least has elaborated and refined them. We have them set out in The New Teacher in School, in Better Schools, in Education Observed 3, and in Quality in Schools.[3] All these are documents that emanated from the Department of Education and Science. Many more contributions came from schools themselves, from professional associations, and from teacher-trainers. What it all amounts to is that if teachers in secondary schools are to do their jobs successfully a very great deal is required of them.

First and foremost, effective teachers develop in their pupils lively, enquiring minds. They stimulate curiosity, sustain motivation, and set high levels of expectation. To achieve this they have to engage and maintain the pupils' interest, which calls for imagination, flexibility, and careful planning. This holds true for pupils of all ages, and the fundamentals of good teaching and learning remain the same throughout the years of schooling, whatever the difference in immediate aims and objectives. The task of the primary teacher is to develop the intellectual, social, and personal qualities of a diverse group of children through a diverse array of learning opportunities. It means advancing learning across a broad front and managing this front in such a way that it matches, with as much exactness as possible, the boundaries the children are capable of reaching at any given time. The secondary teacher has to do all these things, but within an area defined not by its breadth but by its depth. He or she has to operate within a subject or particular area of the curriculum, generating enthusiasm for that subject and relating it to the child's own life, needs, and interests.

This means encouraging speculative thinking and independent learning habits, and recognizing that preparing pupils for examinations does not mean teaching them narrowly. Effective secondary teachers have a shrewd grasp of a wide range of methods. They do not follow fashion blindly, nor cling uncritically to practice that has been found wanting. They apply a professional scrutiny to their work and can judge the truth behind the label. Self-evaluation, so important to all teachers, is not merely a process of judging day-to-day success and failures; it includes the ability to assess the value of developments, to distinguish between the slogans and the facts, and to choose in the full professional knowledge of what is best for their pupils. From this portrait of performance we can itemize the secondary teacher's entitlement:

1 A thorough knowledge of the specialist teaching subject, or area of the curriculum.

2 An understanding of the contribution of this subject to the education of the child, and its relationship with the curriculum as a whole.

3 The ability to conceive and plan a teaching programme designed to meet the needs of the full range of pupils in terms of ability, behaviour, background, and culture, that is in what now constitutes a normal population in many schools.

4 A flexible repertoire of teaching approaches and methods which enables the teacher to make the subject relevant and interesting to a full range of pupils.

5 Confidence in class management and control, and in the ability to organize the work of the class.

6 The ability to assess according to well-informed criteria a pupil's achievement at any given point, related to equally well-informed judgements about his or her potential, and teach to this assessment.

7 A thorough understanding of the importance of language and the way its use in the classroom will influence the quality of the learning.

8 A sensitive response to the personal and social needs of children, and to the concern of their

parents, and an acceptance that the curriculum and its delivery is itself an instrument of pastoral care.

9   A sensible appreciation of the relationship between what children learn in school and the wider world in which they will take up employment.

These relate to a teacher's performance in the classroom and his or her practical contribution to the education of the pupil. They are dependent for their quality on certain professional attitudes and dispositions, which we might define as follows:

1   The ability to analyse from practice, realizing that good teachers have a sense of purpose tempered with flexibility and that they move freely from involvement to objective appraisal.

2   The ability to make decisions, many of them complex, over a broad range of activities.

3   Realism in response to existing practices and conditions, but with the independence of mind to judge whether and how these might be changed and to act on that judgement.

4   A sense of responsibility for continued professional development and therefore a flexibility of mind and an open but critical receptivity to new ideas.

5   The ability to contribute to the development of the school in curriculum and other terms, and to work co-operatively with colleagues from their own and other schools.

This comes close to what we began by saying was risky: a profile of the ideal secondary teacher. Nevertheless, it represents what secondary schools need if they are to be fully effective and if they are to meet the demands which are facing them.

Our knowledge of the quality of what is going on within the schools is derived largely from the reports of HMI. Since Aspects of Secondary Education in England the landscape has changed much. The schools have had to accommodate to falling rolls and to the introduction of GCSE. There have been developments such as the modular curriculum, which though not widespread have prompted many schools to rethink their organization. There have been Education Support Grants, and changes in in-service funding which have placed more responsibility on the schools themselves. There have been pilot schemes of such innovations as TVEI and records of Achievement, which are to be extended to all schools. There have been shifts in the balance of the curriculum, which become apparent when one compares the two secondary staffing surveys conducted by the DES in 1977 and 1984. And now there is the prospect of all the changes in the Education Reform Act, 1988, particularly in regard to the national curriculum, with its percentage allocation of time and the programme of national testing. This is not the place to speculate on how well the schools will respond to these accumulating demands. Nor is it the place to analyse all the strengths and weaknesses displayed by the schools at this present time. But there are some of the latter which are worth isolating because they appear so persistent, and which must therefore command the attention of those responsible for the training of teachers.

Aspects of Secondary Education in England praised the provision for personal and social development, upon which the major influences appear to be teachers' attitudes and the examples they set. But it also pointed out that this was to a much greater extent mediated through pastoral care than through the curriculum. Most schools were judged as needing to take more account of the nature of pupils' individual programmes and their experiences within them. The curriculum with which a child was presented, the processes of teaching and learning, the attitudes and expectations of teachers and the assumptions that lay behind them: all these were presented as features which influenced the personal and social development of individual pupils. There was, moreover, a need to stretch pupils to their full capacity to involve them more fully in their own learning, and to give them programmes of work which achieve coherence. All these points have recurred in HMI reports on individual schools since 1983, when they first began to be published, and in the Education Observed series, the first of which was issued in 1984. Perhaps the most persistent criticism of secondary education is the emphasis on over-directed or 'transmissional' teaching, a style experienced cumulatively by the pupils as they move from subject to subject through the school day. To some extent the problem is inherent in the organizational structure of the secondary school. Knowledge is pursued within subject boundaries, and there is often no overarching awareness of what it means for a pupil to be a 'total learner' in that school. Generally there is no means of studying, for example, a pupil's writing performance across several subjects, the kind of task he or she is being set, or for that matter the sheer volume of what is being required. Nor is there a means of looking at the range of reading demands being made upon the pupil, the levels of density of the texts, and the purposes to which reading is being put. Above all, there is generally no means of knowing how much chance a pupil has to talk, as distinct from listen, in the course of a school day. Yet this knowledge is critically important if teaching and learning are to be at their most productive. The school needs to know whether the transactions through which learning is being acquired are so narrow, so unvaried from one subject to another, that the learning is less efficient than it might be.

These are some of the features of secondary education which continue to leave room for improvement. It is not easy to predict what will be the effect upon them of developments already in train and changes to come. GCSE, with its opportunities for course work and its emphasis on oral work, is already affecting teaching styles. So too will the extension of TVEI, which in its pilot stage has given rise to some enterprising approaches. There is less and less excuse for the kind of practice characterized in reports in examination work as 'over-directive teaching, heavy reliance on dictated or copied notes, and an emphasis of factual recall rather than on understanding'. Nor should the national testing proposals be allowed to encourage such practice. The recommendations of the Task Group on Assessment and Testing, if properly interpreted, should lead no one to teach to narrow specifications.

In the light of what we have suggested about the needs of secondary schools and some of their practices, we might now look at the newly qualified teachers' perception of their own priorities and the quality of their training. In 1981 HMI carried out a survey of 294 newly trained teachers (93 primary and 201 secondary) in their first appointment.[4] In many aspects of their training at least a fifth of the teachers felt ill-prepared, and in some of the aspects this proportion increased to nearly three-fifths. A substantial number believed they had not been adequately prepared in teaching children from different cultural backgrounds and in fulfilling their pastoral role. Comparable lack of confidence was expressed by newly qualified teachers in the survey conducted by University of Leicester School of Education in 1980-81.[5] For example, as many as 40 per cent of all the teachers (primary and secondary taken together) said that syllabus planning had not been included in their training. This compared closely with a finding in the HMI survey, where 42 per cent said they had had insufficient preparation in planning a programme of work. Both findings can be read alongside the conclusions in Quality in Schools, of which more below, that students on teaching practice lacked confidence about long-term planning and the progressive development of knowledge, concepts, and skills.[6] Of particular interest in the Leicester study was the insight into the newly qualified teachers' view of what they considered to be their priorities. The emergent teachers listed in rank order the abilities they saw as 'highly desirable' to do their job successfully. Their top ten were:

1   enthusiasm for the subject to be taught
2   the ability to keep control of classes
3   patience in dealing with pupils
4   the ability to use a variety of teaching methods
5   detailed knowledge of the subject to be taught
6   clear diction
7   sympathy for the problem of pupils
8   punctuality
9   teaching from material prepared in advance of lessons
10 willingness to participate in extra-curriculum activities.

Some of these shifted position a little in the priorities of teachers at the end of their probationary year, but on the whole the rankings remained the same. Perceptions such as these, and views on the quality of their training, need to be read alongside judgements on the training while it is in progress, and on the performance of teachers in their first year of service. The best source of these is Quality in Schools, the report of a survey of initial teacher training carried out by HMI, and The New Teacher in School, the report of the survey of newly appointed teachers referred to above. As a general conclusion, the latter report found that the majority had been well trained and had been given teaching programmes which put to good use their skills and knowledge. Their most common weaknesses lay in the assessment of pupils' work and in the matching of teaching methods and materials to the pupils' needs, particularly where there was a wide range of ability of cultural background. It is perhaps significant that Quality in Schools, which reports on teacher-training in the period 1983-5, also identified the two weaknesses referred to above. In respect of secondary training courses it had this to say:

> Only about half the institutions were dealing effectively with the assessment of pupils' progress. ... Only about half the subject method courses in either BEd or PGCE were providing students with an understanding of the variety of individual pupils' needs or helping them to make the teaching of their subject relevant to the full range of pupils they would meet.

These observations are singled out here from what in general are favourable reports because taken together they represent a very important dimension of the secondary teacher's task: to assess according to well-informed criteria a pupil's achievement at any given point, and to teach to that assessment, taking account of the pupil's individual needs and knowing the methods and materials that will best serve them. This is a feature of the teacher's work that is going to become even more important. The report of the Task Group on Assessment and Testing recommends a complex system of assessment and moderation, closely related to practice in the classroom.[7] One of its recommendations alone has far-reaching implications for the training of the teacher: 'We recommend that a mixture of standardized assessment instruments including tests, practical tasks, and observations be used in the national assessment system in order to minimize curriculum distortion'. We could go on exemplifying at length to illustrate the central argument. The needs of secondary schools, and the skills required of their teachers, have always been many and complex. They are going to become more so, and the changes will mean radically modifying some long-established practices and developing new ones. And what happens in schools will have to be reflected in the way teachers are trained.

What is the situation in which teacher-training institutions find themselves, and how are they to meet these demands? Apart from a relatively small number of specialist subjects, all initial training for secondary teaching is now conducted by way of postgraduate certificate courses (PGCE), and 61 per cent of these are provided by university departments of education. In 1983 the White Paper <u>Teaching Quality</u> had reflected the advice of ACSET that the Secretary of State should establish criteria which he would consider when deciding on the approval of initial teacher training courses.[8] On further advice from the same source the Secretary of State decided to set up a Council for the Accreditation of Teachers (CATE) to advise him on this approval process. The Chairman of the Council was Professor William Taylor, an intelligent and far-sighted appointment, and the vigour with which that body has pursued its work needs no recounting here. The criteria to which CATE works, published in DES Circular 3/84 could be seen taking shape well before they appeared there.[9] As long ago as 1982 in a speech at Durham University, Sir Keith Joseph, at that time Secretary of State, flagged some concerns that eventually formed up into criteria. He focused on selection procedures, on the content of courses, and on the need for lecturers to refresh their experience of teaching in schools: 'I want to ensure that every teacher of pedagogy is a practitioner with as much recent experience as possible in the classroom'. And the substance of what became the criteria was also to be found in <u>Teaching in Schools: The Content of Initial Training</u>, an HMI discussion paper which was issued in 1983.[10] The succession of documents filled out, some would say alarmingly, the inventory of what should be in a teacher-training course if its products were to be properly equipped to do their job.

As far as secondary courses go, the difficulty is an obvious one from the start. Given that a minimum of fifteen weeks of a PGCE course must be spent in schools, how is everything to be encompassed in the remaining weeks, which are nominally twenty-one but in practice are commonly rather fewer? Obviously the major concerns of the course find root and expression in school-based work, but there is the question of specific study within the institution itself. There are few who would argue for short discrete units, each handling one of the issues. The assumption is rather that they should be 'contextualized', finding expression in such major elements of the course as subject method. Those who do the job are the only ones who know how difficult this is to achieve without carefully organized support within the institution. The subject method tutor has a major task on hand to equip the students in so short a time with all that they need to become good teachers of the subject. And yet it must be acknowledged that the students will feel most confident in taking account of these wider professional issues when they are presented in the context of the subject, and are seen as an essential aspect of the teaching of it. This points to the need for members of staff with a designated responsibility to advise and work alongside colleagues within subject method courses at appropriate times. There are institutions which still do not even relate education studies and subject method courses, for example, in any systematic way. It is left to the student to draw the links. Coherence between the different strands and elements of a teacher-training course remains a major priority. Only in this way will students be assured of the importance and relevance of all the features of their training. In every generation of teachers in training there is a large body of impatience with education studies, which in the minds of many appears to lack practical value. This is a false view of a key element in the preparation of a teacher, and no teacher-training course can be seen as successful where the students see it that way. Some of the most successful practice is found where education study tutors as well as subject method tutors work alongside students in the schools, relating theory to practice at all points.

In many teacher-training courses at least half the time is spent in schools, in a combination of weekly attachments and block practice, or in such patterns as three days a week in schools for almost the whole duration of the course. Classroom experience has to meet very high expectations on the part of student, institution, and school, and it can generate as many strains as opportunities. For the students it is that part of the course where they realize themselves as teachers, and where they expect to acquire classroom skills and confidence. For the tutor it is the proving ground, where everything the course has to offer takes practical shape. The school has its own expectations, which can be a source of support and illumination to the student or one of undermining discouragement. Unless mutual understanding between institution and school is kept at a continuously high level, the student will be the point at which the friction is most acutely felt. The tutors need to know the school and the department thoroughly, to share its aspirations, and to be confident that the student is likely to see the teaching of his or her subject at its best. The school staff, for their part, need to understand the overall objectives of the course, and the specific objectives of any part of school experience, and they should share some aspects of the planning of it with tutors and students. There is a long history of concern for closer involvement of teachers in the training process. As long ago as 1971 the NUT, in its policy statement The Reform of Teacher Education, advocated teacher-tutor and dual appointment schemes, saying that 'the involvement of the practitioner in the education of those who are to enter the teaching profession is the keystone to a new approach to teacher education'. A year later the James Report envisaged a scale of involvement through which 'the teaching profession of this country would have a share in training its own members and establishing its own standards which would be almost certainly greater than that enjoyed anywhere in the world'.[11] In 1977, Education in Schools: A Consultative Document called for 'a policy for much greater exchange of teachers between schools and colleges so that each has a better understanding of the other's role'.[12] And we have already referred to the resolve of the then Secretary of State in 1982 to refresh the classroom experience of teacher-training lecturers. A lot had already been achieved before CATE began its work, and the pace of development has accelerated since then. It is now fairly standard practice for teachers to be involved in the selection and assessment of students, consulted in the planning of courses, invited to become teacher-tutors, and so on. The IT-INSET project disseminated some valuable thinking, and certain institutions have given a particularly strong lead. The most successful practice recognizes that simply putting students into schools for longer periods of time will not necessarily and of itself bring about improvement in their performance. Unless the partnership is properly conceived there is the danger that students will encounter bad or indifferent models rather than the best. And there is surely little to be said for the argument that since this reflects the reality in schools, the students should be exposed to the whole range during their training. Quite the contrary. They should emerge from the formative stage with a clear picture of what can be achieved in teaching at its best. They should have their horizons extended, and this means that only the best practitioners in the schools should be involved in their training. The LEA adviser should be involved in this process, advising the tutors on good practice in the schools, supporting the teachers in their developing role, and contributing to the students' training in such elements as subject method courses.

It is now taken for granted, at least in the utterance if not in the fulfilment, that the professional development of the teacher should occupy the whole span of his or her career. The first stage of this long journey is the induction process, to which every LEA is in principle committed. In practice it is not what it might be. In a survey conducted in 1982-3 it became clear that few probationers can count on being released from their classrooms for the kind of time that is needed to continue their training and to build up confidence by sharing their experience with others.[13] It is now common for young teachers to be pitched straight into teaching GCSE courses based on 100 per cent course work which generate complex tasks of setting and assessing assignments. This is only one example of a variety of demands for which their initial training may not have fully prepared them, and which become the concern of those responsible for induction. It is equally important to recognize that these newly qualified teachers have a great deal to offer their schools from the outset. The local authority and the schools themselves should not only provide them with support but also take full advantage of the ideas and enthusiasm they bring with them. There is no doubt that many of the young people entering teaching are impressive in their qualities of personality, their commitment, and their resilience. The institutions from which they come have selected them well and have sustained their motivation through a training process which demands a lot and of which a lot is demanded. We owe them a great deal.

NOTES AND REFERENCES

1   DES, Aspects of Secondary Education in England, London, HMSO, 1979.
2   DES, Teacher Training and the Secondary School, London, DES, 1981.
3   HMI, The New Teacher in School, HMI Series: Matters for Discussion 15, London, HMSO, 1982; DES, Better Schools, Cmnd 9469, London, HMSO, 1985; HMI, Education Observed 3: Good Teachers, London, DES, 1985; HMI, Quality in Schools: The Initial Training of Teachers, London, HMSO, 1987.
4   HMI, 1982, op. cit.
5   G. Bernbaum, H. Patrick, and K. Reid, The Structure

and Process of Initial Teacher Education within Universities in England and Wales, University of Leicester School of Education, mimeo, 1982.

6   HMI, 1987, op. cit.
7   DES, National Curriculum: Task Group on Assessment and Testing: A Report, London, HMSO, 1988.
8   DES, Teaching Quality, Cmnd 8836, London, HMSO, 1983.
9   DES, Initial Teacher Training: Approval of Courses, Circular 3/84, London, HMSO, 1984.
10 DES, Teaching in Schools: The Content of Initial Training, HMI Discussion paper, London, DES, 1983.
11 DES, Teacher Education and Training, James Report, London, HMSO, 1972.
12 DES, Education in Schools: A Consultative Document, London, HMSO, 1977.
13 Survey of Local Authority Arrangements for Induction and In-Service Training of teachers (the INIST survey) Conducted by the DES, 1982-3.

5

EXPERIENCE OF PROBLEMS RELATIVE TO CURRICULUM CONTINUITY AND SCHOOL TRANSFER IN TEACHER-TRAINING COURSES

Brian T. Gorwood

In his opening address to the 1986 UCET conference, David Hargreaves, then ILEA's chief inspector, speculated on aspects of initial preparation he would wish to pursue more vigorously were he to return to a teacher-training institution. Among some five or six matters for attention he suggested school transfer and curriculum continuity as presenting particular cause for concern. He implied that transfer from primary to secondary schooling was the cause of something more than transitory disruption. Within teacher-training courses, the problem should be addressed and ways sought to effect some improvement. It would seem that two issues need to be explored: the impact of school transfer on a child's total educational experience and the potential for improvement in school transfer procedures and curriculum continuity of more attention being given to these issues in teacher-training courses.

SCHOOL TRANSFER PROBLEMS

Disaffection from school is a mainly secondary phenomenon. Does it follow therefore that transfer from primary school must be potentially hazardous? Delamont and Galton argue that school transfer produces only very temporary problems for nearly all children. The difficulties which pupils experience are, within a very few weeks 'schooling problems' not 'transfer problems'.[1] Yet, for a sizeable minority, school problems become manifest because secondary schools are so different from primaries. A main cause of some pupils' persistent truancy, it is claimed, is inability to adjust to the internal organization within comprehensive schools. Disturbed by having to move classrooms and change teachers every lesson, they feel less attached to their secondary than their primary school and opt out of education.[2] It can be argued that the majority of pupils make the transition from primary to secondary schooling successfully. Several researchers, but most notably Youngman and Lunzer, have pointed out that something like 70 per cent of new secondary school pupils are very happy with their change of school.[3] However, 10 per cent of pupils actively dislike secondary schooling, showing serious disturbance long after transfer. At least half the pupils display some anxiety for a shorter period. Nor is this solely a British problem. Studies in other parts of the world suggest a growing international awareness of a relationship between school transition problems and alienation from schooling.[4] Attainment, too, can deteriorate after transfer. During their primary schooling, children in the ORACLE study made continuous progress. After transfer, not only were average levels of progress a good deal lower than they were during the primary years:

> but for the first time substantial numbers of pupils made losses in absolute terms, that is, they achieved lower scores in the tests of basic skills at the end of their first year in the transfer school than they had at the end of their last year in the feeder school.[5]

Evidence from several studies suggests antipathy towards education and under-achievement by at least a quarter of the pupils in first-year secondary classes. Even if this is merely a manifestation of the 'humpback bridge' effect suggested by Stead and Sudworth, it is a matter of grave concern.[6] For some pupils, however, after the transfer 'humpback', adjustment to a different set of conditions is never achieved. Although social and psychological circumstances underlie many of the problems of secondary schooling, there are also educational and institutional factors. Too often, ascription of difficulties to pupils' poor home backgrounds and low ability leads to abrogation of responsibility for trying to rectify institutional and organizational failures. Many teachers have, of course, made valiant attempts to respond to exhortations in recent documents to improve transition between schools but their efforts have been mainly confined to smoothing the passage of pupils from one institution to another. Strategies to alleviate the trauma of transfer are undoubtedly easier to devise and put into effect than those concerned with achieving the long-term aim of curriculum continuity. In addition, by seeming to confine the problem to a narrow age-band around the transfer divide, they lead to the fallible notion that continuity can be left to a few teachers concerned with the transfer age-range. It is the contention of this writer that the achievement of educational continuity should be an important aim of all teachers.

DISCONTINUITIES

The importance of seeking continuity between educational institutions is not accepted universally. Indeed, there are those who argue that discontinuities are beneficial. Disturbance associated with a sharp break is functional in promoting personal and social development. It marks a 'going out' and a 'coming in' from one stage of life to another.[7] There are pupils who are stimulated by a new environment, new subjects, a different system of organization, and changes in teaching style. 'Discontinuity', if such is the proper term for this phenomenon, may thus help promote maturation. Though change of school may benefit those of average and above-average ability, its effect on some pupils has been shown in study after study to be quite harmful. Particularly at risk are children from deprived backgrounds and those of low ability.[8]

Discontinuity is scarcely acceptable even on grounds of pupil development but it can never be justified merely because it is difficult to resolve. Yet that seems to be the position taken by some educationalists. Marland has commented that attempts to create a close liaison between educational institutions can consume considerable time to little effect.[9] Several local authorities, while accepting that lack of continuity is a cause for concern, make little attempt at improvement because there are more pressing issues to absorb their slender resources.[10] The Isle of Wight study by Stillman and Maychell revealed several constraints to liaison. Most teachers supported the theoretical ideal but many found it to be impossible. Their reluctance to become involved in inter-sector continuity has been explained by the researchers as being rooted in 'attitudes generated by sector hierarchy, poor experience of the other sector, and professional isolation'.[11]

TEACHER COMMUNICATION

Continuity cannot be achieved entirely by LEA or central government fiat; it must involve communication between teachers in different phases of schooling. An atmosphere of suspicion, lack of knowledge, and misconceptions can make such communication difficult. Tension between teachers in different phases of education was evident from my own research into transfer between middle and upper schools at age 13. Teachers in the receiving schools complained that the unity of secondary courses had been impaired by having an inadequate start in the pre-transfer school to what was essentially a five-year course. Contributory schools argued they were being used as a convenient scapegoat for upper-school deficiencies. Seldom was censure based on evidence. An upper-school head of department's assertion that many middle schools lacked teachers with a qualification higher than O level in their subjects had clearly not been tested and was, in fact, inaccurate. A middle school's complaint that upper schools 'totally ignored the fact that a common core had been devised in several areas of the curriculum' was supported by nothing more than random comments by past pupils.[12] As Becher and Maclure have commented, 'any attempt to provide continuity between the primary and secondary curriculum, if it is to be at all successful, must include deliberate steps to bring teachers and practices closer together'.[13]

It is understandable that attitudes and practices vary. Apart from their actual contact with pupils, teachers from different phases of education have little in common. The task of the sixth-form teacher is so unlike that of the teacher of an infant intake class that it would be foolish to look for similarities in their ways of working: the one is concerned to introduce students to knowledge in a very narrow field; the other deals with the total spectrum of learning and the child's personal and social development. But to justify 'secondary' and 'primary' modes of learning on the basis of such extremes is unreasonable. As Lady Plowden found, stereotyped attitudes as to appropriate learning in different phases of schooling can lead to marked discontinuities during the middle years:

> In the early stages of working on the Report, I found myself baffled by the difference between what the experts were calling the Primary and Secondary way of

learning. I could not see, in the development of the child, that there was a place for this distinction. But I am now clear in my own mind that there is a difference between the two extremes, in the same way that there is a difference in temperature between 32 degrees and 80 degrees. This difference does not, however, imply any rapid transition. There is not a particular point in time, to continue the analogy, when 60 degrees is cold and 61 degrees is hot. Equally, there is not a moment when it is time for a secondary as opposed to a primary type of education. I think I now see the secondary way of learning as being a study in depth in a limited field. But there must be a gradual transition to this way of learning.[14]

MIDDLE SCHOOLS

At the time of its publication, it was thought the Plowden Report heralded an era of improved continuity practice. One of the reasons advanced for the development of middle schools was their potential for achieving a smooth transition from primary to secondary modes of working. In reality these schools have seldom created a bridge between phases. There are organizational and administrative reasons for this - reasons concerned with optimum size and suitable facilities - but the main cause lies in staffing. In the early years, teachers were recruited to middle schools from primary or secondary schools. They brought with them two cultural inheritances which tended to create an organizational hiatus; there was 'a strong degree of phase match between the training and previous experience of middle school teachers on the one hand and the current age range which they taught within middle schools on the other'.[15]
Middle schools were thought by several educationalists to offer unequalled opportunities for improving curriculum continuity and transfer practice. But when these schools were being developed in the late 1960s and early 1970s, headteachers had to create a new philosophy within which continuity appeared as but one of many matters to be resolved. If they turned to the meagre literature then being published they found no consensus on middle-school orientations. Some advocates proposed an extension of primary schooling; others suggested these schools should avoid too close an alignment with previous practice. After Plowden's belated and tentative recommendation that

transfer should take place at 8 and 12 there was a lack of unanimity about age ranges and ethos for middle schools. Those pressing for a transitional school presented but one of several opinions about what such schools should be trying to achieve. Even when headteachers were convinced of the importance of promoting continuity by means of middle schools they were often defeated by organizational difficulties. The move from general to semi-specialist teaching that was being advocated could work, it seemed, only in generously staffed small schools or those so large that young pupils would find them uninviting.

TRAINING FOR MIDDLE-SCHOOL TEACHING

Middle schools were beset, too, by problems of 'phase match': lower schools were organized along primary lines while upper schools were secondary in orientation. As more probationers graduated from initial teacher-training (ITT) courses specifically designed to serve middle schools, it was thought such problems would be resolved. A new breed of teachers imbued with neither primary nor secondary ideologies would perceive their task as principally concerned with ensuring pupils progressed through an educational continuum. With a few notable exceptions, however, ITT courses labelled 'middle school' offered little that was new. They tended to be an amalgam of elements taken from existing primary and secondary courses and were more inspirational than practical. Students enjoined to consider the bridging function of middle schools were taught by college staff who reflected phase differentiation: primary tutors to proselytize for child-centredness and secondary lecturers whose main interest was in subject teaching. Their first appointment as qualified teachers could well place them in a middle school organized so as to make each year group autonomous, for that was the favoured strategy to promote semi-specialist teaching. As Professor Ross and his middle years of schooling research team found in the mid-1970s, curricular planning could be contained within each year group with very little communication between teachers in the various years.[16] Ten years later, Jennifer Nias reported on middle-school pupils 'enclosed in their own bases and literally shut off from the rest of the school'.[17] What chance continuity between institutions if it cannot be achieved within them! Staff in the early middle schools with primary or secondary experience who looked to newly qualified middle-trained colleagues to help them develop a transitional approach received little support, for their ITT courses had probably addressed the issue superficially, if at all.

Inertia in the educational system in Britain usually allows teacher-training institutions to anticipate new developments. Many years may elapse from original concept to implementation, as ROSLA and GCSE exemplify. The first middle schools existed, however, before the educational community had had time to assess implications of their development. Understandably in the early days of middle schools, teacher-training institutions found it difficult to prepare students adequately for a school existing more as a theoretical ideal than as a practical reality. By the time colleges could recruit middle-school practitioners to run courses, many of the hopes for these schools, including their potential for improving continuity, had been found to be impracticable because of inadequate resourcing and falling rolls.

During the late 1960s and early 1970s, at the time when issues relating to transfer and continuity were receiving considerable attention with the heightened interest in middle years pupils, colleges of education in England were faced with an immense number of organizational and structural problems.[18] The development of the BEd degree, intervention by Secretary of State Short to require teaching-training institutions to examine their practices, the James Report followed by the 1972 White Paper, and Circular 7/73 setting out government intentions that there should be a major reconsideration of the future role of colleges of education both in and outside teacher-training: all kept college staff heavily involved in committee work and activities far removed from the planning of course content. There was little time to devise courses to take account of what was, in any case, a theoretical rather than a practical concept: a school essentially concerned to provide a gradual progression from the young child's general learning to the secondary pupil's disciplined study. Middle-years courses were often extant primary courses with an occasional excursion into what had hitherto been secondary territory. Not enough bona-fide middle-years courses were developed in teacher-training institutions and so was lost an opportunity to make curriculum continuity an issue of import at the very start of a teacher's career.

DIFFERENCES IN PHASE TRAINING

The 'professional isolation' cited by Stillman and Maychell as a major influence making it difficult for teachers to enter into inter-sector continuity discussions has its roots in initial teacher-training. The majority of secondary school teachers have qualified by the PGCE/university route while most primary teachers have followed a BEd or certificate course located in a college. It would be inappropriate here to examine in detail differences between these two patterns of training. Nor should it be implied that a more uniform approach would be in the best interests of the education service. Manifestly the specialist knowledge required to teach at advanced secondary level generates different ITT demands from that required in dealing with young children. It should be recognized, however, that the more extreme the differences between primary and secondary training, the more difficult will it be for teachers from the two phases to communicate about their common task. This issue is embedded in the values of teacher education, a theme considered in depth in Professor Taylor's seminal work, <u>Society and the Education of Teachers</u>. The teacher of the young child is concerned with socialization rather than simply instruction.

> A diffuse commitment of this kind is best secured if the teacher's task is not defined in a functionally specific manner as the communication of a certain amount of knowledge and skill, but in terms of relationships between teachers and pupils; in the jargon of the trade, as a child-centred rather than a subject-centred activity.

Emphasis of this kind permeates the college course throughout its three or four years. In contrast, most graduate teachers will have spent three years in a university academic department before moving on to an education department. During those three years, they will have been exposed to somewhat different value orientations of 'affective neutrality, self-orientation, universalism, achievement and specificity'.[19] The teacher's subsequent classroom behaviour and attitudes are likely to reflect these values. Such rigid delineation of primary and secondary schooling in terms of the higher education and training of teachers takes no account of college-trained secondary teachers or university graduates who elect to teach in primary schools. It is, however, sufficiently indicative of differences in the underlying philosophies of primary and secondary schooling to call into question attitudes which developed during the period of initial training.

COMMON FEATURES OF SCHOOLING

It is axiomatic that primary and secondary schools are different yet in their essential features they are the same. The qualities that Rutter identified as having an influence on secondary pupils' attainments, attendance, and behaviour could apply as well to primary schools: 'Children benefit from attending schools which set good standards, where the teachers provide good models of behaviour, where they are praised and given responsibility, where the general conditions are good and where the lessons are well-conducted.'[20] Similar criteria are used to assess students on teaching practice whether they are in primary or secondary schools. Tutors look for careful preparation of lessons and classrooms in advance, for pupils' active learning, and for a well-ordered environment. The accountability to which teachers are to be subjected in the future will, one assumes, be on the basis of the same standards whether they teach in primary or secondary schools. Wherein, then, lie the differences that generate continuity problems?

BETTER SCHOOLS

The White Paper Better Schools specifies 'areas of substantial weakness in an unacceptably large proportion of schools'. Most of these weaknesses involve curricular issues different in nature between primary and secondary schools. In the primary phase, we are told:

> Many pupils do not appreciate sufficiently the need to exercise such vital qualities as rigour and perseverance. This is partly because teachers do not always insist that pupils should adequately understand the essentials of an area of learning and partly because they underestimate their pupils' potential.[21]

The White Paper acknowledges that primary teachers have to manage a broad curriculum but it urges them to ensure there is 'necessary differentiation'. Clearly the government

79

considers subjects per se should be given greater prominence in primary schools, as has been urged by HMI for almost a decade.[22] Secondary teachers, according to Better Schools, have 'inadequate knowledge and understanding of pupils' individual aptitudes and difficulties'. They direct pupils' work too often, giving them unimaginative work to do. The perceived extreme contrast between the different phases is illustrated by the statement that 'Pupils need more opportunities to learn for themselves, to express their own views and to develop their own ideas through discussion'.[23] How far removed most current secondary practice is from the primary school's encouraging pupils 'to learn by active participation rather than by the passive reception of facts and rote learning'.[24]

CHILD-CENTRED AND SUBJECT-CENTRED EDUCATION

Better Schools seems to be saying that secondary teachers do not know enough about children and primary teachers have an inadequate subject base from which to work. This is hardly an original notion. It is redolent of child-versus-subject-centredness which has been debated for decades. Of recent studies, Alexander's provides the most comprehensive appraisal of this issue. He argues: 'no amount of anti-subject rhetoric at primary level can disguise the fact that the primary teacher operates within curriculum areas sufficiently distinct to merit the term "subjects".'[25] He cites several curriculum projects which demonstrate how 'cultural, epistemological and psychological considerations can be reconciled to produce curriculum experiences which are meaningful and valid by both "adult" and "child-centred" criteria.' Despite the child-centred objection to subjects because they are seen as 'adult' concepts, projects such as Science 5-13, MACOS and Man in Place, Time and Society preserve the key features of the ways of knowing but define these features in 'process' rather than 'content' terms. The skills-based approach at the core of these projects is as acceptable to child-centred theorists as it is to advanced workers in the disciplines concerned.

Few schools, however, make much use of structured curriculum projects.[26] Indeed, many seem not to have made much use of curriculum planning (except in the basic subjects) as the White Paper attests:

A weakness found to a greater or lesser degree in about

three-quarters of primary and middle schools is in curriculum planning and its implementation. Curricular guidelines exist for English and mathematics in about three-quarters of the schools but they frequently do not extend to other important elements of the curriculum, and often do not make explicit the different approaches to learning, and the increasing demands which are needed as children progress through the school.[27]

For a government concerned to raise educational standards quickly, lack of adequate curriculum guidelines in primary schools is intolerable. Teachers who see their task in terms of children learning how to learn are unlikely to develop strong subject commitment or to spend much effort in thinking through curricular issues in terms currently preferred by the DES. If the emphasis is to be changed, if there is to be a stronger infusion in primary schools of the kind of subject study hitherto in the purview of the secondary sector, then the government considers radical measures to be needed.

SUBJECT STUDY IN PRIMARY COURSES

The change agent is to be the ITT course:

Each new primary schoolteacher should be equipped to take a responsibility for one aspect of the curriculum (such as science, mathematics or music), to act as a consultant to colleagues on that aspect, and to teach it to classes other than their own.[28]

Eventually the dominance of class teaching in primary schools will be eroded if the government pursues this aim. In tandem with the ITT initiative, in-service training is to be used to widen the expertise available in schools so that science and mathematics specialists can balance present over-weighting towards the humanities and aesthetic subjects. A primary school with staff competent to teach the full curricular range should be able to offer something more than class teaching. The White Paper clearly sees this as having a powerful influence on continuity for, in the paragraph concerned with transition from the primary to the secondary phase, it states:

In the Government's view, older pupils in the primary

phase should begin to be systematically introduced to teaching by members of staff with expertise in an area of the curriculum other than that which the class teacher can offer.[29]

Though there are continuity implications in what the government recommends for secondary schools, there is nothing as radical as that suggested for the primary sector. Secondary schools are afforded a mere homily:

> The 11-16 curriculum should continue the work of the primary phase in developing personal qualities and attitudes, consolidating pupils' understanding of the values and foundations of British society, and fostering social and study skills.[30]

There is a modest call for a possible change in practice in the first year after transfer when there should be delay in exposing pupils to 'the full range of individual specialist teaching' but there is little to disquiet the secondary teacher. For the primary teacher a gradual change in working situation is envisaged. In addition to undertaking the role of class teacher, those who elect to work in primary schools will have to have the ability and enthusiasm 'to share specialist knowledge with fellow teachers as well as with pupils'.[31] In effect, they will add the advisory teacher role to what they have been accustomed to doing in the past.

ADVISORY ROLE FOR PRIMARY TEACHERS

Advocacy of the advisory teacher mode of curriculum organization can only be based on a hope that it will be effective. What little research there is into this mode of working is inconclusive. It seems to suggest, however, that success depends more on the compatible personalities of givers and receivers of advice than on the availability of subject expertise. Hargreaves asked staff in one of his research middle schools to comment on the influence of their colleagues. Some welcomed helpful guidance but others, mainly the more experienced, clung to their own highly valued sense of independence and autonomy.[32] Though some middle schools have developed a collaborative community in which collegial discussion is the main influence on curricular matters, there is little to suggst that this approach is common in primary schools. Headteachers are the main source of advice on curriculum in the primary sector; despite pressure, mainly from HMI, for over a decade the 'consultant teacher' is little in evidence. Indeed, as Alexander suggests, there may be resistance by headteachers to the very notion of consultation:

> In primary schools the heads, as creators of the philosophy and keepers of the whole curriculum, may regard themselves as the supreme exemplars of such curriculum expertise, and thus the only true curriculum 'consultants'. To argue that class teachers' curriculum needs should be met by other class teachers is thus a fairly considerable threat to heads cast in this mould.[33]

NEED FOR INTERPERSONAL SKILLS

The current strategy of strengthening the subject knowledge of students on initial teacher-training courses is but one aspect of the response to improving continuity and progression. If that subject expertise is to permeate the work of primary schools there will have to be changes in organization but equally important will be the fostering of interpersonal skills needed to influence colleagues. Most primary teachers are concerned almost exclusively with what happens in their own classrooms leaving colleagues to themselves to teach in their particular style and often according to their own notions of the way to deal with curriculum material. A recent series of visits to primary schools has convinced me that autonomy is still the order of the day. In one school, the approach to that curricular area concerned with human beings in place, time, and society provides an extreme example of the issue. Pupils in one class were engaged in thematic work on 'war'; in another they were studying wheatlands of the world. Under another teachers' guidance pupils were conducting surveys of traffic movement, shopping facilities, and recreational possibilities while pupils in a parallel class were using archival material in a study of local history. Lessons on 'war' and 'wheatlands' were essentially content-based and class-taught, the teachers concerned providing most of the information. In contrast, other children working mainly in groups or individually were engaged in enquiry, their teachers being mainly interested in skill development. The teachers accepted that their attitudes were different. The 'expert' in this field strongly disagreed with the way his colleagues were teaching but had had no success in persuading them to change. The head justified a 'laissez-faire' approach on grounds of individual autonomy and his belief that teachers would complement each other in the long run.

RECRUITMENT TO ITT COURSES

Recent government proposals are aimed at strengthening the subject base in primary schools but there is a pressing need to unlock extant expertise. In the near future INSET primary management courses could be influential in changing attitudes and affecting organizational change but in the longer term initial training institutions need to consider how their practice should be modified to accommodate and perhaps even induce change in the primary teacher's role. 'Training institutions should recruit people with ability and enthusiasm to share specialist knowledge with fellow teachers'.[34] Better School's injunction sounds deceptively simple. How can a training institution discern such a quality in applicants? The existence of teachers competent in their subjects, at ease in the presence of pupils but discomfited in interaction with colleagues, suggests that the potential for collaborative or advisory roles has been given low priority in the past. There is, then, a task for course selectors: to attempt an appraisal of a student's likelihood of being imbued with enthusiasm not only for a subject but also for counselling colleagues in its principles and practices. In reviewing procedures for assessing the professional potential, academic competence, and personal qualities of candidates -as the White Paper Teaching Quality requires them so to do - institutions should consider innovative practice of the kind reported by the late Anne Trown.[35] Although of necessity sketchily outlined in a short report, one strategy within an experimental selection day's programme seems to test for the kind of interpersonal qualities needed in a consultancy/advisory role. Candidates were involved in a group activity described as 'a "survival" exercise in which individual priorities are set forth and a group consensus eventually arrived at'. One candidate's response when asked what this revealed suggested:

> This exercise was aimed at revealing social skills, in particular techniques of amicable persuasion, constructive discussion/planning, decision making, a

group interpersonal communication. It also showed how a person reacted to rejection of his/her ideas and opposition.[36]

Traditional approaches to interviewing reported by Dr Trown place little emphasis on discerning qualities of the kind essential in influencing colleagues. Little use is made, either, of standardized tests, those in charge of courses holding 'far more faith in their own, in their colleagues' and in schoolteachers' abilities to tease relevant attributes reliably from among the subtleties of the personal interview'.[37]

'Good working relationships with colleagues are essential for all teachers, for professionalism in teaching is a collective matter, to a degree not always required of other professions.'[38] HMI's acknowledgement of the centrality of teachers' relationships with colleagues in considering professional issues is not reflected in courses of initial teacher-training. Some institutions make use of co-operative projects and encourage group discussion but such practices are by no means general. The need to ascertain individual achievement in a classroom BEd degree and the relative shortness of PGCE courses militates against group activities. But it would seem important for students on initial teacher-training courses to be given more opportunities of group tasks in which they have to defend their own curricular approach. To experience the to-and-fro of curricular planning discussion during training would be excellent preparation for collegiality not only within but also between schools.[39]

EXCESSIVE CONTENT IN ITT COURSES

There is too much to pack into courses of initial teacher-training. Professional preparation, once concerned almost exclusively with subjects to be taught, now has to address cross-curricular concerns: the needs of slow learners, of the very able, and of those from ethnic minorities have to be satisfied. A course cannot be deemed satisfactory unless it attends to relations with industry and the community, to gender issues and to the promotion of economic awareness. Matters relating to curriculum continuity and school transfer have to compete with many other topics for a place in course programmes. As a respondent to my recent survey of teacher-training institutions comments:

The problem of curriculum continuity and transition from one phase to another is one which we have neglected to our shame in our PGCE course. It is one facet of the perennial problem of how to find a place for everything that demands to be let in.

And despite the acknowledged importance of this issue, the likelihood of much more time being devoted to it seems fairly remote, as another respondent affirms: 'We anticipate that with the pressure of the CATE criteria, particularly on the primary BEd, we will be less able to give attention to this issue.'

RESULTS OF A SURVEY OF ITT INSTITUTIONS

The survey of ITT institutions was based on an open invitation to supply information about ways in which students preparing to teach in one phase of education were made aware of approaches to curriculum and different modes of working in another phase. Fifty responses were received from seventy institutions circulated. With a few notable exceptions, institutions admitted to doing very little about school transfer and curriculum continuity. The following give some indication of the kinds of comments from about a quarter of those replying:

- Curriculum continuity is unhappily a somewhat neglected area;
- The topic is not addressed directly in our PGCE course;
- Almost nothing is done about secondary curriculum in our primary course;
- Our course does not deal explicitly with this issue though the subject is embraced in a number of course elements.

A larger group, though accepting that minimal specific attention is given to issues relating to transfer and continuity, maintains that they are considered within a broader framework. A typical response of this kind observes:

School transfer matters receive some modest attention: for example in the contexts of home/school communication and of arguments for a national curriculum framework. They are referred to in lectures and figure in seminar discussions. Curriculum continuity bulks larger in our work. It arises in the context of work on child development; arguments for a national curriculum framework; language in education issues; consideration of relationships between TVEI, CPVE and YTS; tertiary college developments; and detailed work on the curriculum 5-19. These, too, arise in lectures and seminars.

A feature mentioned in several replies from those training for the secondary sector is that continuity may be dealt with disparately by different subject tutors:

> Our maths group are probably more aware of continuity issues than other method areas. They spend much of their serial practice in middle schools prior to continuous practice in a secondary comprehensive.

The reason for different importance being given to continuity according to subject is not clear. It may relate to the linear structure of some disciplines; it may, however, be more a feature of interest being taken by an individual member of staff:

> Chemistry students are exposed to curriculum continuity - probably because the lecturer concerned was heavily involved in Science 5-13.

SECONDARY TRAINEES' EXPERIENCE OF PRIMARY SCHOOLING

Most courses of secondary training start off with some involvement in primary work but the extent of commitment varies widely. Some institutions merely suggest students should gain experience in a primary school near their home before joining a course. At the other extreme, a small number of UDEs and colleges make a primary phase an integral part of their secondary course. Typically students spend a short time in the institution being given essential preparation before going out into local schools for two or three weeks to engage in 'participatory observation'. After a brief period of observation, there is usually more active involvement as confidence is gained, and before the conclusion of the primary phase, students will probably have taken responsibility for the learning of one class or group of pupils. The college or department's tutors visit schools, providing the further advantage that they are exposed to schools with which they may be unfamiliar. Headteachers are often asked to submit a report, not so much to assess but rather to alert tutors to aspects of students' practice needing particular attention. A main aim of such experience is to sensitize students to the need for continuity, as one course handbook affirms:

> We need to pay more than lip service to the notion that education is a continuum. In making experience in primary school an integral part of initial training for those who will eventually teach older pupils, we acknowledge the need for teachers to recognise their contribution within the total span of a pupil's education.

PRIMARY TRAINEES' EXPERIENCE OF CONTINUITY

Secondary trainees, then, usually gain some experience of the primary sector within which they examine transition to secondary schooling. There is little evidence to suggest that intending primary teachers have a similar experience of secondary schooling. Within one primary BEd course, students spend only half a day in four years inside a secondary school and that as part of a general orientation to education in the first term. Course planners argue there is so much to cover when students have to become competent in their specialist subject study as well as the broad general primary curriculum that there is not time for consideration of secondary schooling, which would have to be dealt with so superficially as to be nugatory:

> Continuity and transfer, like special educational needs, multicultural awareness and gender issues, have to be subsumed in general work; they cannot be dealt with as discrete elements.

Yet there is surely a danger that assimilating such important aspects within a broad course framework will result in sparse attention being given to them or even their total neglect.

AGE-SPECIFIC TRAINING

The Secretary of State's inclination to introduce more rigid boundaries and distinctions between training patterns for different age ranges is advanced by some respondents as an influence on lack of reference to continuity in their courses. Though this is usually considered in relation to the primary-secondary divide, some institutions with an emphasis on training for upper-secondary teaching are beginning to meet problems. The demise of the traditional sixth form and the increasing use of colleges by over-16s accentuates another transfer barrier. One university department anticipates difficulties:

> Soon we shall be facing the issue of tertiary education in our locality and we are, at the moment, uncertain what the force of the DES ruling about age/specific training is in an area which has a strong tertiary sector.

Some of those training for a younger age-range have no doubts about the force of central authority 'advice'. 'We are only mandated to train for the primary age-range', one course co-ordinator explains as the reason for minimal reference to continuity. A head of teaching studies writes: 'Our initial training programmes are primary and the HMI directed us to discontinue the secondary component we had planned in the course.' It is right that students should have differential training on the basis of the age-ranges for which they intend to specialize but this should surely not be so constraining as to preclude any but superficial reference to other phases.[40] Surprisingly, even within the primary sector there can be an extremely narrow focus:

> Those on our nursery/infant programmes do not concern themselves specifically with what happens in the junior school. However, those preparing for work with seven-to-twelve-year-olds do pay some attention to what has gone before, particularly in the area of language development.

When HMI argued for sharp differentiation of phase specialism in the content of initial teacher-training courses they surely did not intend to encourage such a degree of exclusiveness.[41]

CROSS-PHASE AWARENESS

A favoured strategy for ensuring a cross-phase perspective

to educational issues is that of students from different courses being brought together on occasions. Some institutions apply this technique widely:

> For all on four-year BEd programmes (primary-early years; primary-later years; and secondary) 'professional perspectives' components in the final two years deliberately bring together students in the different age-range courses, where they explore issues at a common level whilst drawing on their particular experience and interests. Amongst other topics considered are: 'assessment'; 'tradition and change in education'; 'classroom research methods'; and 'equality'. Discussion groups are explicitly arranged to mix students. Lecturers overtly draw on material from different age-ranges for their exemplars.

In other institutions, students are involved in a day's joint study from time to time, such sessions often following periods of school experience when there are heightened perceptions of contrasting practice. In at least one polytechnic, intending secondary teachers and further education lecturers in training attend joint sessions specifically to consider the bridge between compulsory and post-compulsory education. Such procedures, of course, are possible only where training is not confined to a single phase.

ATTENTION TO CONTINUITY WITHIN COURSES

Transfer and continuity are studied in optional courses in some institutions, usually within a very broad framework in which only slight attention can be given to these issues. It is obviously worthwhile that they should receive modest consideration rather than none at all but the rationale for including reference to transition in a course needs careful consideration. One such course considers 'transfer problems' within the context of relationships outside school. Topics addressed include 'how to relate to parents and the community taking particular account of the multi-cultural dimension' and 'introducing industry and commerce into the primary curriculum'. Transition would be more appropriately considered as an 'in-school' issue rather than within a miscellany of 'beyond school' topics, no matter what their importance. Students opting for this course make visits to industrial organizations but not to schools 'since they have recent experience of secondary schooling and visit primary schools for practical work'. Justification for not taking students into secondary schools on grounds that they have only just left them seems inappropriate, particularly when matters relating to transition are under review. A pupil's idiosyncratic view of the school in which he or she was taught is surely an inadequate foundation for making generalizations. The following comment, typical of a few, suggests some future teachers will have intransigent attitudes unlikely to advance the cause of continuity:

> Students are very aware of the different approaches because of the contrast between the way they recall being taught and the way that they are taught to teach. We seem to have a significant number who have selected primary teaching because they do not approve of the way that they were taught in secondary school.

Stereotyped notions of poor practice at the other side of the transfer divide need to be countered rather than reinforced if future teachers are to engage in meaningful continuity arrangements. Research by Stillman and Maychell emphasizes the need for positive attitudes to be encouraged; responses to their Isle of Wight survey revealed that a certain amount of mistrust, especially of primary towards secondary colleagues was a deterrent to successful liaison.[42]

FUTURE PLANS

Several of those conceding that little is being done at present about continuity and transfer in their institutions assert the matter will receive much more attention as courses are redeveloped. In one university department currently redesigning initial teacher education provision, 'a feature of the new arrangements will be a programme of visits to institutions in sectors other than that (secondary) for which students are being chiefly prepared'. Another course revision, still in the planning stage, prefaces a list of objectives with an apposite extract from the HMI document, The Curriculum from 5 to 16:

> Continuity of learning ... is easier if both primary and secondary schools have an appreciation of what each

other is aiming to achieve both in general terms and in specific areas of the curriculum.[43]

There are indications, then, that school transfer and curriculum continuity will appear more prominently in future courses even if their delineation is, at the moment, somewhat sketchy. A director of postgraduate studies writes:

> I shall be retiring at the end of this year and it will become someone else's concern. I don't yet know the name of my successor but I intend to pass on to him or her my feelings about the need to include 'transition' as a regular component. Moreover, I intend to recommend that the students be asked to include a section on it in their school attachment files.

Despite glimpses of enlightened current and future practice, the impression gained from my survey is that the majority of ITT institutions do little to acquaint students with matters relating to transfer and continuity. One course leader's terse comment conveys this point:

> Our course does not deal explicitly with this issue though the subject is embraced in a number of course elements. ... I regret that I am unable to be more helpful - although the brevity of my reply may itself be useful data.

COMPLEMENTARY INSET COURSES

In the opinion of two respondents, this topic falls in the province of in-service rather than initial teacher-training. As Stillman and Maychell have observed, there is need for in-service support when putting curriculum policies into practice. Continuity may require redesigning of syllabuses and development of new courses; such complex activities demand thorough understanding of curriculum structures. Few teachers have experience of planning beyond their own schools and would benefit from in-service guidance to alert them to the main considerations.[44] But support of this kind profits from a firm foundation in appreciation of the issues involved having been laid during initial teacher-training. To use Joyce and Showers terminology, it is better to 'fine tune' existing competence than it is to master new teaching strategies or models.[45] Whatever the qualities needed to promote curriculum continuity, they cannot be acquired 'ab initio' on an in-service course. Most INSET courses are designed for a particular sector, so the bringing together of primary and secondary teachers on the same course can itself be quite an innovation. Further, the trend towards short INSET courses with a specific and sometimes quite narrow focus reduces potential to resolve problems at the heart of curriculum discontinuity. There is not enough time for teachers of different persuasion to reach an accommodation which will allow for the development of more effective practice. A participant in a recent LEA course aimed at improving liaison between primary and secondary schools makes the following telling comment:

> Our adviser seemed to think that by throwing thirty or forty of us together we should come up with solutions to problems the authority have found intractable. What we discovered was that there are deep-seated differences that are going to take a long time to resolve - and then only if resources are made available.

The best prospect for improved continuity must surely be to reduce differences between initial training courses so that future teachers will have a common base from which to work. INSET can then be properly used for 'fine tuning', which will always be needed.

RECENT GOVERNMENT INITIATIVES

The influence of Better Schools on courses of initial training has already been noted. The openly interventionist role of the DES in recent years is further witnessed in the 1983 White Paper, Teaching Quality, and the 1987 consultative document, The National Curriculum 5-16, both of which have profound implications for the way in which the issue of continuity is dealt with in teacher-training courses. On the advice of ACSET, the Secretary of State, in Teaching Quality, gave notice of intent to promulgate criteria against which courses would be assessed before deciding whether to approve them. Of the CATE criteria which resulted, that concerned with subject studies for primary teachers is likely to contribute significantly to the enhancement of specialist expertise in primary schools. The criterion states:

> The higher education and initial teacher training of all

intending teachers should include the equivalent of at least two years' course time devoted to subject studies at a level appropriate to higher education.

Though this has been subjected to astringent criticism,[46] it cannot be denied that future primary teachers should be able to approach curricular issues with a greater depth of specialist knowledge. The rationale for this criterion is stated first in terms of its effect on primary schools:

> Collectively, the staff of a primary school should command a range of subject specialisms covering as much as possible of the school curriculum. This does not imply the replacement of the class teacher by the specialist. It does mean that adequate specialist expertise in each aspect of the curriculum should, when required, be available.[47]

Weakness in curriculum planning in primary schools has already been noted as a contributory factor in impeding continuity. If implementation of the subject studies criterion results in a broadening and deepening of expertise, improved planning should surely effect improved continuity. A second objective for raising the level of primary teachers' specialist knowledge is declared as being to give a higher education experience that is 'both demanding and satisfying'. Intellectual autonomy needed for engaging in constructive debate develops over time but should, I maintain, be stimulated during higher education if primary teachers are to enter into dialogue as equal partners with secondary colleagues, who have studied a single subject in depth.

The government's consultation document on a national curriculum for pupils aged 5-16 was concerned primarily with raising standards. It also maintained that a national curriculum would:

> help children's progression within and between primary and secondary education (and on to further and higher education) and ... help to secure the continuity and coherence which is too often lacking in what they [children] are taught.[48]

The establishment of the national curriculum will undoubtedly have an ameliorative effect in regard to continuity but it will need to advance further into syllabus areas before the kind of coherence government is seeking can be assured. Of course, that increasing movement into course content may well be achieved by assessment procedures, for the regular testing of pupils 'against worthwhile attainment targets in all the essential foundation subjects' is a basic feature of the new proposals. Testing at 7, 11, 14, and 16 is intended to establish 'what children should normally be expected to know, understand and be able to do'. Further, subject working groups appointed by the Secretaries of State will have the task of working out 'programmes of study for subjects, describing the essential content which needs to be covered'.[49] If the reform is fully implemented, much that currently constitutes curriculum courses in ITT institutions will need to be revised. Reference to innovation will be pointless when courses are to be prescribed; emphasis may move from curriculum planning to course implementation. Clearly the next generation of teachers will not have the freedom enjoyed by their immediate predecessors in determining what they teach so it would be irresponsible of ITT courses to present a prospect of bustling participation in curricular decision-making.

It is unlikely, however, that the national curriculum will be developed in terms so specific as to allow continuity issues to fade away. Even if there is to be detailed outline of course content within a subject, problems will continue. When pupils are received from several contributory schools, it is extremely difficult to establish common ground. As the ORACLE project exemplifies, teachers in receiving schools seek to discover not only where pupils are up to in a given course but also how they arrived there:

> If more than one method has been used then the teacher is likely to insist that all pupils 'do it my way' so that some pupils who have enjoyed success through the use of different techniques are forced to abandon their successful method.[50]

Forcing pupils into the mould denies the development of individuality which is so much a part of primary philosophy. It can come as quite a shock to pupils who have previously enjoyed freedom to search for information not only in their own classroom but also in the school library that they must seek permission to move from their desks. Changing demands in presentation style, access to materials and modes of working can be as disturbing to pupils as the boredom and bewilderment they experience because of curriculum mismatch. In following up a pupil whose attainment had regressed after transfer despite close liaison between her teachers, I was intrigued by her comment:

> I was very annoyed having marks knocked off for not getting my margin exactly three centimetres. I don't think I tried much after that.

As Sumner and Bradley suggest, the continuity ideal must embrace pedagogical, material, and social as well as curricular aspects.[51] Emphasis in teacher-training courses tends to be placed on curricular issues but other aspects of continuity deserve attention. Secondary students need to be as sensitized as are their primary colleagues to the essential individuality of pupils.

STUDENT PERCEPTIONS OF PRIMARY AND SECONDARY SCHOOLS

In my own institution, the first month of a secondary PGCE course is concerned with primary schooling. A week of preparation, mainly given by primary teachers, is followed by three weeks' participatory observation in primary schools. Later in the course, after a full term of secondary practice, students are asked to consider whether, and if so how, practice with older pupils has been influenced by the primary experience. Over the last two years, a large majority of the students who responded have found exposure to young children early in the course extremely valuable. A small number, about 3 per cent, fail to see the relevance of such experience. The following is a typical response:

> Two things stand out from the primary practice: bright classroom display and much more lively children. The secondary school seemed barren. I was advised not to leave things on display because they would be vandalised. I did and they weren't. Even first year pupils in the secondary school seemed subdued in comparison with top-class juniors. Perhaps the primary children were too lively but I learnt a lot about class management and organisation from them. Others on the course did not see such extremes but I went to archetypal primary and secondary schools and the

contrast was very marked. I tried to put primary ideals into practice but it's not as easy in the secondary school when you have to switch from class to class through the day. Primary youngsters let you know when things go wrong but in the secondary school you have to probe. I think the primary practice was most valuable in giving me a heightened perception of the need to keep the pupil in mind all the time.

Students questioning the value of a primary preparation to secondary schooling tend to express doubts in terms of subject teaching and class control:

Participation and observation in primary schools gives no sense of the kind of teaching involved when you are dealing with a subject like economics, which is only taught to older pupils.

I enjoyed my time in primary school but it didn't give me any insight into teaching physics to difficult secondary classes.

Though these are representative comments by very few students, they suggest further work is needed to persuade some future secondary teachers to look on education as a continuum experienced by pupils. That secondary teachers need to be aware of pupils' seldom-voiced difficulties is evinced by a heartfelt plea included in a self-assessment record of progress and achievement by a Bradford pupil:

When I am in class and a teacher says 'Do you understand?' everybody says 'Yes'.
I don't but I daren't put my hand up because people laugh. I wish I could ask for help.[52]

Discontinuity is usually considered in the context of problems which are readily discernible but its effects are not always recognized by teachers. Underlying the small group of unmistakeable under-achievers, the confused and the disaffected, there are pupils who passively accept inability to cope. Teachers in training who are allowed to give pre-eminence to their own presentation style rather than pupils' needs are unlikely to recognize the extent to which continuity problems can so frustrate learning.

IMPROVING CONTINUITY

Much of what can be done to improve liaison and continuity lies with local authorities and schools. New funding arrangements for INSET, though disastrous for universities and colleges, could prove beneficial if those to whom resources are devolved, advisers and headteachers, give priority to continuity and liaison in their plans. Initial training, however, must provide the foundation for more successful practice. Government directives to strengthen subject studies in primary courses will have some effect by enabling future primary teachers to speak to secondary colleagues with more authority. By determining the national curriculum in relation to the 5 to 16 age range, the Secretary of State has provided justification for ITT courses to avoid too close adherence to notions of 'primary' and 'secondary' curriculum modes. Students in both primary and secondary courses of training will need to be prepared for new assessment arrangements at ages 7, 11, 14 and 16 and so should cover common ground.

Manifestly there are skills, attitudes, and perceptions applicable to continuity and transfer issues that should be addressed by teacher trainers; Derricott provides a useful checklist.[53] Some may be more appropriately dealt with on in-service courses but there are matters which should receive attention during initial training. Whether they do so or not seems a matter of chance. Some institutions have developed comprehensive strategies to make students aware of the need to minimize pupil disorientation and anxiety at times of transfer; other have done nothing. Unfortunately there is a faction which adopts a 'rulebook' approach to course planning. Because of the Secretary of State's withdrawal of approval for a secondary course, an institution sees itself as 'mandated to deal only with the primary age-range' and therefore, by implication, makes little or no reference to 'matters secondary' in any of its programmes. There are those who appraise courses only in terms of Circular 3/84 criteria. A terse response to my survey makes the point: 'Criterion 5.4 states "Teaching method should differentiate according to the student's intended age range"; that is what we do.' Another respondent suggests the way to ensure continuity is given serious attention is to get it on HMI's checklist. But it must be on HMI's checklist, for most DES and HMI documents in recent years have made reference to liaison and continuity.

Indeed, official documents have been pleading for improved continuity for over fifty years. As Ray Derricott reminds us, however, 'continuity of curricular experience is an idea that is more prevalent at the level of rhetoric than at the level of practice'.[54] General promotion to the realm of reality would require 'continuity' being espoused by some branch of the education service. There is little to encourage individual schools to take the initiative, since curriculum continuity must concern schools in groups. Higher education, and in particular teacher-trainers, can act as facilitators and can give useful research indications of successful practice, but can make little impact on an educational system. It is left to national and local government to move continuity from the level of theory to that of practice. Teacher-training's task will continue to be to provide a high level of professional preparation within which problems relative to curriculum continuity and school transfer should be addressed. But as at all levels, the 'slippery concept' of curriculum continuity is dealt with spasmodically. In the case of some teacher-training institutions, the current report must be: 'Could do better'.

NOTES AND REFERENCES

1   S. Delamont and M. Galton, Inside the Secondary Classroom, London, Routledge & Kegan Paul, 1986, p. 240.
2   K. Reid, 'Retrospection and persistent school absenteeism', Educational Research 1983, 25, 2: 110-15.
3   M.B. Youngman and E.A. Lunzer, Adjustment to Secondary Schooling, Nottingham University, 1977, p. 12; M.B. Youngman (ed.) Mid-Schooling Transfer, Windsor, NFER-Nelson, 1986, p. 2.
4   P.W. Musgrave, 'Some methodological, substantive and theoretical aspects', in B. Fensham (ed.) Alienation from Schooling, Windsor, NFER-Nelson, 1985.
5   P. Croll, 'Pupil performance in the transfer schools', in M. Galton and J. Willcocks (eds), Moving from the Primary Classroom, London, Routledge & Kegan Paul, 1983, p. 81.
6   E. Stead and P. Sudworth, 'The humpback bridge', in R. Derricott (ed.) Curriculum Continuity: Primary to Secondary, Windsor, NFER-Nelson, 1985.
7   L. Measor and P. Woods, Changing Schools - Pupil

    Perspectives on Transfer to a Comprehensive, Milton
    Keynes, Open University Press, 1984, p. 170.

8   See particularly J.D. Nisbet and N.J. Entwistle, *The
    Transition to Secondary Education*, London, University
    of London Press, 1969; B.J. Spelman, *Pupil Adaptation
    to Secondary School*, Northern Ireland Council for
    Educational Research, 1979.

9   M. Marland, *Language across the Curriculum*, London,
    Heinemann, 1977.

10 B.T. Gorwood, *School Transfer and Curriculum Con-
    tinuity*, London, Croom Helm, 1986, p. 160.

11 A. Stillman and K. Maychell, *School to School*, Windsor,
    NFER-Nelson, 1984, p. 118.

12 B.T. Gorwood, *Continuity with Particular Reference to
    the Effectiveness of Middle School Experience upon
    Upper School Achievement in Kingston upon Hull*,
    unpublished PhD thesis, University of Hull, 1981.

13 R.A. Becher and S. Maclure, 'What is curriculum?', in
    Centre for Educational Research and Innovation,
    Handbook on Curriculum Development, Paris, OECD,
    1975, pp. 38-9.

14 Lady B. Plowden, *Children and their Schools*, University
    of Exeter Institute of Education, 1970, p. 3.

15 A. Hargreaves, *Two Cultures of Schooling: The Case of
    Middle Schools*, Sussex, Falmer Press, 1986, p. 140.

16 A.M. Ross, A.G. Razzell and E.H. Badcock, *The
    Curriculum in the Middle Years*, London, Evans/
    Methuen, 1975, p. 41.

17 J. Nias, 'Hinge or Bracket? Middle school teachers'
    views of continuity at eleven', in R. Derricott (ed.)
    Curriculum Continuity: Primary to Secondary, Windsor,
    NFER-Nelson, 1985, p. 105.

18 J. Turner, 'Structure and content in teacher education
    in England', in D.E. Lomax (ed.) *European Perspectives
    in Teacher Education*, London, Wiley, 1976.

19 W. Taylor, *Society and the Education of Teachers*,
    London, Faber, 1969, pp. 275-6.

20 M. Rutter, *et al*, *Fifteen Thousand Hours*, London, Open
    Books, 1979, p. 204.

21 DES, *Better Schools*, Cmnd 9469, London, HMSO, 1985,
    para. 21.

22 HMI, *Primary Education in England: A Survey of HM
    Inspectors of Schools*, DES, London, HMSO, 1978, 8.25.

23 *Better Schools*, op. cit., para. 25.

24 Ibid., para. 5.

25 R.J. Alexander, Primary Teaching, London, Holt, Rinehart & Winston, 1984, pp. 27-30.
26 S.D. Steadman, Impact and Take-Up Project - Interim Report, London, Schools' Council, 1978.
27 Better Schools, op. cit., para. 17.
28 Ibid., para. 162.
29 Ibid., para. 65.
30 Ibid., para. 65.
31 Ibid., para. 163.
32 Hargreaves, op. cit., p. 91.
33 Alexander, op. cit., p. 191.
34 Better Schools, op. cit., para. 163.
35 E.A. Trown, Selection for Teaching, University of Lancaster School of Education, 1985.
36 Ibid., p. 32.
37 Ibid., p. 15.
38 HMI, Education Observed 3: Good Teachers, London, DES, 1985, para. 30.
39 Alexander, op. cit., pp. 182-3.
40 National Association of teachers in Further and Higher Education, Teacher Education - Current Issues, London, NATFHE, 1983, p. 6.
41 DES, Teaching in Schools: The Content of Initial Training, HMI Discussion paper, London, DES, 1983, p.8.
42 Stillman and Maychell, op. cit., p. 126.
43 DES, The Curriculum from 5 to 16 - Curriculum Matters 2, an HMI series, London, HMSO, 1985, para. 131.
44 Stillman and Maychell, op. cit., p. 126.
45 B. Joyce and B. Showers, 'Improving in-service training', in D. Hopkins (ed.) In-Service Training and Educational Development: An International Survey, London, Croom Helm, 1986, pp. 290-1.
46 E.C. Wragg, 'The re-structuring of initial teacher training and its significance for raising standards', NUT Education Review, 1987, 1, 1: 64-7.
47 Council for Accreditation of Teacher Education, CATENOTE 3, August 1985, para. 12.
48 DES, The National Curriculum 5-16 - A Consultation Document, July 1987, para. 9.
49 Ibid., Annex A, 1.2.
50 M. Galton, 'Changing schools - changing teachers' in L.A. Smith (ed.) Changing Schools: The Problem of Transition, University of London Goldsmith's College, 1983, p. 8.

51   R. Sumner and K. Bradley, <u>Assessment for Transition</u>, Windsor, NFER, 1977, p. 9.
52   A. Laycock, 'Liaison and continuity: new forms of record keeping' in F. Findlay (ed.) <u>Moving On</u>, London, National Association for the Teaching of English, 1987, p. 56.
53   Derricott, op. cit., pp. 146-57.
54   Ibid., p. 155.

6

INCULCATING TEACHER AWARENESS OF MORAL EDUCATION, PASTORAL CARE, AND HUMAN DEVELOPMENT

Josephine Cairns

It is commonplace in British education that parents expect the schools to make their children good. The 1988 Education Reform Bill, at the time of writing on its way through Parliament, similarly affirms that a balanced and broadly based curriculum:

> promoted the spiritual and moral development of the pupils at school and of society; and prepares such pupils for the opportunities, responsibilities, and experiences of adult life.[1]

At the moment no formal guidelines exist on how these lofty aims are to be achieved and there is no indication that any such are planned. This situation would seem reasonable, given the keen concern and desire of teachers to continue, as they have in the past, to set their own aims and generally to choose the content and method to be used in the areas for which they have responsibility. Yet the years since 1980 have seen anxiety raised both among teachers and among others concerned with the organization of schools that the area of pupils' development concerned with things moral and personal has been left untended, or at best promoted haphazardly.

THE PROBLEM STATED

In this teachers are reacting to an educational predicament which has not yet been resolved; namely that the schools are being asked to take on two major undertakings with their pupils, the one concerned with the more traditional role of giving information to students and developing skills, the other with offering guidance on questions, issues, and modes of living which were not immediately open to analysis and exploration in traditionally shaped curricula.

This chapter will argue that although many concerned with education are sensitive to the predicament, there needs to be a more thorough-going analysis of the problem than has previously been undertaken, and a resulting reshaping of the professional development of teachers. Current modes of analysis have led education to separate its thinking about the development of pupils other than the cognitive into categories such as personal and social education, pastoral care, aesthetic education, health education, and moral education. In one sense this is helpful, for it has called upon the expertise and knowledge of teachers across a number of curriculum areas to develop aims, content, and resources appropriate to the various categories. In another sense, however, it has obscured the important issue of the role of schools in raising and answering the question of what it means to be human in the changing cultural situation of the latter half of the twentieth century.

The need for some education in what it means to be human arose at the same time as society was wrestling with a new and complex situation. How was it to respond to a bewildering world whose place in the universe and whose potential were daily brought to the attention of ordinary folk through the media, and which now seemed very different as a result of a new understanding brought about by this 'explosion of knowledge'? That new knowledge meant the toppling of traditional perceptions and attitudes in the community's common psyche. A relativism in values emerged and with it an uncertainty about the possibility of meaning in life. As adults grew uncertain so their confidence in rearing their young for adult life decreased. When the underpinning of value judgements is relativity, few adults wish to set themselves as authorities on how the young should respond to their world or behave in it. Consequently in place of the adult community in general and the parent in particular, the schools began to take the responsibility of preparing young people for life in the adult world.

The schools have attempted this work for the last fifteen years or more and it is surely time to evaluate its progress and to ask how far it has been influential and to what extent it needs to be modified in the future. First, the schools, conscious of the shifting grounds of authority in knowledge, personal and social relationships, and the law, saw it as their duty to enable all pupils to make their own way, as far as possible, in acquiring knowledge, in exercising personal skills, and in making moral choices, thus stressing the development of the autonomous pupil. Second, the context for much pastoral guidance and moral education was unquestioningly accepted as multicultural. Briefly, what happened as a consequence was that the schools, overloaded with such new and broad responsibilities, hastily expanded their curricular and pastoral boundaries, often with little time permitted either for the teachers to analyse their new roles or for the pupils to become aware explicitly of the new agenda in which they were participating.

LEARNING FROM THE PAST

It is time now to question the influence of the 1960s and 1970s liberal educational analysis on development in the organization and the curricula of schools and, in turn, on the wider community. Within the formal curriculum there remains a tension between, on the one hand, those activities and areas of learning which give the pupils little room for self-exploration and experimental learning (for example as in mathematics and home economics) and, on the other hand, those learning activities which, although they permit the pupils a great deal of freedom and personal invest-igation, must often seem to be unstructured and weak in content, other than what the pupils bring to them. In other words two styles of teaching are to be found; in one the teacher is an authoritarian instructor and learning is grounded in empirical observation; in the other the teacher is an experimental facilitator and the learning is grounded in experience and reflection. As with teaching styles, so with school organization and pastoral care, there are two modes of operation, one expecting submission and commitment to a given code, the other inducing individual pupil responsibility and participation.

A similar dichotomy can now be seen in society. There are those who are conscious that the traditional cultural underpinning of society has broken down and is being replaced by an emergent culture whose characteristics are ethnic diversity, religious plurality, and moral relativism. Such a view leads to a demand for the widest possible democratic decision-making and complete personal responsibility in the choice of life-styles. There are others who in contrast perceive society's culture as unitary and fundamentally Christian and their concern is to draw the attention of all members of that society to its real roots and to the behaviour which follows. This leads to a commitment to strong and autocratic leadership and less personal responsibility and freedom of choice for individual members of the society.

To offer a profile of the pupils who have participated in this education process would require a lengthy analysis of the state of British society over the last fifteen years. Such is not our immediate task. Rather we might highlight some developments in behaviour and attitudes among the young and not so young which are currently receiving media attention, such as violence in the classroom, vandalism, hooliganism at sporting fixtures and chaos in town centres at weekends. Some look on these phenomena as evidence of the 'anomie' which has seemingly taken a grip of western society and left many hurt and angry by the apparent inability of all except the comparatively elderly to conform to previously held social and legal codes thereby creating a sense of lawlessness and a feeling of vulnerability across the community. Others seek to question the young through means of the ubiquitous opinion polls. From one such recent survey it appears that the young describe happiness as being seen to be successful in employment, acquisition of wealth, and eventual settled relationships. There is, however, evidence that underneath this apparent materialistic hedonism lies a more sensitive approach to life. For instance Robinson and Jackson in their research into values at 16-plus found that no more than 10 per cent of their 6,576 subjects rated a high standard of living, a good job, and good sexual relationships as 'most important'.[2] They further comment that over 5,200 of them claim to have had some kind of transcendent experience, which may suggest that the young have an untapped sensitivity which they hide behind their professed attachment to the pursuit of success and pleasure. Which of these two views seems better to reflect experience of the young depends on the position of the viewer in the continuum mentioned above between liberal pluralism and autocratic traditionalism.

SETTING AN AGENDA FOR TEACHER EDUCATION

It is clear, then, that teachers, both in the classroom and when responsible for the organization of schools, should feel able to perceive and analyse the attitudes and behaviour of their pupils with sensitivity and from an adequate theoretical base. Those engaged in teacher-training and in in-service work are becoming increasingly conscious that the teachers are able to offer valuable insights into the problems and questions which pupils raise but frequently lack the resources and the formal expertise to make these insights available to the public generally. They are further perplexed by confused messages from vociferous minority groups, Parliament, the government, parents, certain school governors, and so on, as to what is required of them by the wider community, some of which ask for liberalism and some for a return to traditionalism.

So far it has been argued that much of the confusion about personal, pastoral, and moral education results from the present inability of the community to decide what kind of people it wishes its young ultimately to become. If the schools are to continue to take responsibility for these areas of the curriculum then all teachers need guidance in the following:

1   Knowledge and understanding of the values and attitudes which their pupils have and how they acquire them, become conscious of them, and develop them.

2   A more explicit consensus from the community as to which values and types of behaviour it wishes them to commend and develop.

3   An awareness of how a school's organization, ethos, and curriculum, both hidden and explicit, shape and develop the attitudes and values of its pupils and is likely to influence their subsequent behaviour.

4   Content for reflection on the human condition and the formation of some ideal of the true potential of the human individual.

The achievement of these insights will necessitate a change of awareness in teachers and a shift of emphasis in professional development, since much of the received educational wisdom of the 1960s and 1970s will tend to militate against them. For in that period the proponents of moral education were advocating something different from the sort of moral education that was being given in the home, and was unlikely to be understood by many of the parents. Pupils were being subjected to one approach to

107

morality at home and another at school, a situation that was more likely to confuse than to help them.

Advocates of formal explicit moral education then suggested two ways forward: the first was to take the area of moral reasoning as a separate and important aspect of human life which ought to be treated educationally. This involved an exploration on the part of the pupils of the moral realm, with its central questions and its methods of dealing with those questions, and also the provision of simulated situations in which the pupils were required to articulate how they would act and why.[3] The second was to specify the method of handling morality in a plural society. That was to argue that all people have a right to determine their own moral values and to decide for themselves how they are going to behave. Pupils were, therefore, invited to become familiar, either across the curriculum or in separate curriculum spots, with a wide range of possible moral codes and ways of life, and then, against knowledge of them, to choose how they would react in any given situation. Thus pupils were to be given the tools of moral reasoning, but the judgement of which codes were most valuable for the individual or for his or her community was to be left to the pupil.[4] The canon of reason in moral choice and subsequent action was all that the educational system could offer in a plural society by way of moral education.[5]

Herein lay the reason why moral education appeared to be making little headway; for the canon of reason to take hold as the measure of what was good in the community, the schools needed to foster specific kinds of development in pupils. Those pupils needed not only the cognitive understanding of the moral realm, but also the potential to choose the humanist tradition of morality as their own. This proved to be the stumbling block and showed the inadequacy of the liberal humanist tradition's analysis of the potential of schools to set about educating the pupils of a plural and multi-cultural society in the area of morality. That analysis has presumed that an inevitable consequence of a philosophically sound moral education would be the acceptance by the pupils of the liberal humanist vision of the nature of humanity and of the nature of society. Thus it was thought that a morality based on the potential good of the human being would foster a sensitivity in the young to be concerned about others and how they were treated and engender a respect for the world which gave rise to such human beings. In this way society at large would be enlightened and enriched with a sense of common purpose. What the advocates of moral education had hoped was that the young would see that there was a sensible way for a society in flux to proceed. Therefore when pupils were faced with the practical questions which follow from 'How should I treat my neighbour?' and 'What kind of person do I wish to be?' they would wrestle with them and seek to achieve a wider vision of a society in which all are treated fairly and all are concerned to develop their humanity in a reasonable and discerning fashion.

MEETING THE AGENDA

The community, the school, and moral education

At the heart of the exercise of education concerning the question of what it means to be human there should, then, be some attempt to exercise the young in exploring possible visions of their universe and their place in it as human beings. The followers of the liberal tradition therefore set themselves the work of fostering interest and of developing skills in the process of becoming a person. They failed to recognize that the end of educational activity should be widened to allow time to explore first the underlying perceptions and visions which inform differing concepts of 'person'. The question which arises from this muddle is what are the schools to do and how are they to do it?

> First they must make a clearing through the dense landscape they have created along with their partners in the education process, the parents, politicians and the wider society they all share. This involves examining the wishes of parents and teachers to make the children good. Is it possible to make children good in a confused and complex situation? Does education contain within itself the potential for creating an ethos, among pupils of all backgrounds, to which the pupils will submit themselves for training and for which all parents will offer support?
>
> Second, given that such a definition of 'good' might be arrived at by social consensus, we must ask whether the young will accept this definition on such authority, since they frequently require stronger evidence that something is good than that it is demanded by their elders.

If these conditions were realized, and the question faced, we should have a strong and powerful vision of a self-regulating nation; that vision then might be achieved by a call to education to provide a consensus definition of what it means to be good, since within the bounds of education we find a human concern for growth and stability both from parents and teachers. There can be, too, a reasoned conversation between pupils and those teachers who are living out definitions of the moral life which can be open to their pupils' analysis. Moreover, there will be pupils who, in a secure framework, may share and argue about their individual ideas of morality with their papers. To strive towards a necessary definition, and at the same time be aware that your effort will have some influence on the future shaping of society, will surely highlight the potentially exciting nature of education in a democracy.

Equally in a literate and articulate society it will be necessary both for adults and pupils to take seriously and sympathetically the conclusion to which modern scientific inquiry can lead, that human beings 'are the temporary occupants of a cooling solar system; that all the ages, from the first down on earth to its extinction, will amount to no more than a brief parenthesis in the endless night of space'.[6] In this way discussion around the question, What does it mean to be human? will be informed by references to the prevailing cultural and philosophical influences in society and at the same time respond sensitively to the ideas, emotions, and questions of the young who have grown up in a plural world with few certainties offered them; a world so different from that in which many of their teachers grew. The coming together of those two different backgrounds, (the one which teachers in the 1970s and 1980s created where agnosticism rather than commitment was favoured, in order to cope with plurality, and the other, the world of the pupils, where commitment and dogma had not usually been encountered) in schools in the 1980s has led to the present painful awareness of a need to assist pupils in their personal development and the potential for some exciting developments in this aspect of education.

Mindful of the restrictions placed on the schools by a community which cannot offer a consensus view of what it means by 'promoting the spiritual and moral development of the pupils at school' it is still possible to offer a tentative definition of educating in human development in the schools of a contemporary plural society. If that society takes seriously plurality, scientific understanding, and the responsibility of the individual in his or her own development, it will be:

1   Sensitizing pupils to the variety of possibilities of interpreting the experience of being human.

2   Encouraging pupils to engage in the wide-ranging experiences which may elicit an emotional or personal response in the individual, thereby enabling them to reflect on the potential thought or action that may follow.

3   Offer in the school community, through its teachers and its organizational structures, examples of moral human beings, thus encouraging the pupils to engage with teachers and peers in a conversation about the good life.

The place of the young in the process

The internal foundation of any genuinely adult maturity is the acquisition of a series of identities or selves unified by a general concept of who one is and by what standards one is prepared to live.[7]

Most teacher-training courses include some reference to psychologists who have noted that adolescence is a time of increasing maturity triggered by participation in a number of 'growth tasks'. Most psychologists, along with Wall, would include in their list the following aspects of the self as demanding reflection and promoting growth:

1   The physical self
2   The sexual self
3   The vocational self
4   The social self
5   The philosophic self.

We have noted above that one's understanding of the behaviour and attitudes of the young is in part, at least, affected by one's views of the place of the individual in society. It therefore follows that teachers involved in this aspect of personal development must have available to them accurate means of analysing the individual pupil's perplexities and experiences in all of the five areas.

To facilitate such development and to encourage the provision of teachers' insight in the ways of human growth the following activities need to be undertaken:

1   Extensive reflection on the part of teachers on the context of pupils developing their personal identity while at school.

2   Precise and communicable aims should be formulated when this kind of work is undertaken, which can be made available to pupils, parents, colleagues, and school governors.

3   Classroom research to be initiated, in which teachers would participate, into the extent to which pupils are making links between the content and experiences offered by the teaching and their own perception of change in themselves. The results of this research, perhaps in package form, might be shared and form the basis of further course planning and resourcing.

4   An acquaintance with the developmental perspectives on human growth offered by Piaget (consciousness of morality), Selman (taking the perspective of the other), Kohlberg (moral judgement), and Loevinger (ego development) quoted by Pring in Personal and Social Education in the Curriculum.[8]

Such sensitivity to the pupils' potential development should assist in creating an environment in the school where the pupils become implicitly, and sometimes explicitly, involved in making choices which will affect the way the community chooses to define the nature of humanity. But, of course, the school cannot alone ensure a positive interest on the part of the pupils. For that the wider community must play its part and all concerned in the process must continue to be aware of the uncertainty caused in the process by the unpredictability of human response.

The pupil's self-evaluation of his or her response to the process will depend on the place of the particular school in a continuum stretching from those which chart pupils' progress by success in external examinations and vocational achievement to those which are concerned to mark and celebrate the individual progress of the pupil across a wide spectrum of achievements in personal and social skills, assessing skills, decision-making skills, patterns of self-awareness, reliability, and participation in many curricular activities.[9] Schools on the latter end of this continuum promote, on the whole, programmes of assessment through schemes based on a joint evaluation by profiling based on agreement between the teacher and the pupil. More important within the process of evaluation will be the possible findings of classroom research which may form the basis for a more succinct and comprehensive framework in which the pupils may perform their necessary tasks of (1) meeting with experience, (2) reflecting on it, (3) asking questions about it and receiving information, (4) reconsidering their response to the experience and choosing how it will affect their future thought and action.

Recognizing the human

To a large extent both the response of the individual pupil to all encouragement to think around the question of what it means to be human, and those skills which we may delineate as central to the teacher's role in assisting the pupils, are dependent on the knowledge and experiences which have to be provided and it is to an examination of these that we now turn.

At one level HM Inspectorate address this issue in the document Curriculum 11-16.[10] They ask that all pupils be enabled to share in a number of 'areas of experience', such as the physical, the moral, the aesthetic, and the spiritual. Thus pupils cannot be counted educated, and thereby sufficiently mature to enter society, unless they have been involved in ways of looking at the world which differ according to the basic insights from which the areas of experience arise. The context of these documents was rightly educational, but they were responding to wider questions about what kind of people are most valued by a rapidly changing community. It was to encourage the promotion of this view of the curriculum that the movement towards personal and social education emerged. This placed emphasis on defining and expanding the concept of person as a means of dealing with the question of what kind of human being we value and which the education system might assist to evolve. Attempts have been made to describe that sort of person who is seen as one knowledgeable and informed about personal and social relationships and the ideals of others. What is not made clear is how those others have come upon their ideals, and, more importantly, how pupils might become conscious of their own ideals which seem verified by their own experiences.

The problem for the teacher then is to decide what experiences should be provided to help the pupils discover and become conscious of the ideals which are going to motivate them. This may be what the inspectorate is referring to when it speaks of the spiritual. In a less multicultural world than the present it would involve enabling pupils to grasp and to endorse the shared vision of the community. But at present there are many visions of what a human being at best should be and the teacher must allow wide freedom to the pupils to make up their own minds which each of them is to accept. It is to be hoped that at the end of the process each pupil will be conscious of what they wish to become and be understanding and tolerant of their fellow pupils who have come to differing conclusions.

This raises the question of how those visions or, if that word is thought too precious, those ideals, are raised, thought about, and communicated. If the findings of Robinson, Paffard,[11] and others are reliable it is probable that most people are mainly influenced in forming their ideals from some kind of transcendental experience. How they interpret and communicate that experience depends on their prior assumptions and convictions. Those from a religious milieu, whether eastern or western, will describe and interpret them in metaphoric, symbolic, and myth-ological language. Those with a secular background will think and speak of them more diffusely and with less recourse to symbolism and story. This diversity creates both a difficulty and an advantage for teachers; the difficulty is that they must select from a wide range of material concerning spiritual experience in such a way as to do justice to the multicultural and plural nature of the community and, at the same time, provide learning experiences which are fitted to the pupils' backgrounds; the advantage is that whatever the background of the pupils, teachers will be able to offer illustrations of spiritual experience that will be of meaning to them. In connection with this it may be necessary for representatives of the wider community to invite teachers to initiate all pupils into the experiences of one western monotheist tradition, one eastern religious tradition, and one tradition without transcendental reference.

From the above we find it possible for education to take a positive lead in redefining what it means to be human at the present time. It is equally possible, however, that it may be responsible for obscuring some essential aspects of human nature in a bid to recall the community to more traditional ways of learning. For example, the 1988 Education Act focuses the energies of the educational process on leading children through acquisition of information and development of specific technical skills. Assessment of the pupils in these areas will then rely on a series of tests at given ages and through nationally directed methods. This could lead to a concentration on education as essentially information giving, putting at a premium the exploration and personal interpretation of experience. Education in personal development and appreciation of the human might suffer.

Skills of the teacher

Effectively to counsel pupils and to help them in their personal and moral development in the complex situation examined above, teachers need continuously to be assessing the kinds of sensitivities and skills which they will need. In initial training it may be useful if the following skills and sensitivities were promoted:

1   A sense of the complexity and mystery that surround the ideals and accompanying values both of the individual and of the community.

2   A consciousness of, and reflection on, the role of education in shaping the development of the pupils' sense of what it means to be human.

3   An ability to understand and respond to pupils from differing cultural, ethnic, religious, philosophical, and social backgrounds.

4   An ability to promote viable interpersonal skills in classrooms and tutor groups.

5   An ability to help the pupils grow increasingly conscious of their individual identity and its role in inspiring certain values and attitudes to their community and peers.

6   A consciousness of their place in the continuum,

analysing the nature of society as pluralistically liberal or traditionally autocratic, thus ensuring adequate understanding of their personal commitments and perspectives, and how they influence their professional work.

MORAL EDUCATION, PASTORAL CARE, AND HUMAN DEVELOPMENT IN SCHOOLS

Despite the difficulties and complexities challenging the schools as a result of our present plural and multicultural society teachers recognize their duty to assist pupils in important aspects of their personal development. Most of us are conscious of the often personal and individual nature of this work, which makes it difficult to give prescriptive suggestions as to how it should be attempted. Yet it is important that some guidance is offered to teachers in this increasingly central part of their professional lives. On this basis we offer a tentative outline of the aims which they may wish to try and achieve. They would be:

1   To acquaint pupils with, and offer guidance in, the basic question of human existence, 'Does human life contain the potential for finding meaning and purpose?'

2   To discuss the subsequent questions which arise from this, such as, 'How should I treat other human beings?' 'How can I most usefully spend my life?' 'What, if any, are my responsibilities to the environment?'

3   To relate the answers and methods of dealing with those questions to underlying belief and value systems.

4   To compare nihilism with the belief and value systems which arise from both eastern and western perceptions of reality.

5   To explore and analyse the concept of authority which is found in those systems.

6   To work towards a system of morality which permeates the whole curriculum and takes seriously the need for a stage theory of moral development.

A CALL TO THE COMMUNITY

Society is demanding as never before that schools shoulder, almost alone, the responsibility for educating pupils in personal development, values acquisition, and moral insight. There are, however, two difficulties about this. One is that school is not the only influence to which children are subjected. Outside school they meet a diversity of values and conflicting attitudes, some of which may impede the pupils' development as persons, militate against the formation of a clear and coherent system of values, and negate what teachers in school are trying to do both for the community and for the pupils separately. The other is that the diversity of values in the wider community means that the teachers, as representatives of that community, find it difficult to know what precisely the community wants them to do and what should be the direction and objective of their teaching. The difficulty is compounded by the fact that within the ranks of the teachers themselves the same uncertainty about ultimate values is to be found. Moral education and personal guidance in schools is consequently very much a matter of what individual teachers feel they ought to do and are capable of undertaking. It is likely to remain uncoordinated and haphazard, sometimes idio-syncratic, until there is a consensus among teachers about its aims and desired outcome. That consensus depends in turn on the community knowing what it wants taught in the moral and spiritual field, making clear to the teachers what that is, and acknowledging its own part in supporting that work and influencing the young through its attitudes, customs, and mores.

This chapter has reflected on both a felt need for guidance in human development through the schools and a confusion in attitudes and values in the community which makes it difficult to define precisely and to meet consistently that need. A study of history suggests that from time to time the human race goes through such periods of doubt and unsettledness, but that such times may be succeeded by ages of greater consensus and shared vision. The question which education must now ponder is whether its role at such a time is to temporize, do the best it can in the mean time, and wait for society to find again a common vision, or whether its obligation is to give its pupils the capacities and perceptions to participate in the finding and sharing of a common vision, in the hope that they will, as a result, make a more integrated, morally just, and more human society.

NOTES AND REFERENCES

1   DES, Education Reform Bill, London, HMSO, 1987, Clause 1 1/2.
2   E. Robinson and M. Jackson, Religion and Values at Sixteen Plus, Alister Hardy Research Centre, Oxford, 1987. Michael Paffard has similar findings in his Inglorious Wordsworths, London, Hodder & Stoughton, 1973.
3   J. Wilson, Approach to Moral Education, Oxford, Farmington Trust, 1967.
4   P. McPhail et al., Moral Education in the Secondary School, London, Longman, 1972.
5   P.H. Hirst, Moral Education in a Secular Society, London, University of London Press, 1974.
6   J. Carey, in Times Literary Supplement, 22 February 1980, quoted by D. Holbrook in Evolution and the Humanities, Aldershot, Gower.
7   W.D. Wall, Constructive Education for Adolescence, Windsor, Harrop/UNESCO, 1977, p. 39.
8   R. Pring, Personal and Social Education in the Curriculum, London, Hodder & Stoughton, 1984, p. 53.
9   B. Wakeman, Personal, Social and Moral Education, Tring, Herts, Lion Publishing, 1984, pp. 68-9.
10 DES, Curriculum 11-16, HMI Working Papers, London, HMSO, 1977.
11 Paffard, op. cit.

TRAINING FOR MULTICULTURALISM

Sally Tomlinson

The training of teachers to teach effectively in a multicultural society is a partial success story of the 1980s. Those who remember the 1960s, when suggestions that teachers might actually have some training to prepare them for teaching in multi-ethnic schools were often met with blank incomprehension, now feel that there have been distinct advances along this front. In 1987 it is no longer acceptable for any teacher in any school to assert that because 'we do not have those sort of children here',[1] teachers do not need training to teach effectively in a multicultural society, and to understand the place of Britain in an interdependent world.

The awakening of the teacher-training system to these ideas has been a long slow process: a 'catalogue of tardy and grudgingly miminal reactions'.[2] As recently as 1981 the House of Commons Home Affairs Committee wrote with some asperity that:

> the issues involved have been kicked around by interested parties for so many years now, that it is no longer acceptable to wait for the complex administrative structure to come to terms in its own good time with the challenge presented by the multiracial classroom. It is against a background of justified weariness and impatience that we consider how teacher training must now tardily adapt to this challenge.[3]

Changes have occurred quite rapidly since 1980 - 1981 being something of a watershed year - and by 1985 the Swann Committee was confidently asserting that 'all schools and all teachers have a professional responsibility to prepare their pupils for life in a pluralist society and in the wider world which has changed so dramatically over the last 30 years'.[4] It is mainly a belated acceptance that training for multiculturalism is a professional responsibility that has brought about recent changes and development in teacher-training in this area.

This chapter documents the way in which, after twenty years of indecision, the issues, pressures, and problems of teacher-training for a multicultural society have begun to be incorporated into initial, in-service, and postgraduate teacher education. A major message to emerge, however, is that new developments are merely a beginning: it will be well into the next century before all teachers are equipped with the skills, techniques, knowledge, empathy, and confidence to prepare effectively all pupils for life in a multicultural world.

TEACHER-TRAINING 1960–70

A brief but succinct account of early attempts to train those who were teaching or intended to teach in 'immigrant' areas is offered in Colour and Citizenship, an extensive report on race relations in Britain in the 1960s.[5] This report had a good deal to say about a variety of racial and cultural issues, but discussion of teacher training took up barely two pages. The major problem, as perceived by all educationists in the 1960s, was that of teaching English as a second language (ESL), to help immigrants 'assimilate' into society. The Ministry of Education published English for Immigrants in 1963 which contained an excellent statement on the necessity for teaching ESL.[6] Unfortunately at this time there were very few teachers of ESL in Britain and no in-service courses, and those who trained to teach English as a foreign or second language usually found work abroad. A few local education authorities began to employ minority teachers to teach immigrant children,[7] but by and large the opportunity to use the skills of ethnic minority teachers trained overseas was not taken up in the 1960s. Birmingham Local Education Authority set up a special language department in 1960, and an Association for Teaching English to Pupils of Overseas Origin (ATEPO) was established in the Midlands in 1962. Pressure from this association and the National Council for Commonwealth Immigrants resulted in the setting up of a one-term, in-service ESL course at the London Institute of Education in 1965. Edge Hill College of Education at Ormskirk (a constituent college of University of Lancaster School of Education) was the next teacher-training establishment to set up ESL courses; by 1968 it was offering the first course in the 'Education of Immigrants' in the three-year certificate and BEd course. Other colleges followed suit, and a few LEA's, notably the Inner London Education Authority, began to run in-service courses.[8] However, preparation of teachers going into multicultural classrooms was minimal. Rose noted that 'in 1967 it was not impossible for a probationary teacher to find herself, without warning or preparation, placed in charge of a reception class of forty children of "immigrants" ', a situation which persisted for many years after 1967.[9] A Schools Council survey published in 1970 confirmed the lack of preparation by colleges of students who did intend to work with minority group children.[10]

Such training as there was during the 1960s was very much oriented to the 'special needs' of immigrants and disadvantaged pupils, along the lines of the compensatory education models then popular in Britain and the USA.[11] There was a strong assumption, underpinned by assimilationist ideologies, that only teachers of immigrant or minority children would need preparation for teaching in a multicultural society. An exception to this way of thinking was the House of Commons Select Committee on Race Relations and Immigration, which recommended in 1969 that all teachers be equipped to prepare children for life in a multicultural society.[12] However, this plea went unheeded for ten years or more, and those teacher-training institutions that did develop option courses at the BEd or PGCE level intended these only for students whose missionary zeal would lead them to teach in inner-city multicultural classrooms.

TEACHER-TRAINING TO 1980

The 1970s were a period of exhortation and recommendations for the inclusion of multicultural elements in both initial and in-service teacher-training rather than action. Craft wrote in 1981 that 'it is profoundly depressing to find the same kinds of recommendation for action appearing again and again'.[13] From 1971 the Department of Education and Science had committed its inspectorate to offering 'practical help and advice to teachers faced with the challenge of teaching immigrant children' but there was no central directive or finance forthcoming.[14] The Home

121

Office had, by the Local Government Act, 1966, become committed to paying for extra teachers in areas of 'high commonwealth immigration concentration' but there had never been any co-ordination with the DES to offer special training to these teachers, or indeed to see that they actually were employed to teach 'immigrant' children.[15]

Teachers themselves throughout the 1970s felt the lack of professional preparation for multiculturalism, and while central government and teacher-trainers prevaricated, some teachers directed attention to the need for curriculum reform. A grass-roots movement aimed at the elimination of eurocentric stereotypes and a negative presentation of other races and cultures in the curriculum was the result of teacher initiatives.[16] However, without a general acceptance and clarification of the aims of multicultural education many teachers in multiracial schools found themselves frustrated, and teachers in 'all-white' schools did not consider the issues relevant to them. Townsend and Britten carried out a survey into organization and curriculum in multiracial schools in 1972 and concluded that lack of adequate teacher-training was a major problem of staffing in the schools.[17] Teachers lacked knowledge of the background of the minority children they were teaching, and lacked teaching techniques appropriate for multiracial and multilingual classrooms. Townsend and Britten also raised the issue as to whether teacher-training courses should reflect the fact that 'all teachers will teach in a multi-racial Britain', an issue which was still being debated in the 1980s.[18]

The committees and researchers who recommended improved teacher-training for multiculturalism during the 1970s found difficulty in specifying just how this should be done. The Select Committee on Race Relations and Immigration, in their 1973 report on Education, suggested that sociology of education courses were probably the best vehicle for teaching student teachers about multiculturalism.[19] However, sociologists employed as teacher-trainers never really gave the multi-ethnic nature of British society, and racial inequality, the same attention which they devoted to class inequalities, and an opportunity to help students locate racial and cultural issues within wider issues of social justice was lost. The DES replied to the Select Committee in 1974 that consultation on initial and in-service training for multiculturalism had been initiated but by 1977 were forced to conclude that 'too many entrants to the teaching profession have inadequate experience and understanding of the world outside education, including its multicultural and multi-racial aspects'.[20]

An HMI inquiry into BEd courses in fifteen institutions, published in 1979, reported that courses relating to education for a multiracial society were 'superficial or non-existent', and the catalogue of findings criticizing minimal teacher preparation in this area reached a peak in the late 1970s.[21] A further HMI survey of forty-six public sector institutions in 1979/80 found that twenty-one of them considered that the issues of a multicultural society were not relevant, and a further twelve were uncertain![22] Eggleston and his colleagues at Keele University carried out a survey of in-service education for a multicultural society in 1979/80, starting from the premiss that as new entrants to the profession had diminished considerably, the existing teaching force had an inescapable responsibility to inform itself of the issues. However, this survey concluded that 'our investigation left us in no doubt about the fragmentary and incomplete provision of in-service education for a multi-cultural society. Indeed, it is non-existent in many areas and in none is it wholly adequate'.[23] Dunn has elaborated on some of the early in-service courses examined in this research and has documented the confusion of aims, reluctance to admit to problems and to change practice which characterized the courses. Some teachers who attended courses, as Dunn noted, 'can be adept at ignoring racial conflict between their pupils, utilizing a variety of devices to put the blame elsewhere'.[24] He also commented that in-service courses which ignored racism and 'disappeared in a tangential celebration of cultural diversity' did little to change participants' views or understanding.

By the end of the 1970s more teachers were becoming aware of the need for in-service training in multicultural issues. The Commission for Racial Equality reported the views of a sample of teachers they interviewed who felt that they were inadequately trained for their work in multiracial schools, and felt that they received insufficient support and guidance from their LEA;[25] however, there was still no clear understanding as to what kind of training for multiculturalism was available.

An attempt to provide a comprehensive picture of all initial teacher-training courses which included race, ethnic, and cultural issues was made in 1979 by Cherrington and Giles, who circulated all college, polytechnic, and university teacher-training departments.[26] They reported that in colleges, only fourteen out of sixty-four were offering courses in multicultural education, but a further forty-six courses were offered in the colleges which were described as containing elements of multiculturalism. Eighteen courses were offered in nine polytechnics, and four courses at four universities, although a further nine offered multicultural elements in some courses. Cherrington and Giles also reported that the courses tended to present multicultural education as a way of dealing with a problem, rather than as an educational concept valid for all children in a multicultural society.

ENTERING THE 1980s

Given this catalogue of complaint and inadequacy, it may well be asked what teacher-trainers thought they were doing in training for multiculturalism up to the 1980s. Why did they not respond to pleas for such training, or not consider the issues important enough to warrant the development of more courses? One answer to these questions may be that teacher-trainers during the 1970s were too busy responding to continuous change in institutional structures, pedagogy, curriculum, modes of assessment, decline in teacher-training entrants, and new national policies to devote much time to multicultural issues.[27] Other answers may be that teacher-trainers themselves had little experience of teaching in multiracial classrooms, lacked knowledge of basic issues in race relations, immigration, and cultural diversity in Britain, and had little idea about the kinds of new knowledge, skills, and techniques which would be required by teachers for teaching in a multicultural society. During the 1970s the Association for Teachers in Colleges and Departments of Education had produced, in conjunction with the Commission for Racial Equality, only one report on teacher education for a multicultural society. This was a brief but comprehensive report outlining the ways in which 'preparation for a multiracial society can be incorporated into the experience of all students', but it made little impact upon teacher-trainers generally.[28] The report did, however, initiate a debate carried into the 1980s as to whether optional specialist provision, or the 'permeation' of all courses with multicultural awareness was the most appropriate way of raising multicultural issues, and it did stress the importance of in-service training as a priority.

The year 1981 can be located as something of a watershed, after which it became impossible to ignore training for multiculturalism, although hesitancy and inadequacy continued to be apparent. In April 1981 the Commission for Racial Equality Advisory group for Teacher Education, under the auspices of Professor Maurice Craft, organized a seminar on 'Teaching in a Multicultural Society: The Task for Teacher Education' at Nottingham University, the proceedings being published.[29] The participants were teachers, teacher-trainers, LEA advisers, HMI, and academic researchers, and a major theme of this conference was the need to prepare all children for life in a multicultural society and the need for compulsory multi-cultural elements in all initial training, in addition to specialist options and in-service work. Conference members were influenced by developments overseas, particularly in the USA, where teacher-educators had become more sensitive to their responsibilities in this area. Multicultural requirements had been laid out in teacher education accreditation programmes in the USA in 1976, and in 1980 the American Association of Colleges for Teacher Education had produced a series of documents on stereotypes for implementing multicultural teacher education.[30] Information on teacher education in other multicultural education systems had also begun to filter through to some British teacher-educators, in particular from Australia and Canada.[31]

Further influences on teacher-educators in 1981 were provided by three major reports on multicultural education which were produced in that year. The Home Affairs Committee published its report on Racial Disadvantage which, as already noted, heavily criticized the failure of teacher-educators to respond to issues of race and cultural diversity.[32] The Rampton-Swann Committee of Inquiry into the education of ethnic minority pupils, set up by the government in 1979, published an interim report which referred to an 'overwhelming picture of the failure of teacher-training institutions to prepare teachers for their role in a multi-racial society', and blamed the absence of guidance from the Department of Education and Science for the situation.[33] This committee made thirteen recommendations for improvement in teacher-training and the advisory services, the first being that 'the governing bodies and maintaining authorities of all teacher training institutions in the public sector, and University Departments of Education should institute a fundamental reappraisal of their policy towards multicultural education'.[34] A third report came from a survey set up by the Schools Council to review national and local policies in multicultural education. Thirteen of the sixty recommendations of this report on Multi-Ethnic Education - The Way Forward recommended action to be undertaken by teacher-educators and professional associations.[35]

These reports, surveys, and exhortations to action were by the 1980s influencing local education authorities, who, following the initiatives of the Inner London Education Authority in the later 1970s began to produce policy statements and guidelines on multicultural education, which usually included recommendations for in-service training. Local authorities in multiracial areas were certainly galvanized into action following the 1981 racial disturbances which occurred in most major British cities, and teacher-training institutions were undoubtedly influenced by the view of Lord Scarman, investigating the Brixton riots, that 'there is a clear need for improved training of teachers in the particular needs, the cultural background, and the expectations of minority group children and parents'.[36]

EXTERNAL PRESSURES

From the early 1980s all teacher-training institutions were subject to a variety of external pressures, some subtle and some more direct, to translate the exhortations of the 1970s into action. Pressures were exerted by teacher unions and associations, the Council for National Academic Awards, the Council for the Accreditation of Teacher Education, set up in 1984 by the DES, and Lord Swann's Committee of Inquiry into the education of ethnic minority pupils.[37]

The National Union of Teachers had adopted low-key but consistent policies on issues of race and multi-culturalism from 1967, when it published a report, The NUT View of Immigrants.[38] This report contained the novel suggestion that day colleges be opened in areas of high minority settlement to offer training and research facilities to both native-born and immigrant teachers, a suggestion which was never taken up. The NUT concentrated on suggestions for combating racism and for curriculum change, and at its 1980 conference passed a motion expressing concern at the propagation of racialist ideas in Britain and calling for a multicultural curriculum and more relevant induction and in-service training for all teachers in multicultural issues. The Avon branch of the NUT, after 'race riots' had occurred in Bristol in April 1980, produced a report accepting the heavy burden of responsibility placed on teachers in a multi-ethnic society and called on their local authority and teacher-training institutions to improve teacher-training for multicultural education. One secondary-school teacher interviewed for this report noted that 'at my school we had ONE in-service training day on this theme with no follow-up that I am aware of - an empty gesture'.[39]

A more direct plea to teacher-trainers was made in 1984 by the National Association for Multi-Racial Education (NAME), a liberal teachers' association created in 1974, which during the 1980s became more militant in its stance on racism in Britain.[40] In a short but powerful statement NAME urged all bodies involved in teacher education to adopt an anti-racist approach in their professional activities, asserting that 'multicultural education' could become tokenist and did not tackle issues of unjust racist structures and processes in education.[41] The statement proposed wide-ranging changes in the management and staffing of teacher-training institutions, in the recruitment and assessment of students, the provision of courses at initial and in-service level, the evaluation of courses, and the levels of resource offered. There is some evidence that the NAME statement did have an important effect on teacher-trainers, and larger numbers of teacher-trainers did begin to attend the annual conference run by this organization.

More direct pressure on teacher-training institutions in the public sector was exerted by the Council for National Academic Awards (CNAA) which through its validating activities began to require all institutions presenting or re-presenting courses for validation, to demonstrate that some degree of 'permeation' of multicultural elements had taken place, in addition to specialist option courses.[42] Although the initial reaction of some institutions to this requirement was to pay lip-service to 'permeation', many teacher-trainers who had previously rejected multicultural ideas were forced to give them some consideration.[43] One college validated by CNAA and described by Arora produced a comprehensive academic policy with a declared commitment to multicultural education and a responsiveness to the needs of the local (Bradford) multi-ethnic community.[44]

In addition, the CNAA set up a working group to examine ways of promoting good practice in teaching for multiculturalism in January 1982, and in 1984 the group produced a discussion document suggesting principles of multicultural and anti-racist education and a checklist of possible items for inclusion in teacher-education courses. This document had wide circulation in colleges and polytechnics, and caused the University Council for the Education of Teachers (UCET), which represents all university teacher-training departments, to set up its own working party to produce a similar discussion document. The four-page document was included in the Swann Report on the education of ethnic minority pupils,[45] and was summarized by Lynch who noted that it 'espoused expansive and by then largely acceptable commitments' to a variety of multicultural and anti-racist perspectives.[46] However Lynch's judgement was premature: in 1986 the CNAA's Committee for Teacher Education reviewed the document and, without the knowlege of the working party, deleted the term 'anti-racist'. Several members of the working group protested and one resigned from the Committee for Teacher Education.[47]

This incident illustrated a further possible reason for the slow development of teacher-training courses for a multi-ethnic society. The whole area of race and education had by the 1980s become heavily politicized; multicultural, anti-racist education had moved centre-stage as a focus for racial tensions. Opposing ideologists of the left and right were attempting to influence the development and content of teacher-training in the area, and the CNAA was responding to these external pressures.

Further external pressures on initial teacher-training in both public sector and university institutions came via the Council for the Accreditation for Teacher Education (CATE) the body set up in 1984, under the chairmanship of Professor William Taylor, to advise the Secretary of State on the approval of all teacher-training courses in England and Wales. Criteria for such approval were, according to the DES circular announcing the Council, to include the requirement that:

> students be prepared through their subject method work and educational studies to teach the full range of pupils whom they are likely to encounter in an ordinary school, with their diversity of ability, behaviour, social

background and ethnic and cultural origins. They will need to learn how to respond flexibly to such diversity and guard against preconceptions based on the race or sex of pupils.[48]

However, the guidance notes issued by the new Council between 1984 and 1986 as to how it intended to carry out its remit did not deal with multicultural issues or requirements.[49] However, in practice the Council does not insist on all courses' including some work on multiculturalism.

The creation of new secondary-school examinations during the 1980s also constituted external pressures on institutions, as the examination boards preparing guidance on the new General Certificate of Secondary Education (GCSE) syllabuses decided to include a requirement that multicultural criteria were met in both subject matter and examinations. For example, the criteria for the acceptance of a subject for an examination includes as one element:

> Recognition of cultural diversity: In devising syllabuses and setting question papers, examining groups should bear in mind the linguistic and cultural diversity of society. The value to all candidates of incorporating material which reflects this diversity should be stressed.[50]

It slowly became apparent that all secondary-school teachers would need to be properly prepared by teacher-trainers for this aspect of their work.

However, the biggest single external pressure on teacher-trainers and local authorities planning in-service courses was undoubtedly the final report of Lord Swann's Committee of Inquiry into the education of ethnic minority pupils. The report included a whole chapter on teacher education, with sections on initial training, in-service training, and the employment of ethnic minority teachers.[51] A section in the previous chapter on 'Religion' also included a section on the supply and training of religious teachers.[52] Chapter 9 contained thirty-three main conclusions and recommendations, which were condensed to nineteen in the Report's final conclusions. The Swann Report illustrated conclusively the official acceptance that Britain is a culturally plural multi-ethnic society and that assimilationist assumptions could finally be jettisoned:

> We believe that all initial teacher training courses, both PGCE and BEd., should be permeated with the principles underlaying a genuine pluralist approach to education.
>
> All providers of in-service training should ensure that the courses they offer have this pluralist perspective.[53]

The committee was of the opinion that much of the lack of progress in training for multiculturalism had come about because of confusion among teacher-educators who did not know whether they were preparing students for teaching in multi-ethnic schools or a multi-ethnic society. They firmly supported the notion that 'all schools have a responsibility to offer their pupils an education which reflects the realities of life in today's multi-racial Britain'.[54] However, they warned that the notion of 'permeating' all teacher-education courses with multicultural perspectives had to be carefully thought through.[55] Indeed 'permeating', as Gaine has pointed out, has become a catch-word without necessary consideration being given to what exactly is being 'permeated', and why.[56] There is a danger that 'things can become so well permeated that they disappear altogether'.[57] Trainers, pushed to include multicultural perspectives in their courses, may be embracing the concept of permeation in the absence of detailed knowledge or understanding of what these perspectives are. This is understandable, as few trainers have themselves received any training to help them to such knowledge.

TRAINING THE TRAINERS

By the early 1980s it had become very obvious that whatever the reasons for the lack of response from teacher-trainers to training for multiculturalism, some kind of training-the-trainers programme would have to be initiated, but only on a voluntary basis. The Home Affairs Committee had in their 1981 report advocated that 'the D.E.S. produce as a priority a programme for training those intended to train teachers in multicultural education'.[58] The DES had been further encouraged to take action on the teacher-trainers, by an HMI survey on The New Teacher in School published early in 1982.[59] Over half the young teachers questioned in this survey said that their courses had given them no preparation for teaching minority pupils or for dealing with issues of race and culture. They felt that the ethnocentric base of teacher-training had barely shifted. One new teacher reported that:

> my training had prepared me for teaching in a small, suburban primary school in a middle class area, but not for the special priority area, urban, multicultural school.[60]

With DES encouragement therefore, the first training-the-trainers programme was set up in 1982 at Nottingham University by Maurice Craft, who, from the innovative work he undertook at Edge Hill College in the 1960s, has been a committed and active exponent of training for a multi-cultural society. Craft obtained funding from DES regional in-service funds, from Shell UK and the Boots Charitable Trust, and one-term or two-term courses were set up at six institutions: Birmingham, Manchester, and Sunderland Poly-technics, and Nottingham, Liverpool, and London Universities. By 1986 over forty colleges, polytechnics, and universities were running training-the-trainers programmes, either singly or on a regional basis, and the DES had funded an evaluation study which indicated that the programmes did have a positive impact on participants.[61] Each institution planned and organized the courses, mostly choosing a model of workshop sessions and invited speakers, and all the programmes tackled issues of race and racism and were emphatically not simply geared to issues of cultural diversity. Craft also commissioned a series of short booklets to help course participants.[62] Thomas produced a Lifestyles Pack, which became a popular teaching tool for the trainers' courses and the courses they subsequently organized.[63]

At the present time it is difficult to evaluate the long-term impact of programmes of training the trainers. The Swann Committee had noted that as participation was on a voluntary basis, such courses could become specialized 'option courses' attracting only those teacher-trainers who were already committed to change and to action. The committee was concerned that if the senior staff in institutions were not involved, change would be minimal.[64] Latham, in a perceptive article in 1982, had pointed out that the 'academic structures and internal politics of higher education institutions' had to be taken into account before the content of any multicultural courses and their impact could be discussed.[65] Latham was particularly concerned that the complexities of multiracial education were such that courses could easily become trivialized and distorted. He advocated that trainers should be equipped to offer student teachers a broad indication of the range of pedagogic, political, and theoretical issues which constitute education for a multiracial and multicultural society.

FURTHER DEVELOPMENT

Although the Rampton Committee in 1981 criticized the Department of Education and Science for its failure to encourage teacher education for a multicultural society,[66] the DES has, over the past few years, exerted more pressure on the teaching force, training institutions, and local authorities to run courses and projects which would help teachers to prepare all pupils for life in a multi-ethnic society. Better Schools made the link explicit between professionalism and the changed attitudes needed to carry out this task effectively.[67] The message is now clearer that having 'trained for multiculturalism' is part of a teacher's professional repertoire, not an optional extra. The provision by the DES of Education Support Grants and other special finance for LEAs to run in-service courses and curriculum development projects has made it possible to put rhetoric into practice. Circular 6/86, which set out the grant-related in-service training arrangements for 1987/88, included a list of nineteen national priority areas for training, the seventh of which was 'training in teaching and planning the curriculum in a multi-ethnic society'.[68] With the help of grants a number of local authorities, including some in 'all-white' areas, have begun to undertake in-service work and curriculum development projects.[69] The aim of these projects is to encourage all teachers to review their professional activities, giving consideration to how best to reflect a culturally and ethnically diverse Britain, challenge stereotypes and racism, and help pupils become realistically aware of the rest of the world, and to provide relevant curriculum materials.[70] These kinds of activities go some way to making up for the lack of appropriate training for multiculturalism which currently affects serving teachers.

Developments at the in-service level, it is to be hoped, will do much to change the attitudes and practices of serving teachers over the next few years. Indeed Craft considers that schools and LEAs may now be ahead of initial teacher-training institutions in reviewing and changing their practices.[71] Such evidence as there is suggests that some initial teacher-training institutions may still be engaged in what Lynch has described as 'evasion strategies': attempting to ignore what is 'nothing less than the moral, intellectual, social, cultural and professional re-jigging of a whole generation of teacher educators'.[72] But other institutions are taking the whole area of training for multiculturalism very seriously.

In addition some institutions are still engaged in the option course versus permeation debate and some are still undecided whether they are preparing teachers only for multi-ethnic classrooms or preparing all teachers. There is still confusion and lack of clarity over the aims, objectives, and content of courses.

There is now, however, some literature available to suggest what the content of courses training for multiculturalism could include.[73] But what is currently lacking is a theoretical conceptualization as to how staff development for teacher-trainers, the courses the trainers produce, and the effects of the courses on intending teachers, can be best understood. Lynch has attempted the production of a typology of staff development needs for teacher education,[74] and rightly notes that while 'it is now becoming urgent for British teacher education to reverse the long history of inertia in responding to the democratic cultural pluralism of British society', a commitment to professional dialogue and discourse, which rules out authoritarian strategies, has to be the basis for good multicultural teacher education.[75]

Lynch's own institution (Sunderland Polytechnic) has begun, in 1987, to teach the first master's degree wholly concerned with multicultural education, and there are now a variety of institutions which offer a component of training for multiculuralism in their higher degree programmes.

ETHNIC MINORITY TEACHERS

No discussion of teacher education for a multicultural society can ignore the situation of ethnic minority teachers in Britain. Ideally a multiracial, multicultural society should employ a substantial number of teachers of ethnic minority origin, who have similar opportunities to all other teachers for promotion and a good career structure. The Swann Report pointed out that the educational justifications for increasing the number of ethnic minority teachers were varied. In particular, people staffing an educational service should reflect the make-up of the population, people from ethnic minorities should have equal opportunity to take up educational training, and ethnic minority teachers could act as role models for minority children and as sources of cultural expertise for all children. Even in 1985 there was little statistical information available to the Swann Committee on numbers of ethnic minority teachers employed by local education authorities, few of whom noted racial or ethnic origins of their staff. The Select Committee on Race Relations and Immigration had noted in their 1973 report that 'like the DES, we do not know the numbers of immigrant teachers, but we agree with the majority of our witnesses that there should be more'.[76] Reasons for the small percentage of minority teachers in schools are not hard to find. During the 1960s some immigrant teachers were issued with employment vouchers and the DES offered some letters of 'possible employment', but mostly the DES insisted that teachers trained overseas, undertake further training in Britain, and LEAs were equivocal in their willingness to employ 'immigrant teachers'. The National Union of Teachers reported in the late 1960s that even where immigrant teachers found posts, some had found difficulty with probation and promotion. Ethnic minority teachers and potential teachers certainly had a clear message as to their possible second-class status in the profession. In the later 1970s there was little indication that young people from ethnic minority backgrounds were seeking to enter teacher-training institutions, even when qualified to do so. The Special Access Courses, begun in 1979 and designed to prepare minority group students for higher education and professional courses, did have some success in recruiting more teachers of Afro-Caribbean origin, but smaller numbers of students of Asian origin are attracted to teaching.[77]

In response to the Swann Committee recommendations, in July 1985 the DES issued a consultation paper on Increasing the Supply of Ethnic Minority Teachers and considered possible ways of improving the supply.[78] Action proposed included improved promotional material for the teaching profession, LEAs to ensure that their teacher recruitment and promotion procedures operated without discrimination, careers advisers at schools encouraging young people from minority backgrounds to enter teacher-training, and teacher associations taking up the issue. The paper also suggested that teacher-training institutions should improve their recruitment and selection procedures and make their courses more attractive to minority students. The DES has also recently supported the idea of supplementary training for teachers trained overseas, to bring them to qualified teacher status, and a pilot course has been set up at Manchester University.

Information on the (small) number of ethnic minority teachers employed in Britain in the mid-1980s was provided by a survey carried out by the Commission for Racial Equality which recorded that out of 20,246 teachers in 1,189 schools surveyed, only 431 (2 per cent) were of ethnic minority origin. These teachers were disproportionately on the lowest scales, concentrated in certain subject areas and on average were older than their white peers, suggesting that a decline in the number of minority teachers, rather than an increase, was likely.[79]

Certainly if an increased number of ethnic minority teachers in the profession, adequately trained and offered equal opportunities for promotion, is part of teacher-training for multiculturalism, there is currently a significant failure in this area.

CONCLUSIONS

This chapter has explored some of the issues, pressures, and problems of training for multiculturalism in Britain over the past thirty years. Any survey, however brief, cannot fail to confirm that the response of teacher-training institutions over the years has been characterized by hesitancy, indecision, and slowness to respond to official recommendations and suggestions. However, the progress made over the past six years does now make guarded optimism possible. Teacher-trainers and local education authorities are beginning to recognize their key role in educating the teachers who will prepare all pupils for life in a multi-ethnic society and an interdependent world more appropriately. There certainly are significant omissions and failures, but having recognized their responsibilities, it is no longer possible for all those concerned with teacher education to evade their role in training for multi-culturalism.

NOTES AND REFERENCES

1   This remark by a headteacher was documented in
    H.E.R. Townsend and E. Britten, Organisation in
    Multiracial Schools, Windsor, NFER-Nelson, 1972, and
    typified the attitude held by many teachers in Britain
    up to the 1980s.

2   J. Lynch, 'An initial typology of perspectives on staff
    development for multi-cultural teacher education', in S.
    Modgill, C.K. Verma, K. Mallick, and C. Modgill (eds)
    Multi-Cultural Education - The Interminable Debate,
    Sussex, Falmer Press, 1985, p. 149.

3   Home Affairs Committee, Racial Disadvantage, Vol. 1,
    London, HMSO, 1981, p. lix.

4   DES, Education for All, Swann Report, London, HMSO,
    1985a, p. 560.

5   E.J.B. Rose et al., Colour and Citizenship - A Report on
    British Race Relations, Oxford, Oxford University
    Press, 1969.

6   Ministry of Education, English for Immigrants, London,
    HMSO, 1963.

7   Rose et al., op. cit., p. 274.

8   On a personal note, it took me over a year in the early
    1970s to persuade the teacher-training college in the
    West Midlands at which I was employed to allow me to
    run a six-lecture course for students about to begin
    teaching practice in multiracial schools.

9   Rose et al., op. cit., p. 280.

10 Schools Council, Immigrant Children in Infant Schools,
    Working Paper 29, London, Evans, 1970.

11 M. Craft (ed.) Teaching in a Multi-Cultural Society -
    The Task for Teacher Education, Sussex, Falmer Press,
    1981, p. 4.

12 Select Committee on Race Relations and Immigration,
    The Coloured School-Leaver, London, HMSO, 1969.

13 Craft, op. cit., p. 2.

14 DES, The Education of Immigrants, Education Survey
    13, London, HMSO, 1971, p. 15.

15 This situation did not change until 1982 when the Home
    Office undertook a review of 'Section Eleven' teachers
    (Home Office Circular 97/1982).

16 J. McNeal and M. Rogers, The Multi-Racial School,
    Harmondsworth, Penguin, 1971.

17 H.E.R. Townsend and E. Britten, Organisation in
    Multiracial Schools, Windsor, NFER-Nelson, 1972.

18   Ibid., p. 138.
19   Select Committee on Race Relations and Immigration, Education, London, HMSO, 1973.
20   DES, Education in Schools - A Consultative Document, London, HMSO, 1977, p. 27.
21   DES, Development in the BEd Degree, London, HMSO, 1979, p. 6.
22   I. Ambrose, 'An HMI perspective', in M. Craft (ed.) Teaching in a Multicultural Society, Sussex, Falmer Press, 1981.
23   S.J. Eggleston, D.K. Dunn, and A. Purewal, In-Service Teacher Education in a Multi-Racial Society, University of Keele, Staffordshire, 1981.
24   D.K. Dunn, 'In-service miseducation', in R. Arora and C. Duncan (eds) Multicultural Education - Towards Good Practice, London, Routledge Educational, 1986, p. 188.
25   Commission for Racial Equality, Teacher Education for a Multi-Cultural Society, London, CRE, 1974, repr. 1978, p. 7.
26   D. Cherrington and R. Giles, 'Present provision in in-service teacher-training', in Craft, op. cit.
27   W. Taylor, 'The national context 1972-82', in R.J. Alexander, M. Craft, and J. Lynch (eds) Change in Teacher Education, London, Holt, Rinehart, & Winston, 1984.
28   Commission for Racial Equality, op. cit., p. 8.
29   Craft, op. cit.
30   G. Gay, 'Why multicultural education in teacher preparation programmes?', Contemporary Education 1983, 5: 79-85; Lynch, op. cit.
31   B. Bullivant, The Pluralist Dilemma in Education - Six Case Studies, London, Allen & Unwin, 1981; K.A. Moodley, 'Canadian multicultural education: promises and practices', in J.A. Banks and J. Lynch (eds) Multicultural Education in Western Societies, London, Holt Educational, 1986.
32   Home Affairs Committee, op. cit.
33   DES, West Indian Children in Our Schools, Rampton Report, London, HMSO, 1981, p. 60.
34   Ibid., p. 82.
35   A. Little and R. Willey, Multi-Ethnic Education - The Way Forward, Schools Council Pamphlet 18, London, Schools Council for Curriculum Development, 1981.
36   Lord Scarman, The Brixton Disorder 10-12 April 1981, Harmondsworth, Penguin, p. 165.

37 DES, 1985a, op. cit.
38 National Union of Teachers, The NUT View of Immigrants, London, NUT, 1967.
39 Avon National Union of Teachers, After the Fire - A Report on Education in St Paul's, Bristol, Bristol, 1980, p. 54.
40 In 1984 NAME became the National Anti-Racist Movement in Education, and based some of its policies on the Marxist-oriented writings of Mullard. C. Mullard, Anti-Racist Education: The Three O's, London, National Association for Multi-Racial Education, 1984.
41 National Association for Multi-Racial Education, Teacher Education, London, NAME, 1984.
42 CNAA, Multicultural Education - A Discussion Document, London, CNAA, 1984.
43 The danger of lip-service to 'permeation' was pointed out by the National Union of Teachers in their evidence to the Home Affairs Committee on Racial Disadvantage, 1981.
44 R. Arora, 'Initial teacher training: a case study of a decade of change in Bradford', in R. Arora and C. Duncan (eds) Multicultural Education - Towards Good Practice, London, Routledge Educational, 1986.
45 DES, 1985a, op. cit., pp. 636-9.
46 Lynch, op. cit., p. 151.
47 Times Higher Education Supplement, 'Lecturer quits CNAA in anti-racist row', 5 December 1986, p. 1.
48 DES, Initial Teacher Training - Approval of Courses, Circular 3/84, London, DES, 1984, p. 8.
49 Council for the Accreditation of Teacher Education, The Council's Approach to Accreditation, CATENOTE 1, London, DES, 1985a; CATE, Subject Studies, CATENOTE 3, London, DES, 1985b; CATE, Links Between Initial Teacher Training Institutions and Schools, CATENOTE 4, London, DES, 1986.
50 DES, GCSE - The National Criteria, London, DES, 1985, p. 4.
51 DES, 1985a, op. cit., pp. 541-648.
52 Ibid., p. 493.
53 Ibid., p. 611.
54 Ibid., p. 551.
55 Ibid., p. 559.
56 C. Gaine, No Problem Here - A Practical Approach to Education and Race in White Schools, London, Hutchinson, 1987.

57 Ibid., p. 171.
58 Home Affairs Committee, op. cit., para. 145.
59 HMI, The New Teacher in School, HMI Series: Matters for Discussion 15, London, HMSO, 1982.
60 Ibid., p. 35.
61 M. Craft, Teacher Education in a Multicultural Society - An Introduction, National Programme for Training the Trainers, University of Nottingham, 1986.
62 Craft, 1986, op. cit.; D. Houlton, Teacher Education in a Multi-Lingual Context, National Programme for Training the Trainers, University of Nottingham, 1986; J. Lynch, Multicultural Education - Approaches and Paradigms, National Programme for Training the Trainers, University of Nottingham, 1986; S. Tomlinson, Ethnic Minority Achievement and Equality of Opportunity, National Programme for Training the Trainers, University of Nottingham, 1980.
63 D.G. Thomas, Lifestyles Pack, University of Nottingham School of Education, 1985.
64 DES, 1985a, op. cit., p. 598.
65 J. Latham, 'Exceptional children or exceptional teachers? - An alternative policy for teacher education in a multi-racial society', Journal of Further and Higher Education 1982, 6, 2: 40-7.
66 DES, 1981, op. cit., p. 61.
67 DES, Better Schools, Cmnd 9469, London, HMSO, 1985b, p. 44.
68 DES, Local Education Authority Training Grants Scheme - Financial Year 1987/88, Circular 6/86, London, DES, 1986.
69 For example, curriculum development projects funded by ESG grants have been set up in Cumbria, Shropshire, Wiltshire, Derbyshire, and Northumberland.
70 See for example the pamphlet produced by Cumbria, Education for Life in a Multicultural Society, Curriculum Paper 14, Cumbria County Council, 1987.
71 Craft, 1986, op. cit., p. 27.
72 Lynch, 1985, op. cit., p. 154.
73 CNAA, op. cit.; Craft, 1986, op. cit.
74 Lynch, 1985, op. cit., p. 157.
75 Ibid., p. 161.
76 Select Committee on Race Relations and Immigration, 1973, op. cit., p. 32.
77 K. Millins, Special Access Courses - An Evaluation, London, Ealing College of Higher Education, 1981.

78 DES, <u>Increasing the Supply of Ethnic Minority Teachers - A Consultation Paper</u>, London, DES, 1985c.
79 C. Ranger, 'Main findings of the CRE research', in <u>Black Teachers - The Challenge of Increasing the Supply</u>, London, Commission for Racial Equality, 1986.

8

TEACHER AWARENESS OF THE ECONOMIC FOUNDATIONS OF A FREE SOCIETY

Pauline Perry

> It is a duty incumbent on statesmen and churchmen alike to provide that there be a due supply of men qualified to educate the youth of the nation. It is a public obligation in no way inferior, say, to the ordering of the army.[1]

Thus Erasmus, 450 years ago, declared his view of the importance of the training of teachers to the preservation of the interests of the State. It is said that, until recently, successive governments in Britain have shown little recognition of the truth which Erasmus argues, that the quality of teachers and the nature of the teaching force are as important to the defence of society's values and goals, and as inherent to its economic prosperity, as the nature of the armed forces is to its physical defence. Most governments have discharged their duty only by attempting to provide adequate numbers of teachers; indeed the forecasting of required teacher numbers has been a major exercise, consuming time and great energy and performed with varying degrees of success by the Department of Education and Science and its advisory committees over past decades.

History teaches us that education is one of the most powerful instruments of social change. It also teaches us that changes in the education system, and in the expectations of society, require fundamental changes in the nature of the teaching force, and yet throughout the changes in educational provision throughout the 1950s and 1960s this urgent need seems to have gone unrecognized. The restructuring of schools from the mid-1960s and the long-running debate about the system of examinations were undertaken with minimum regard to the changes in the teaching force which were needed to deliver those new ideas effectively.

The most glaring example of this was the lack of consideration given, at national level at least, to the production of a comprehensive force of secondary teachers to staff the secondary comprehensive schools. The 1944 Act had divided children at secondary age into groupings which assumed an economic structure already long out of date. The secondary modern schools were to be schools for the majority of children, providing them with a liberal education as a gift from the State, but in no way preparing them to be participants in an educated and skilled work-force. The assumption was that the British manufacturing industries would still require a vast unskilled labour force, for whom education was a gift rather than a vocational necessity; I describe this as 'soup-kitchen education'. Despite the recognition that this form of education was no longer appropriate, the former grammar-school specialist graduate teachers, many of them with no training as teachers beyond their degree, were moved into the new comprehensive schools alongside the former secondary-modern non-specialist certificated teachers. These were the teachers who, in very large numbers, were trained throughout the 1950s, 1960s, and early 1970s before Margaret Thatcher's 'all-graduate entry' policies tried unsuccessfully to produce a more unified secondary teaching force. In most cases, the two groups of teachers continued to provide two classes of secondary education under the roof of the comprehensive school, representing two often irreconcilable schools of thought about the needs of secondary pupils, and indeed the aims of secondary education.

Successive Secretaries of State for Education have explored the powers available to them to impact on an education system administered, and largely controlled, by local education authorities. The powers available are by themselves formidable: no change in the structure of schools, including the opening of new ones or closing existing ones, can take place without the Secretary of State's permission; the form and nature of public examinations are the direct responsibility of the Secretary of State; power over the curriculum has been carved out of the duty imposed on the Secretary of State to promote education; directly and explicitly, the Secretary of State gives recognition as a teacher qualified to serve in state schools to every individual student successfully completing an approved course of teacher-training.

Despite this array of powers conferred by the 1944 Act, Secretaries of State during the decades following seemed set on policies of delegating as many of these powers to others as could decently be arranged. The reform and restructuring of secondary education which began in the 1960s was an exceptional use of the powers over school structure; but the slow progress of the following twenty years, while local authorities resisted, hastened, altered, and debated their response to the process of comprehensivisation, says perhaps more about the restrictions on central powers than it does about their efficacy. Power over the structure of examinations, played with timidly by the setting up of interminable working parties and committees, has again never been fully exercised until very recent times, though it was urgently needed at least two decades ago. The Secretary of State's involvement in the curriculum is a power newly tested. Despite the vocal opposition of the education establishment, it is a power any sensible tax-payer and parent would expect the Secretary of State to have and to exercise, and the move towards national agreement on the curriculum, provided proper safeguards are attached, is much to be welcomed.

During the three decades which followed the 1944 Act, Mrs Thatcher in her period as Secretary of State for Education was the only minister to pick up and examine the possibilities of the powers her office held over the qualifications of teachers. Strangely even she, like her successors of the Wilson and Callaghan years, failed to exploit the potential within them. The committee under Lord James of Rusholme, which reported in 1971, farsightedly saw that the demographic dip, reducing the demand for high numbers of entrants to the teaching profession, offered an opportunity to forget the quantity and concentrate on the quality.[2] Their recommendations, in the light of this opportunity, were that all new entrants to the profession should be graduates, and that the existing teaching force, who would continue to form the over-whelming majority of its number for the next two decades, should be provided with increased and strengthened in-service training.

The recommendations of the James Report were, in themselves, unarguable, and it is to the credit of the government of the day that attempts were made to ensure that the opportunity for improvement in quality was not allowed to slip. Unfortunately the magic prescription of 'graduate' was thought to be sufficient on its own to be effective, without anyone examining whether the nature of the BEd degree, as proposed and practised, was appropriate. Neither Lord James's committee, nor the government in its 1972 White Paper, attempted to lift the lid on the quality of the existing teacher-training system.[3] The recommendations for a 'two plus two' degree as it was called, that is to say a BEd which consisted of two years of general higher education, followed by two years of professional training, was an attempt to reconcile the conflict between academic study and professional training which was seen as a major problem of the structure of the BEd at that time. The government chose to accept the recommended introduction of the DipHE as a two-year general higher education qualification, but left the choice of whether the professional training element should be concurrent, that is to say woven alongside the higher education content or consecutive and separate from it, to the individual institutions and their validating bodies. The Secretary of State's direct powers to inquire into the quality of individual courses were once again delegated to the validating bodies, which increasingly meant the Council for National Academic Awards (CNAA). As area training authorities (ATOs) based in universities were disbanded, universities moved out of the validation of teacher-education, and more colleges moved into the polytechnic sector or merged into larger institutions validated by CNAA.

In retrospect, it seems strange that Margaret Thatcher as Secretary of State should have shown such touching faith in the ability of academic validating bodies to be guardians of the national interest in relation to the quality and nature of the teaching force. Apparently there was still no real understanding that the nature of the teachers' training and qualifications determined the most fundamental aspects of the internal workings of schools. In the event, the CNAA system of peer review ensured that the educationalists took over responsibility for the validation and accreditation of all BEd courses in the CNAA sector, and almost no input from academics in other disciplines was brought to bear on the consideration of the quality of the courses, nor of their fitness to provide for the needs of children in schools in the 1980s and 1990s.

Things might have taken a different turn, if it were not that the 1970s and early 1980s were periods of sharp contraction in the teacher-training system, when not only were whole institutions closed, but also those which remained were greatly reduced in size. Such a period does not encourage the development of course content into areas which would be taught by members of staff outside the beleaguered departments of education. The understandable wish to preserve the maximum number of jobs in schools and departments of education, as they merged into polytechnics and other large higher education institutions, led to an increase in the academic educational aspects of the course, together with a watering down of the academic subject content, which in the 1960s, particularly in university-validated institutions, had often constituted the degree-worthy component of the BEd course. It is not appropriate in this chapter to open up the debate of whether this was beneficial or not, but it was certainly the antithesis of what the 1972 White Paper's policies had intended, and led directly to the 1983 White Paper Teaching Quality,[4] and the initiatives which culminated in the publication of the criteria for initial training in Circular 3/84.[5]

The recognition in the 1972 White Paper of the need for increased training for the teaching force already in post was, in retrospect, most far-reaching and far-sighted. It was a policy admired and imitated by many other countries in the western world, and enabled the growth of award-bearing courses at both BEd and master's degree level, upgrading the qualifications of the existing teaching force on a very wide scale. As many of the BEd and MEd in-service programmes focused on the specific needs of schools, while others provided particularly for strengthening and updating in the subjects which the teachers were teaching, the value of much of the early provisions was very high indeed. Of course, it is possible to point to examples of higher education institutions offering courses which were inappropriate to the needs of the education system or indeed to the individual teachers who attended them, and the abuses of the financial provision for secondment, through the in-service pool, grew in number in the early 1980s.

Nevertheless, the generous provision of a right of access to higher education for teachers, many of whom had and still have only a three-year certificate built on O Levels, was an important move in the direction of quality. It would be tragic if, as Prime Minister, Mrs Thatcher were to preside over the destruction of in-service training provision in higher education. Policies for the provision of a teaching force adequately trained and fitted to the philosophies and needs of society are as vital for those already in service as they are for those undergoing initial training. It is therefore remarkable that the government should have removed the responsibility for determining the needs of teachers from the teachers and higher education institutions (who certainly did not always get it right) to the local education authorities, many of whom will interpret those needs very differently from the government's overriding priorities.

There were therefore clear signs, throughout the 1970s, that governments were beginning to realize that the quality of the teaching force was a central plank on which to build not only education policies, but also the broader social and economic policies which they were pursuing. Mrs Thatcher's recognition of the need for a unified force of academically well-qualified teachers was the first move, albeit not wholly successful, to move the British education system into the modern world.

The 1944 Act had provided that the teachers who staffed the secondary modern schools were to be trained in a broad liberal manner, two years following O Level or School Certificate, through a course with an academic content not expected to rise greatly above Higher School Certificate or A Level standard. Margaret Thatcher's call for graduates as the sole entrants to the teaching profession was thus a welcome recognition that the tradition of 1944 was dead. She sought to produce a teaching force which was itself educated well enough to produce the educated population a modern economy demands. Britain was indeed already far behind its competitors in the education it offered, and judged by the most direct of standards, that is to say the number of pupils who were prepared to stay on after the end of compulsory schooling, ours was the least successful secondary education of the advanced and civilized world.

Mrs Shirley Williams as Secretary of State built on the foundation which Mrs Thatcher had laid. During her period at the DES she too strengthened the priority for in-service training, and added to Mrs Thatcher's all-graduate entry requirements the further requirement of O Level Maths and English. To her eternal credit, she wrestled for the first time with the supply problems of shortage subjects in secondary schools. In launching the education 'Great Debate', Mrs Williams included sharp questions about the nature of the teaching force, and its adequacy for the nation's needs. She also voiced concern about a problem which had already become acute: the gap in teachers' knowledge of science, technology, industry, and commerce, on which the modern world is built.

Shirley Williams and James Callaghan articulated these concerns very clearly, and further raised public awareness of the inadequacies of the education system to meet the demands of modern society. The Education Debate, however, raised an even more important awareness in the public and political mind, which the government of the 1980s and particularly Sir Keith Joseph and Kenneth Baker have translated into action. This awareness was not only that the education system was failing to deliver the kind of educated adult population which a modern economy requires, but also that the country's schools, and that above all means its teachers, were no longer fulfilling their role as transmitters of the values and beliefs of the majority in society.

It was perhaps a uniquely British tradition which assumed that teachers would perform their role as transmitters of values without its requirement being explicitly stated. Perhaps too the origins of such a tradition lie in the days when there was a much greater consensus amongst the adult population as to the values which were to be handed on. Nevertheless, we have long accepted that Religious Education, with a syllabus approved by government, should be a mandatory element of the school curriculum, in contrast to the USA, where it is statutorily banned from the curriculum.

Outside the vexed area of Religious Instruction however, the record is less clear. The 1860 revised code, which some of its critics regard as an assertion by the State of its right to control education, rather than the Church, laid down very precise rules for the conditions on which the State was prepared to provide money for schools. HM Inspectors, charged not to interfere with Religious Instruction, discipline, or the management of schools, were sent to 'verify the fulfilment of the conditions on which grants are made'.[6] In what was perhaps an over-reaction to the value for money and payment by results era, the British system enjoyed for almost half a century a remarkable absence of any control over the content of education, not only at national, but even at local authority level. The responses to Shirley Williams' Circular 14/77, which asked authorities what arrangements they made for supervision of the curriculum, produced some historically remarkable responses, underlining the fact that the curriculum had become a very secret garden which the teachers both in their individual classrooms and collectively in their schools, or through their national teacher associations, tended and guarded for themselves.[7]

It would however be simplistic to suppose that public concern with the content of education, and in particular with the nature of the teaching force which delivered that content to pupils in the privacy of the classroom, stemmed solely from a move towards greater 'accountability'. The concern was more complex than that, and arose from a perception of attitudes of the teaching profession. These attitudes too often implied that society, including both parents and the future employers of pupils, had no right of interest or involvement in the content of what was taught. These attitudes were disguised under the acceptable form of professionalism, and the professionalization of the teaching force, most of which stemmed from the lengthening and strengthening of the pre-service and in-service training in the hands of educationalists, became a barrier which precluded the dialogue which society expected to have with its teachers about the education of its children. It is over a decade since I first heard a Swedish professor say 'our most important task is to de-professionalize the teachers': and at the time I resisted what he was saying. Since then, many of us recognized the danger of professional barriers between the general public and those activities which are central to our social policies and aspirations. Education is perhaps the major tool of social policy, and those who deliver education, the teachers, must reflect and respond to the philosophies, values, beliefs, and aspirations of the society they serve.

This analysis perhaps makes clearer the context in which Circular 3/84 was produced. In particular, I hope it sets in its immediate historical context the requirement that student teachers should acquire:

> a basic understanding of the type of society in which their pupils are growing up, with its cultural and racial mix, and of the relationships between the adult world and what is taught in schools, in particular, ways in which pupils can be helped to acquire an understanding of the values of a free society and its economic and other foundations.[8]

The call for pupils' awareness of the economic foundations

of the values of a free society is not just a call for the teaching of economics as a discipline, difficult as it is to separate that from ethical and social issues; nor is it a call for industry links, though these might be one of the many strategies for teachers to employ. It is rather a call for social and moral values to be specifically addressed. In other words, teachers are asked to explore with their pupils value-laden concepts such as profit; wealth distribution; exploitation; the right to work; the dignity of labour; pollution; state ownership; capitalism - and so on. What is more, the wording of the Circular suggests that the value-laden nature of such concepts should in no way be addressed in a neutral fashion, but that they should be taught in a way which directs the young towards the predominant values of their own society, and how these relate to its economic structures.

To those who lived through the educational ideas of the 1960s, embracing the Stenhouse theory of the neutral chairman, who left pupils free to reach their own conclusions about moral and social issues, some of this still comes as a surprise. Those days are however long past, and perhaps we have learnt to be wary of moral neutrality, and of an educational system which fails to make explicit to the young the values of their own society. Certainly the concept of education as a transmitter of society's values, with the elected government as guardian of those values, is not new. Aristotle argues:

> nobody would dispute that the education of the young requires the special attention of the law giver. Indeed the neglect of this in States is injurious to their constitution: for education ought to be adapted to the particular form of constitution ... and in so much as the end for the whole state is one, it is manifest that the superintendence of [education] must be public.[9]

In his concern for the transmission of the values considered desirable for the rulers or Guardians of the State, Plato argued for total censorship over what children were to be taught:

> Our first business will be to supervise the making of fables and legends, rejecting all which are unsatis-factory; and we shall induce nurses and mothers to tell their children only those which we have approved. ... Most of the stories now in use must be discarded.[10]

149

In more recent times, it was no accident that Hitler closed the universities at the beginning of his power in Germany in the 1930s, or that secondary and higher education were the first objects of attack in the tragic period of the cultural revolution in China. Plato wished for a controlled and censored education to ensure the correct educational 'product' fit to rule at the end of the process: while Hitler and the Gang of Four, like many other totalitarian regimes over the centuries, recognized the dangers in any form of extended education, however carefully controlled. They relied on curtailing all opportunties for the development of free and critical thinking. Both extremes however, in their way, demonstrate a recognition that every State depends, for the survival of its values, on the nature and content of the education system.

Common sense would lead us to believe that a society which believes passionately in its defence of freedom of thought, of speech, and of ideas, should take whatever steps are necessary to safeguard that freedom. These steps logically must include making explicit to the young those elements in their society which guarantee their freedoms, and these must surely include the economic structures of their society.

It was not the monetarists of the 1980s who first emphasized the dependence of social structure and values on the economic foundations of any society. Karl Marx's belief that all culture was merely the superstructure of economic life was redefined by the historian Engels, writing in the 1888 preface to The Communist Manifesto. He asserts:

> In every historical epoch, the prevailing mode of economic production and exchange, and the social organization necessarily following from it, form the basis upon which it is built up, and from which alone can be explained the political and intellectual history of that epoch.[11]

No one today, whether capitalist or communist, would question the relationship between the economic foundations of society and its current social and political values. There however the agreement would end. Many, for example, would argue that in a capitalist society no worker is truly free: others would argue that in a communist society none is free. The simple truth is that if teachers are to be asked, as Circular 3/84 suggests they should be, to teach pupils about the economic foundations of a free society, they are being asked to declare explicitly the political convictions and beliefs they hold. This, I do not doubt, is not precisely what was intended.

To sum up so far: I believe there are ample historical justifications for believing that schools should teach children about the values of their society, and that there are powerful historical arguments for the involvement of democratically elected governments in the content of what is taught, and therefore more specifically, in the nature and character of the teaching force. In British education the powers of the Secretary of State for Education to control the training and selection of teachers are well established, even though until recently they have been little used. If the government of the day, democratically elected, has a right to concern itself with the way in which social and economic values are transmitted through the schools, then undoubtedly it also has a right to concern itself with the way in which teachers are trained to pass on those values. The inescapable danger of such an approach, however, is that it opens the doors to political indoctrination: either beyond the control of government, if the teacher-training system continues to teach about the economic structures of society in ways which are politically uncontrolled; or through direct intervention in the content of what is taught about economic and social structures in the initial training of teachers. Of all the criteria for initial training promulgated in Circular 3/84, this one opens what is unquestionably the most frightening Pandora's Box of them all.

Faced with these difficult issues, it is not surprising that teacher-trainers, like the schools, have tended to take the simple approach of providing information about the economic structures of our society, rather than wrestling with the issues of political and moral controversy. Not only is this criterion the most controversial of those in Circular 3/84, it is also, on the evidence of the HMI survey of initial training, the one most ignored. In reporting on the training of secondary teachers, HMI comment:

> The world of work received imaginative coverage in only a few institutions. ... In general, however, the industrial and commercial relevance of the school curriculum was receiving scant attention. Little seems to have changed since the visits by HMI in 1980 and

1981 to find how students were acquiring the necessary skills to help their pupils prepare for adult life.[12]

The findings were the same in relation to primary training. Here HMI report: 'There were only isolated instances of institutions extending the students' understanding of industry and the world of work, and relating this to the education of children in primary schools.'[13]

This is all the more surprising, not only in view of the many initiatives which have been set up to foster and encourage work on economic awareness in initial training, but also in view of the great increase in the work in schools. Holley and Shelton, reporting in 1980 on the NFER project Economics Education 14-16, found that only 2 per cent of the school population received any formal education in economic awareness.[14] By 1987, when HMI conducted their own survey, they reported:

> an encouraging level of awareness in schools of the importance of economic understanding for all their pupils. This existed not only among teachers of economics, but also at senior management level and among those teachers responsible for mounting courses in personal and social education.[15]

In their survey, HMI not only examined the various activities which schools were offering for their pupils, but also pursued with pupils and through their written work the level of awareness and understanding which they had achieved. Here the results were often disappointing, and HMI found that the pupils' understanding tended to be 'at a descriptive rather than an analytical level'. Overall however, the most worrying feature of the HMI findings is the absence of any clear definition of what is to be achieved by education in economic understanding. In view of the very controversial and difficult nature of the topic, and yet its key importance to society's expectations today of what schools are doing, it is particularly worrying that schools themselves appear to have failed in so many instances to achieve a clear definition of what they are doing and why.

HMI were careful to assess whether there was any evidence of implicit or explicit bias in the teaching of economics and economic awareness. While there is congratulation for those many schools which avoided bias and demonstrated 'the utmost professionalism' HMI rightly expressed concern about the examples of teachers who deliberately side-stepped any controversial issues. They cite the example of a geography lesson dealing with the fall in the demand for coal and the subsequent decline of the coal-mining industry, where there was no reference to the miners' strike or the economic and social issues which it raised. It is noteworthy that the teacher described her reason for avoiding such an issue by saying she wanted to 'stick to the facts'. The example is a poignant reminder of the difficulty of presenting facts in any meaningful way, without some political and social assessment of the facts themselves, and exhibits clearly the inescapable dilemma of economic awareness as a feature of the school curriculum.

One of the initiatives designed to support the trainers of teachers in introducing such issues into the initial training courses was the Industrial and Commercial Perspectives in Initial Teacher Education Project (ICP) based at Bath and Southampton Universities. This project is jointly funded by the DES and the Department of Trade and Industry (DTI) and is due to present its final report in 1988. ICP has done some excellent work in producing resourcing materials and syllabuses for use within courses of secondary initial training. The project's aims are to promote in tutors an awareness of the potential of the industrial context for presenting educational issues, and in students a command of the skills needed to foster industrial awareness and understanding in pupils. Some discouraging evidence of the level of interest and commitment to economic awareness is illustrated by the fact that the response rate of institutions to the ICP was very low indeed: only 33 per cent of PGCE courses and 27 per cent of BEd or concurrent courses replied to their initial survey.

However, a particularly useful feature of the project has been its commitment to that aspect of the Circular 3/84 criteria which calls for 'adequate attention to the methodology of teaching the chosen subject ... and of relating it ... to the everyday life and work of the community'.[16] This criterion related the initial training requirement of teachers to the requirement of the 'applied curriculum' which they will have to deliver in the schools. At first sight this may seem a long way removed from the broader and more troubled waters of awareness of the economic foundations of a free society; nevertheless the ways in which knowledge is used and applied in the day-to-day business of the adult community is a central path

153

towards the real understanding of why we have schools, and of what the education system is funded by society to do.

In this broad context we can perhaps feel less dismay that the schools HMI visited were concentrating on delivering economic understanding and economic facts, rather than dealing head on with the political, social, and moral issues attached to those facts. Education is a central, cultural, and social institution: the vehicle through which society passes on its values, skills, and knowledge from one generation to another. Any move which encourages teachers to pass on the facts of history, mathematics, geography, and science, as well as the skills of music, dance, art, poetry, and the appreciation of literature, in a way which relates these academic subjects to the overall activities of society, seems to me to be a move in the right direction. Of course facts cannot be left by themselves: you cannot tell children about the facts of poverty without exploring the reasons for it, nor can you tell children the facts about industry, international trade, or the welfare state without exploring the ways in which the success of one interrelates with the success of the others. In exploring the reasons behind the facts, perhaps some teachers will fail to avoid controversy, and that may be no bad thing. One of the freedoms which all of us should cherish is the freedom of speech, and teachers should not be exempt from this, although their professionalism, in the right sense of that word, must safeguard them from the temptation to indoctrinate.

So from the evidence of what is happening, both in the schools and in initial teacher education, we can draw both comfort and concern. Concern because as yet not enough is happening: the economic foundations on which our society is based, with its strengths and its weaknesses, are not being fully communicated to and understood by all the young people growing up in our society. In this regard the criterion is wholly justified. We are a free society in so many ways, but our freedom cannot be safeguarded unless all members of our society understand what it is that gives or denies them their freedom. A free society has a responsibility to ensure that children growing up understand this, and cherish and respect those aspects of freedom which their ancestors have won for them.

Concern there is too, for the absence of a commitment to the serious issues in initial teacher education means that teachers are unprepared in themselves to tackle the important aspects of economic awareness and understanding in their teaching, and therefore they may tackle them badly or not at all. The initial training system has for far too long lagged behind developments in the schools, and the development of economic awareness amongst teachers themselves is too key a requirement in these uncertain times to be allowed to go by default.

Comfort there is also in the findings of the various surveys in that examples of good practice exist, free from unacceptable bias, and yet designed to increase pupils' understanding and awareness. These examples provide a model for others to copy, and can be a more widespread and generalized experience, particularly within the vehicles now available through TVEI and similar curricular initiatives.

Bias and mishandling of controversial issues will always be found in some teaching. I however have great faith in the resilience of pupils, provided that they are exposed to a wide range of views and opinions, and this surely argues for economic, moral, and social issues being openly discussed by all teachers, at the level that this is appropriate within the subjects they teach. Slowly but surely the framework of our education system is moving into the modern age, as we attempt to provide a common curriculum for all abilities, a common system of examinations, and a broad and balanced curricular experience, on which we hope an increasingly large percentage of young people will build further and higher education opportunities. Such a better-educated population must understand their society, what makes it work, and what bestows upon them the freedom and opportunity they enjoy, as well as those aspects of society which deny such freedom and opportunity to others.

To deliver such a curriculum we need teachers who are themselves educated and aware: able to debate openly and intelligently with their pupils: but most of all able, open, and willing to debate with the community outside the school about the kind of education it expects. We have still a long way to go. Too many teachers are afraid of the criticism from outside - and they have been bruised understandably by the public debate of the last twelve years - and they retreat into Professionalism (with a capital P) which acts as a barrier between them and those who could well be their allies. The majority of the teachers who will staff the schools of the twenty-first century, throughout its first decade at least, are already in our schools today. The demand for new teachers through the 1990s will greatly exceed any possibilities of supply through the conventional

18-plus graduate route, and we have yet to see how the government will respond to that numerical dilemma. What is certain is that in addition to the measures taken in initial training, appropriate in-service training, geared very closely to the aspirations and priorities of the majority of the nation as a whole and not just to any individual local authority, will be needed if we are to maintain a national teaching force, reflecting in its teaching the national purposes and goals of education.

We, by which I mean all of us in the education service at whatever level, exist to serve the needs and aspirations of the whole nation. At our peril do we fail to remember or pay attention to that one central truth.

NOTES AND REFERENCES

1   Erasmus, Desiderius: Opera Omnia, vol. 1, trans. W.H. Woodward, New York, Macmillan, 1904.
2   DES, Teacher Education and Training, James Report, London, HMSO, 1972.
3   DES, Education: A Framework for Expansion, Cmnd 5174, London, HMSO, 1972.
4   DES, Teaching Quality, Cmnd 8836, London, HMSO, 1983.
5   DES, Initial Teacher Training - Approval of Courses, Circular 3/84, London, DES, 1984.
6   Board of Education, Minutes and Regulations of the Privy Council on Education, Reduced to the Form of a Code, London, Board of Education, 1860.
7   DES, Local Education Authority Arrangements for the School Curriculum, Circular 10/77, London, DES, 1977.
8   DES, 1984, op. cit., p. 26, para 12.
9   Aristotle, The Politics, book 8, trans. H. Rackman, Cambridge, Mass., Harvard University Press, 1932.
10   Plato, Fragment 12, trans. J. Burnet, in Early Greek Philosophy, London, Black, 1920.
11   F. Engels (ed.) 'Preface' to The Communist Manifesto, 1888.
12   HMI, Quality in Schools: The Initial Training of Teachers, London, HMSO, 1987, p. 125.
13   Ibid., p. 102.
14   B.J. Holley and V. Shelton, Economics Education 14-16, phase 1, Final Report, Windsor, NFER, 1980.

15 HMI, <u>Economic Understanding in the School Curriculum</u>, London, DES, 1987.
16 DES, 1984, op. cit., p. 26, para 8.

9

TRAINING FOR SPECIAL NEEDS

Robert Povey and Peter Abbotts

Chairman: We have to decide on the allocation of hours to courses in Professional Studies by 4 o'clock. So perhaps we'd better make a start? Brian, since you drew up the discussion paper perhaps you would take us through it?

Brian: Thank you, Chairman. The document is, I think, fairly self-explanatory. We have the same number of competing demands for inclusion in the primary BEd timetable as last year - mathematics, language, RE, movement studies, etc. - but we also have to find space for a larger special needs component this year.

Chairman: But wasn't it only last year that we renegotiated the timetable to provide more Bullock hours (or was it Cockcroft hours - I forget)? Anyway we have certainly been under pressure to provide a thick spread of language and mathematics across the curriculum.

Brian: Quite so, Chairman, but now we need some Warnock hours. The Principal has been nattering on at me about this for some time, waving DES circulars and asking what we are doing about it. So I have tried to re-shuffle the hours yet again in a way which accommodates the increased special needs component, and I hope we shall be

able to reach an acceptable compromise
solution with our usual degree of flexibility.

Anyone who has been involved in negotiating the curriculum
in a college, polytechnic, or university Department of
Education is likely to recognize something familiar in this
dialogue since discussions about what should be included in
initial training courses feature as both annuals and
perennials in the world of teacher-education. The annual
(and more frequent) discussions of teaching programmes
take place against the backcloth of perennial white-papered
documents from the DES and its associated advisory bodies
offering advice and directives; in the last few years this
stream of DES-inspired opinion and advice has built up from
a slow trickle to an almost irresistible flood. In recent years
discussions about in-service provision have also been
subjected to similar pressures from DES and LEA training
proposals culminating in the recent TVEI and grant-related
training initiatives (TRIST and GRIST). The first part of this
chapter deals with this historical backcloth and the rest of
the chapter discusses recent research on development in
special needs teaching within the context of teacher-
training. We conclude with a report of an hitherto
unpublished survey carried out as part of our research for
this chapter.

FROM JAMES TO WARNOCK

The committee which produced the James Report argued
that all students in initial training should receive a general
introduction to the problems of children with learning
difficulties but they also hinted that many of the skills
involved in the teaching of handicapped children could
probably be developed most effectively on the basis of some
experience of teaching.[1]
    In many respects these recommendations in the James
Report probably reflected the status quo in teacher
education since many training establishments in the pre-
James era had been providing courses with special needs
components for both initial training and in-service students.
Some of these teaching programmes were offered as
'common core' courses dealing with individual differences in
general and covering certain basic aspects of special needs;
others were optional courses covering specific areas of

special needs (e.g. the education of slow-learning children). Thus the recent upsurge of interest in special needs courses may be mistakenly interpreted as an indication that these are entirely new elements in the curriculum of student teachers; whereas they might be more accurately described, in many contexts, as developments of existing strands of the curriculum. Indeed we have experience of teaching (and being taught) on such courses, and can testify from first-hand knowledge that they frequently tended to be over-subscribed - even without the pulling power of DES endorsements! It is perhaps salutary to note at this point, therefore, that previous generations of teacher-trainers had recognized the importance of special needs courses in the Teachers' Certificate, BEd, and PGCE curricula well before the advent of the Warnock Report, which provides the next significant stage in the development of special needs teaching in teacher-education.

If the James Report could be described as taking a 'cool' position on the inclusion of special needs courses in initial teacher training, the Warnock Report could be said to be distinctly 'hot'.[2] The Warnock Committee adopted what Mittler has called an 'integrationist' approach to the provision of courses in teacher-training.[3] A 'special education element' was to be included in all courses of initial teacher-training, taught within the general context of child development. The aims of this element should be:

1   to develop an awareness that all school teachers, whatever the age group of their pupils or level of their work, are likely to be concerned with helping some children who have special educational needs;

2   to enable teachers to recognize early signs of possible special educational need;

3   to give teachers knowledge of the part which they can play in the assessment of a child's educational needs and in the execution of any special measures prescribed;

4   to give teachers knowledge of what special education is like, together with knowledge of the range of various forms of special educational provision and of specialist advisory services;

5   to provide some acquaintance with special schools, classes, and units;

6   to give teachers some understanding of how to communicate effectively with parents and an awareness of the importance of appreciating parents' anxieties and encouraging their continued involvement in their child's progress;

7   ABOVE ALL, to give teachers knowledge in general terms of when and where to refer for special help.

The Warnock Committee recognized that it would be difficult to accommodate their proposals within the already congested timetable of existing initial training courses. They regarded it as essential, however, that the special education element:

should be explicitly covered in all initial teacher training courses for teachers of all subjects and age ranges, including postgraduate courses, as part of a coherent and well co-ordinated plan drawn up by each college and department of education.

In the mean time in order to meet the needs of the teachers already in schools a crash programme of short in-service courses was recommended, equal to about a week's full-time study.

A government White Paper, Special Needs in Education, followed slowly on the heels of Warnock.[4] The new, broadly based concept of special educational needs was accepted; in a splendid piece of government rhetoric, the principle that handicapped pupils should be integrated into the normal school wherever possible was also embraced like a cold piece of wet cod, at arms' length and wrapped in fine print! The government intended 'that the process of planned and sensible integration of handicapped children into ordinary schools should continue'. It did not, however, 'propose to bring into force section 10 of the Education Act 1976' (which provided for the integration of handicapped children). 'Special educational needs' had been replaced, as someone remarked at the time, by 'present economic circumstances'. Nevertheless the government had accepted the new concept of special educational needs and this carried the implication that something like 20 per cent of the school population would have special needs at some time in their school careers. They further recognized that this new concept:

puts a premium on the teacher's skill in recognizing each child's characteristics, noticing special needs where they emerge, and responding to those needs. This should be progressively reflected in teacher education and training, as resources permit.

With the Education Act, 1981, a start was made on the conversion of words into legislative action (or inaction if emphasis is given to the fact that the Act did not come into effect until 1 April 1983). The Act did not receive universal acclamation, however, and as Margaret Peter reported in an editorial in the British Journal of Special Education, 'it has been variously described ... as "a step in the right direction", "a dead mouse" and like Brighton pier "good as far as it goes but ... not much of a way to get to France".'[5] It did nevertheless give a strong (if belated) nudge to the integration movement and LEAs now had a duty:

to educate children with special needs in ordinary schools provided that educating the child in an ordinary school is compatible with:

(a) his receiving the special educational provision that he requires;
(b) the provision of efficient education for the children with whom he will be educated; and
(c) the efficient use of resources.

The 'let out' clauses are likely, of course, to dent the efficacy of the Act in practice, and the evidence for the post-1981 period is not very encouraging. Swann, for example, reports that:

overall, there is no evidence of a trend towards integration. ... There is evidence of integration in the case of children with sensory handicaps, but in the case of children with learning difficulties and those termed maladjusted, there is clear evidence of a trend towards increasing segregation, especially in the primary age group.[6]

Mary Warnock has also expressed disquiet at the way in which the Act is operating in practice and wonders 'where we went wrong'.[7] The Warnock Committee had envisaged that 'recorded' (later 'statemented') pupils would constitute a very small fraction of the total school population (probably less than the 2 per cent of children who were in special schools at the time the Report was being compiled). She notes how the numbers of statemented children were becoming much greater than the Warnock Committee's expectations and laments the fact that some schools appeared to have decided 'that only children with statements could be treated as having special needs'. In other instances, it is clear that statements were being written in accordance with available provision rather than the pupil's individual needs. As Smith puts it, 'to talk of "statementing" children reduces what should be a sensitive appraisal of personal needs to a bureaucratic procedure'.[8]

The proliferation of 'bureaucratic statementing' is also illustrated by Peter, who provides examples of how statementing has jammed up the works in some school psychological services.[9] In relation to the 1981 Act and its effects in practice she argues that the:

> creature has a voracious appetite for paper in all forms. It takes a long time to goad into action and it needs far too many educational psychologists, teachers, administrators and other staff to keep it up to scratch.

Such problems, indeed, led to the setting up of a House of Commons Select Committee in February 1987, to inquire into the Act's operation. The report of the Committee, which was published in mid-June 1987, admonishes the DES for its very limited monitoring of the implications of the 1981 Act and for failing to disseminate examples of good practice.[10] It notes the confusion which has been evident in the interpretation of terminology used in the Act and the widespread variations in practice relating to 'statementing', and recommends that the DES should investigate ways of improving the functioning of the Act. We shall have to wait and see what effects the comments of the Select Committee will have in practice.

The scene for teacher-trainers had, however, been set by the implementation of the 1981 Act and it was clear that in the post-1981 era student teachers and classroom teachers would increasingly be expected to possess the skills necessary to deal with children with special needs within the ordinary school. The HMI discussion paper, Teaching in Schools: The Content of Initial Training, stated the case unambiguously as far as initial training is concerned:

> An effective course of training should include those aspects of the teacher's skill which relate to ... the recognition of children with special needs in the ordinary classroom. ... While some students may wish to pursue further specialist options in these concerns, they should be part of the basic professional preparation of all teachers in relation to the subjects they will teach to the children of any 'normal' classroom.[11]

As far as in-service training is concerned the 1981 Act (and the earlier Warnock recommendations) could be seen as a catalyst for revised in-service training opportunities in special educational needs. The claim that 'every teacher [is] a special needs teacher' was intended to strike hard and the development of an integrationist policy had clear implications for the further training of teachers.[12] In the pre-Warnock era there had been an inevitable over-representation of special school teachers on in-service training courses epitomized by the Diplomas in Advanced Special Education to be found in most training establishments. The philosophy of Warnock and the 1981 Act, with the move away from categories of handicap towards the concept of 'special needs' and integrationist policies, meant that mainstream teachers would increasingly become the targets of in-service courses in special needs.

The change could be characterized somewhat crudely, perhaps, as a move away from the handicap-based, medically inspired view of special education towards the type of initiative which placed curriculum issues first. This approach sought to encourage teachers to consider pupils' needs primarily in terms of their implications for the mainstream curriculum and to avoid an over-emphasis on stereotyped groupings, an approach clearly articulated in the 1985 Fish Report.[13] The transition from the pre-Warnock philosophy in special education to this newer thinking, emphasizing the modification of mainstream curricula, the development of whole school policies and new professional competencies, has taken place at a breathless pace but its progress has been clearly discernible and the revised patterns of delivery well documented.[14]

Two further watersheds have confronted those of us involved in in-service training. First, there is no doubt that the DES Specific Grants Scheme initiated in 1983 through Circular 3/83, not only provided a favourable financial fillip for one-term training opportunities in certain areas (of which special educational needs in mainstream schools was one) but also threw out the challenge to those training establishments which felt suitably equipped for the task to contemplate the initiation of new modes of INSET. The specific task for training course tutors was quite clear: to develop, with the local authorities as active partners, one-term programmes in which awareness of the range of children's special needs in ordinary school situations was the initial focus. The demand for such 'awareness courses' was considerable and their provision helped to emphasize the importance of special needs provision. It also seems likely that these courses helped to confirm the position of special needs in the financial pecking order of many local authorities; it is interesting that this area is still seen by Circular 6/86, marking the coming of the Grant Related In-Service Training Initiative (GRIST), as a national priority area. The difficulties of balancing the financial equation presented by the post-1981 Act priorities, however, are highlighted by Taylor, who suggests that a national advisory body might be set up to help in the co-ordination of such activities.[15] Such a body would be charged with the duty of providing guidance on 'such fundamental matters as the proper pace of integration, the proportion of the total school population which might eventually warrant state-ments and the appropriate development of post-school education and training'. The Report of the 1987 Select Committee is circumspect about the establishment of such a body. It supports instead the setting up of a 'multi-disciplinary national development group' which would contribute to the development of good professional practice in special education and would have to focus on certain aspects of professional practice which had been selected as priority areas 'in consultation with the Government and other interested parties'.

Second, the new criteria which emerged in 1984 from the Advisory Committee for the Supply and Education of Teachers (ACSET) had far-reaching implications for in-service training, notably the criterion that in-service training in special needs should be offered to those teachers who already had good experience in teaching across the full range of pupils.[16] Furthermore, ACSET introduced a major shift of emphasis, suggesting that it is inappropriate in initial teacher-training to include courses aiming to inculcate skills for teaching pupils with very specific educational needs. ACSET recognized the importance of 'awareness courses' as part of initial training but argued against the continued provision of the small number of ITT degrees offering professional qualifications in the teaching of children with special needs (e.g. mentally handicapped children). Such courses, it was argued, should not be introduced until the in-service stage. The immediate effect of this policy would be, of course, to reduce the supply of teachers to the key areas of severe learning difficulty and sensory impairment; it is debatable whether a sufficient supply of adequately qualified teachers could be maintained via the in-service/short course route. A strong case can certainly be made for retaining some four-year training provision for those individuals who are clearly committed to working with children with special needs. The benefit which such four-year-trained teachers can provide in our overall SEN teaching provision may well outweigh any disadvantages related to their limited experience with non-handicapped pupils. Leaving aside this debate for the moment, however, what evidence is there that teacher-training courses have implemented the various special needs recommendations since the 1978 Warnock Report?

RESEARCH SURVEYS ON DEVELOPMENTS IN SPECIAL NEEDS TRAINING

Studies by HMI, Sewell, and Labon

The provision of special needs courses in initial training has been somewhat patchy and this is revealed very clearly in a report on developments in the BEd degree course.[17] Fifteen non-university-sector institutions were visited by HMI during 1977 to assess the quality of their BEd courses. They reported that:

> the compulsory elements of most courses did not ... bring students towards much awareness of the special needs of certain categories of children, in particular those with a cultural background different from that of the majority or those whose learning was otherwise handicapped. ... Expertise in both areas was usually present among a college's staff but it was made available chiefly in optional courses.

As far as PGCE courses are concerned, Sewell investigated the provision of special needs within the university sector in

England and Wales.[18] Since only about half the university departments replied, it is not possible to draw any clear conclusions from the evidence about the state of university education departments in general. It is possible, however, to distinguish certain trends and there is no strong reason for thinking that these trends are unrepresentative of provision in the university sector at that time. Only nine (50 per cent) of the departments had a compulsory special needs element and in four of these cases the compulsory element amounted to one lecture session only. Of the departments replying, 83 per cent did, however, provide optional courses in special needs with a time allocation ranging from two to sixteen hours. The proportion of students taking option courses was only between 10 per cent and 25 per cent of the student body in departments offering such courses. Despite the paucity of provision and the limited number of lecturers qualified to teach in the sphere of special needs, however, there did appear to be a clear enthusiasm amongst the students for the courses on offer (a point we have noted earlier).

A more recent inquiry into the state of special needs provision in university-based PGCE courses is that of Labon, whose project was based in the Department of Education at the University of Southampton and organized by the Department of Educational Studies in the University of Oxford.[19] Thirty-one of the thirty-two English and Welsh university departments of education supplied information on their special needs provision either by completing a questionnaire or by incorporating such information in a letter to the research officer. Despite the inexact nature of the response data and the differences in sample size between the Sewell and Labon inquiries, one or two tentative comparisons are possible. It appears, for example, that the degree of overall activity in the special needs area was rather more energetic in 1982-3 than in 1980-1. (To what extent this was 'cosmetic energy' is, however, less easy to determine.) Labon reports:

> at least 30 of the 32 university education departments in England and Wales are making some provision broadly along the lines recommended by the Warnock Report ... [but] whereas explicit provision is extensive in a few universities, in the majority it is relatively small.

Thus the median provision of 'common core' special needs

elements in which all PGCE students participated appeared to be five or so staff-student contact hours in the form of lectures by two departmental staff and visiting contributions from LEA or another university department.

As far as optional programmes are concerned at least twenty-seven of the thirty-two university courses included a form of special education option. The median departmental picture was that of about three staff, one of whom may be co-opted on a visiting basis, offering a single option which takes up twenty or so staff-student contact hours and recruits something like 25 per cent of the students in that year group. Labon noted:

> a relative shortfall in coverage of support services ... use of micro-teaching techniques, organised school visits and practice in developing observation skills [and] marked under-representation of content designed to enable students to communicate effectively with parents.

Amongst practices receiving a commendatory comment, on the other hand, was one in which a whole cohort was engaged for a block of time (e.g. for a week) 'in a focused study of special needs'.

Oxford Educational Research Group studies

In 1984-5 a postal survey was conducted, under the auspices of the Oxford Educational Research Group (OERG), to reassess provision in university departments of education since Labon's survey.[20] Twenty-five out of thirty-two departments responded. The replies suggested that special needs provision in university departments had been subjected to some reappraisal since 1982-3, 40 per cent having increased the amount of whole-cohort provision, 8 per cent reporting the developing of optional courses in special needs, and 28 per cent indicating that special needs teaching was being carried out within the context of curriculum method work. Just over half of the departments responding (52 per cent) made the point that they had begun to concentrate their special needs curriculum on the skills required in teaching pupils with special needs rather than on 'awareness courses'.

This latter development is likely to have been influenced by the 1984 ACSET report, which argued that 'subject specialist teachers should be equipped to take account of special educational needs in the planning and development of their curriculum areas'.[21] The message here was clear for those organizing initial teacher-training, that institutions should be preparing subject specialists to consider special needs within their own curriculum, not as an adjunct (and in some cases an 'optional extra') to their professional preparation. 'Special educational needs' (SEN) was clearly a concept best suited to 'permeation'. No longer would the 'special needs person' be marshalled to do the annual block on special needs for the BEds and the PGCEs but an examination of approaches to the teaching of children with special needs would be seen as an integral part of the content of 'method' courses.

This is a conclusion reinforced by the findings of a number of other studies undertaken by OERG (under whose auspices Labon's 1984 study was also carried out). Summaries of these findings can be found in a booklet produced by OERG in 1987. The group argue that curriculum work in teacher education should incorporate a concept of special needs which stresses that:

> teaching techniques available to the mainstream teacher can help to relieve pupils' learning difficulties and should provide insights into a range of such techniques. This work should be embedded in the curriculum programme and not handled as a separate issue, to be dismissed in one or two specific sessions.[22]

'Permeation' would thus enable students on initial training courses to consider the learning and behaviour problems faced by SEN pupils, in the context of their method courses. As Smith has demonstrated, student teachers see such issues as immediately relevant to their teaching activities in schools.[23] Permeation would also tend, on the other hand, to preclude detailed consideration of the aetiology, identification, and treatment of severely handicapping conditions (such as Severe Learning Difficulties and various physical handicaps) within general courses of initial teacher-training. It could be argued, however, following the 1984 lead of ACSET, that most future mainstream teachers are unlikely to come into frequent teaching contact with such pupils and that some 'awareness' teaching would be sufficient in this context.

Furthermore it is clear from the OERG studies that too

much emphasis on 'special needs' pupils as an additional, as opposed to an integral, part of subject teaching, tends to reinforce the notion of the separateness of such pupils. The provision of option courses and the excessive use of 'outside experts' to provide the special needs input, usually relating to pupils at extreme ends of the range of needs, can also have the same effect. Indeed, in one of the early OERG studies it was found that students attending a special needs option course were not very idealistic about integrating special needs pupils into mainstream classes and 'saw "withdrawal" into special classes as the most suitable form of provision'. Such evidence supports the view that a curriculum-led approach adopting permeation as a key-note feature is likely to provide a firmer basis for the development of courses in teacher-training than the more traditional 'apartheid' approach in which special needs courses are partitioned off for separate development.

The adoption of such an 'integrated' approach also draws attention to the importance of developing criterion-referenced assessments in relation to special needs work, so that problems and curriculum programmes can be identified in specific skill-related terms. With this teaching approach in mind the OERG has produced a series of materials designed to assist the student teacher in preparing for teaching in mainstream schools. The series is entitled Special Educational Needs in Mainstream Schools and covers such areas as classroom responses to learning difficulties, classroom responses to disruptive behaviour, and organizing a school's response.[24]

For primary schools, the Special Needs Action Programme (SNAP) developed in Coventry is, of course, already well used.[25] This concentrates on increasing the teacher's initial identification and intervention skills; in organization it employs a 'pyramid' approach in which teachers who have attended preparatory SNAP courses then develop school-based in-service courses for colleagues. A recent appraisal of the impact of SNAP by Muncey emphasizes not just the active involvement of all teachers in early identification but the goal of active learning through multi-media modules, as if to chastise those who may have considered that SNAP was a rigid package concerned with identification and assessment alone.[26]

Povey and Abbotts' survey

Our own survey was carried out in relation to provision for the academic year 1986/7. A questionnaire was distributed to a sample of lecturers responsible for special needs courses in universities, colleges, and polytechnics. The sample was drawn from lecturers attending two DES conferences in the summer of 1986 and the spring of 1987. Participants were asked to complete a short questionnaire and a response rate of over 70 per cent was achieved. The lecturers were asked for details of the courses taught (including numbers of hours devoted to compulsory and optional courses) and of teaching methods and modes of assessment used in relation to PGCE, BEd, BA/BSc and diploma/higher degree courses. They were also asked about staffing levels and about the strengths of their courses and problems associated with special needs teaching.

The final sample included responses relating to seven university departments of education, five polytechnics, and sixteen colleges. This represents about 20 per cent of university and polytechnic departments, and 40 per cent of education departments in colleges of higher education in England and Wales. The findings are likely to offer, therefore, a reasonable (though not necessarily representative) indication of current practice in colleges, polytechnics, and university departments of education. Since the institutions had been invited to attend or had decided to attend the conferences because of their involvement in special needs work, however, it can be assumed that the findings represent a substantially accurate picture of life in education departments which are active in the sphere of special needs in England and Wales.

Some course tutors claimed that special needs teaching followed the 'permeation' model and in these instances 'hourly returns' were not produced. In most cases, however, tutors did provide estimates of contact time on an hourly basis. From the responses for PGCE courses it is clear that the majority of institutions still include only a small number of hours on common core courses. Of the institutions offering such courses 61 per cent, provided only nine hours teaching or less, with a maximum of twenty hours. This includes a rise in the median number of hours on the university courses sampled from five to six hours when compared with Labon's 1984 study, but the number of universities surveyed in the present research is, of course, much smaller and this finding may not be entirely representative of British universities generally. As might be expected, because of the longer period of teaching time available on the BEd courses, the number of common core hours for such courses tended to be somewhat higher, over half being between twenty-five and fifty hours. The great majority of institutions offered optional courses in special needs in both BEd and PGCE contexts.

In general, these courses were extremely popular and the usual proportion of the student cohorts electing to take them was between 20 per cent and 50 per cent. The courses tended to be more popular in the BEd than the PGCE setting. In relation to BEd courses all courses attracted at least 20 per cent of the student cohort (apart from one course which was selected by only 10 per cent of the student group) whereas the majority of PGCE optional courses were attended by fewer than 20 per cent of the total student cohort. Very little provision was made for special needs courses in BA/BSc degrees, despite the clear attraction of such courses when they were on offer. This paucity of provision presumably reflects the view amongst lecturers in higher education that special needs courses are most suitably placed within an essentially professional rather than academic context.

In relation to staffing provision, it is interesting to note that the 'median' picture drawn by Labon of about three staff per department seemed to be roughly the same in our survey, even though the range of courses on offer is greater in many cases than it appeared to be in the earlier study. The range in staff provision (based on the numbers of staff having special needs as their main teaching commitment) extended from 0 to 8. In 6 per cent of the institutions responding there were three or fewer staff engaged in special needs courses as their main teaching commitment; in 15 per cent of the institutions there was no lecturer at all in this category. The best-staffed institutions appeared to be the polytechnics with 80 per cent having five or more special needs lecturers; the colleges had 31 per cent in this category but none of the seven universities responding had more than four members of staff with special needs as their main commitment.

Joint LEA/college of department appointments were conspicuous by their absence. If one excludes university departments offering professional training for educational psychologists, for which course joint LEA appintments are often an essential component, there were only three institutions with staff operating on the basis of joint funding. The majority of institutions, of course, involve LEA support services (such as educational psychologists, advisory teachers, special school staff) in taking sessions or supervising practical placements on special needs courses. In one institution 30 per cent to 40 per cent of the teaching on special needs courses was carried out by such individuals. Nevertheless, the lack of jointly funded posts is still somewhat surprising. The establishment of joint appointments by LEAs and colleges/departments is a practice which has much to commend it, as Moore has argued; our experience in Kent suggests that it can work most effectively provided the college and LEA have closely identified objectives.

In relation to the content of courses, these range widely with perhaps most emphasis (following the lead of the 1981 Act) on learning difficulties. In the INSET context the courses dealing with Special Educational Needs in the Ordinary School (SENIOS) appear to be the cornerstone of the teaching programmes on offer. These are essentially those courses initiated originally by Circular 3/83. One of the aspects of special needs work which these courses often attempt to address is that of the need to effect and manage institutional changes, that is changes in school organization and teaching strategy.[27] What are required, perhaps, are programmes of systems management for teachers to complement attempts to modify pupils' behaviour, to which end methods of applied behavioural analysis are already well used.[28] Increasingly, courses have organizational changes as one of their primary objectives, in addition to the 'awareness-raising' component which still emerges strongly in the course descriptions.

The methods of teaching (or 'delivering the service' in the current inelegant, mechanistic terminology!) ranged in our survey from the traditional lecture-based 'awareness course', through seminars and tutorials to the increasingly common 'school-focused', practical, and workshop approaches. (In partial defence of the odd group lecture it is worth mentioning that the OERG studies found that lectures were effective in transmitting information about special needs but that they did little to alter attitudes.) The policy of permeation was mentioned by several respondents and in at least one instance there was evidence of collaborative teaching between special needs and method tutors. One of the difficulties of the permeated approach is often the lack of permeated 'special needs' expertise within the method departments. It seems likely, therefore, that this pattern of collaborative teaching is one which will become quite common in teacher-education until the skills of special needs teaching become more widely dispersed throughout the subject departments.

Observation exercises and the keeping of practical diaries or notebooks during school-based experiences were reported by several respondents and there was some evidence of student-centred learning,[29] and one mention of action research and self-evaluation.[30] There was no direct reference, however, to skill-based teaching. This does not mean that skill-based teaching is not being carried out, of course, but, unlike the conclusion drawn by the OERG survey, it is clearly not one of the features of special needs courses which stands out. Similarly apart from one institution which was heavily involved in this area, there was very little evidence of any major involvement of computer software in special needs courses.

The organization of courses appears to be increasingly modular in order partly to cater for the demands of LEAs for flexibility in the provision of courses to meet changing needs. For example, the problems engendered by the removal of recognized professional training courses for teachers of pupils with special needs at the ITT stage has created a pressure for INSET courses, particularly in the sphere of severe learning difficulties.[31] Indeed, the fact that recent DES guidelines have identified the areas of sensory and severe learning difficulties as priority areas for INSET suggests that this is now being recognized at government level. This would still appear, however, to leave the special schools for emotional and behavioural difficulties, moderate learning difficulties, and speech and language difficulties with an undesirably low proportion of teachers having advanced qualifications.

On the assessment of course, the lecturers' responses showed a wide range of approaches being employed, from the traditional three-hour unseen paper through 'revealed' papers to course work, school-focused projects, and dissertations. One feature worth commenting upon is the clear demise of the traditional three-hour paper in the examination of special needs courses. This type of examination is still fairly prevalent in the BEd degree (58 per cent of such courses being examined this way); only 11 per cent of PGCE courses were assessed by written papers and only 14 per cent of in-service courses.

Finally, tutors were asked about the strengths/ innovations in their courses and about teaching/ organizational problems. Strengths ranged from the one centre in which computer software was being developed to the introduction of problem-solving elements, permeation, and, frequently, school-focused work. A number of special needs tutors engaged in regular exchange arrangements with teacher colleagues in schools, thus ensuring that the lecturers have 'recent, relevant teaching experience' and that the students benefit from a rich cross-fertilization of ideas between schools and colleges/departments. A type of 'European dimension' was also evident in some responses to the 'strengths' section of the questionnaire. In some cases this took the form of reciprocal arrangements in which staff and students attend European conferences or study programmes and, in other cases, lecturers were contributing teaching sessions in other teacher-training institutions in Europe.

Problems ranged from the common 'under-staffed/over-worked' variety to 'the wide spread of expertise needed to match student need' variety. The uncertainty created by funding arrangements meant that courses could not be planned with sufficient time or care. Although most tutors organized visits for students without undue difficulty they did sometimes find difficulty in making sufficient contact visits with schools themselves. The increasingly common 'off-site' teaching arrangements in which courses are 'delivered to the consumers on their home territory' are already giving rise to considerable difficulties in relation to the demands on staff travel time, non-availability of resources, and lack of suitability of premises. The constantly changing requirements of in-service training for special needs also demands a great degree of adaptability in tutors responsible for special needs courses. Flexibility is required in relation to teaching approaches as well as in content and delivery of courses. Stamina is also required (at least within the public sector of higher education) to withstand the 'paper-devouring' validation exercises necessary to produce the modified courses in such a way that they meet with the approval of both the LEA and university or CNAA masters. The need to be able to respond sensitively and rapidly to constantly changing demands in the special needs field suggests that we ought to plan more carefully for an 'in-built' flexibility within ITT and, more particularly, INSET course programmes in order to obviate the need for over-frequent involvement in the apparatus of formal course approval.

A final plea related to the 'massive decline in full-time secondments [which] could threaten the existence of our [university] centre'. This move against the long course has been noted with regret by a number of commentators recently.[32] Buffeted about in the currently choppy TRIST and GRIST-related waters, educational institutions have had to abandon their long award-bearing ships for the immediate safety of short LEA-shaped modular life-boats. Perhaps in the days ahead we can hope to keep a few big ships afloat amidst the flotilla of little boats?

NOTES AND REFERENCES

1   DES, Teacher Education and Training, James Report, London, HMSO, 1972.
2   DES, Special Educational Needs, Warnock Report, London, HMSO, 1978.
3   P. Mittler, 'The challenge of teacher training: doing more and more with less and less', Secondary Education Journal 1984, 13,2: 22-3.
4   DES, Special Needs in Education, London, HMSO, 1980.
5   M. Peter, 'Editorial - The Education Act 1981', British Journal of Special Education 1981, 8,4:5; London, HMSO, 1980.
6   W. Swann, 'Is the Integration of children with special needs happening?', Oxford Review of Education, 1985, 11,1: 1-18.
7   M. Warnock, 'Personal' column, Times Educational Supplement, 11 November 1983.
8   C.J. Smith, 'Let's stop "statementing" children', British Journal of Special Education 1985, 12,4:142.
9   M. Peter, 'A hard Act to follow', Times Educational Supplement, 30 March 1984.
10   House of Commons, Report of Commons Select Committee on Education, London, HMSO, 1987.
11   DES, Teaching in Schools: The Content of Initial Training, HMI Discussion paper, London, DES, 1983.
12   D. Mongon, 'Patterns of delivery and implications for training', in J. Sayer and N. Jones (eds) Teacher

Training and Special Educational Needs, London, Croom Helm, 1985.

13   ILEA, Educational Opportunities for All? Report of Committee Reviewing Provision to Meet Special Educational Needs, Fish Report, London, ILEA, 1985.

14   S. Wolfendale, Primary Schools and Special Needs: Policy, Planning and Provision, London, Cassell, 1987; C. Robson, 'A modular in-service advanced qualification for teachers: children with special needs', British Journal of In-service Education, 1984, 11,1:32-6; E. Cowne and B. Norwich, 'Training with a school focus', British Journal of Special Education, 1985, 12,4: 167-70; J. Moore, 'Innovations from Kent', Special-Children 1, 29.

15   B. Taylor, 'Wanted a sense of direction', Times Educational Supplement, 6 February 1987.

16   ACSET, Teacher Training and Special Educational Needs, London, DES, 1984.

17   DES, Developments in the B.Ed. Degree Course, London, HMSO, 1979.

18   G. Sewell, 'The Warnock Report and university P.G.C.E. courses: possibilities of change', unpublished paper, University of Durham Department of Education, 1981.

19   D. Labon, 'Special education aspects of university P.G.C.E. courses'. Journal of Further and Higher Education 1984, 8,1: 29-39.

20   OERG, 'Programme of research on children with special educational needs', Oxford Educational Research Group, University of Oxford Department of Educational Studies, 1987.

21   ACSET, op.cit., p.3.

22   OERG, op.cit., p.21.

23   C. Smith, 'Special education aspects of P.G.C.E. courses', unpublished research report, Birmingham University, 1983; D. Thomas and C. Smith, 'Special needs in initial training', in J. Sayer and N. Jones (eds) Teacher Training and Special Educational Needs, London, Croom Helm, 1985.

24   Macmillan have, so far, published three titles in their Special Educational Needs in Mainstream Schools series. They are: K. Postlethwaite and A. Hackney, Organizing a School's Response, London, Macmillan, 1988; B. Raban and K. Postlethwaite, Classroom Responses to Learning Difficulties, London, Macmillan, 1988; J. Gray and J. Richer, Classroom Responses to

Disruptive Behaviour, London, Macmillan, 1988.

25   J. Muncey and M. Ainscow, 'Launching SNAP in Coventry', British Journal of Special Education 1983, 10,3: 8-12.

26   J. Muncey, Meeting Special Needs in Mainstream Schools, Coventry Education Department, 1986.

27   R. Burden, 'The educational psychologist as instigator and agent of change in schools: some guidelines for successful action', in I. McPherson and A. Sutton (eds) Reconstructing Psychological Practice, London, Croom Helm, 1981; M. Newton and D. Hill, 'Special educational needs in the ordinary school - a new initiative', Remedial Education 1985, 20,4: 159-62.

28   K. Wheldall and F. Merrett, Positive Teaching: the Behavioural Approach, London, Allen & Unwin, 1984.

29   D. Brandes and P Ginnes, A Guide to Student Centred Learning, Oxford, Blackwell, 1986.

30   S. Hegarty and P. Evans, Research and Evaluation Methods in Special Education, Windsor, NFER-Nelson, 1985.

31   P. Mittler, 'From Warnock to GRIST', Times Educational Supplement, 24 April 1987.

32   Mittler, 1987, op. cit.; P. Mittler, 'A new look at in-service training', British Journal of Special Education 1986, 13,2: 50-1; R. Gulliford, 'The training of teachers in special education', European Journal of Special Needs Education 1986, 1,2: 103-12.

10

THE IN-SERVICE EDUCATION AND TRAINING OF TEACHERS

J. Geoffrey Mattock

The consequences of recent changes in the funding arrangements have demonstrated the considerable importance which organizational issues have on the provision, delivery, and quality of the in-service education and training of teachers (INSET). It is largely for this reason that much of this chapter will focus on such matters as the organization, funding, and management of INSET.

In order to put these issues into a professional context, the first section of the chapter looks briefly at justification and need for INSET. Most of the rest of the chapter is divided into two main parts: the first dealing in some detail with the development of INSET in the early 1980s, the second part attempting to analyse some of the consequences of the new funding arrangements instituted in April 1987. Finally, there is brief review of past and present arrangements for co-ordinating INSET.

THE CASE FOR INSET: JUSTIFICATION AND NEED

Although the need for INSET provision has never been in serious doubt, hard evidence to substantiate the intuitive support for it offered by most experienced educators is difficult to find. Indeed, Lord James commenting on the recommendation of the Report of the Committee on the Education and Training of Teachers,[1] that new scope and emphasis must be given to in-service training, suggested:

> to ascribe such a priority to this element involved to some extent an act of faith, for surprisingly little hard information exists as to what effects various kinds of post-experience training actually have on teaching the teacher: how long these effects last, what are the most

appropriate kinds of education to accomplish ends which may be quite different for different individuals and what effect on the schools themselves the in-service education of their staff has.[2]

Although some sixteen years later it is very difficult to answer these and many other questions with any real certainty, it is the case that the majority of INSET providers are now making serious attempts to evaluate the effectiveness of their offerings, particularly for purposes of course development. LEAs have also been urged to monitor and evaluate the effectiveness of the various aspects of training included in their INSET plans.

Further evidence supporting the need for INSET comes in most of the important reports concerned with teaching in schools. Perhaps two examples will suffice to reinforce this well-known situation. The Cockcroft Report, entitled Mathematics Counts, in discussing the need for in-service support, states:

> It should not, however, be supposed that in-service support is needed only to remedy the deficiencies of those who lack suitable qualifications. However good their initial training and induction may have been, all those who teach mathematics need continuing support throughout their careers in order to be able to develop their professional skills and so maintain and enhance the quality of their work.[3]

In the DES White Paper, Teaching Quality, the following reference is made: 'The LEA, as the employer of most teachers, must bear the primary responsibility for providing in-service training - including school-based training - to meet the changing needs of the school system'.[4]

It is generally recognized that INSET provision should take account of the needs of the nation, the LEA, the school, and the individual teacher. What is more problematical is achieving an appropriate balance between these. Attention to the need for balance was drawn in the following extract from the White Paper, Education: A Framework for Expansion:

> Underlying any such programme (that is, a substantial expansion of in-service training) is the problem of striking a balance between the teacher's personal

interest in his professional development and the employer's concern with the current needs of particular schools and of the pupils in them.[5]

The long course type of INSET, particularly the course which leads to a named award, has generally been accepted as best serving the personal needs of teachers - a fact which is well borne out by the large numbers of head-teachers, LEA education officers, and advisers who have followed such courses in higher education establishments.

The broad categories of INSET need which can usefully be identified include: induction, dissemination of curriculum developments which in some cases involve new examinations, LEA and school reorganization, teachers' change of role, updating of subject knowledge, acquiring new skills, retraining for the shortage subject areas, dissemination of educational research, and general enrichment. These are now well-known needs but in order to illustrate the links between INSET and the development of our education system, I propose to consider two of them in a little more detail.

Developments in the content and structure of the curriculum are likely to be implemented effectively in schools only if appropriate programmes of INSET for teachers are initiated. Back in the 1960s and early 1970s this obvious link between development and training was not fully recognized and many of the earlier Nuffield and Schools Council national projects were not very well disseminated because of a lack of sustained INSET programmes. An appreciable part of this problem arose because both the Nuffield Foundation and the Schools Council were not seen as in-service providers but rather as curriculum developers and at that time there were lines of demarcation to separate the two functions. As the work of the Schools Council progressed, this situation changed to a certain extent and nearly all projects were expected to build in from the outset a strategy for dissemination. However, even with those projects which were generally well received, their impact was invariably reduced by the lack of resources available for providing teachers with sufficient training to be able to utilize the new ideas and materials with confidence. More recently it has been acknowledged that development of the curriculum most effectively arises when it is closely integrated as a part of the INSET process.

In terms of the broad aims of INSET listed above, the category which has probably seen the most emphasis in recent years relates to changes of a teacher's role. In particular there has been a considerable focus on training in organization and management in the context of the responsibilities of senior teachers in schools including headteachers, deputy heads, heads of departments in secondary schools, and subject co-ordinators in the primary school. The most obvious explanation for the expansion of this area of INSET is that national resources were made available through the Training Grants Scheme much at the same time as many LEAs were realizing its considerable importance. The recognition of the particular need for headship training led a consortium of LEAs in Yorkshire and Humberside to set up a Headship Unit, based on Woolley Hall, near Wakefield, to provide a continuing programme of six-week courses for headteachers of primary, middle, and secondary schools. No doubt other groups of LEAs have taken similar initiatives. In order to co-ordinate this considerable activity, the DES funded the National Development Centre for School Management Training based on the University of Bristol School of Education.

THE DEVELOPMENT OF INSET in the EARLY 1980s

Long award-bearing courses

The need to classify the more substantial programmes of INSET - as long courses - has arisen because full-time courses of twenty days' duration in aggregate or longer and part-time courses of more than sixty hours were funded separately from the rest of INSET by means of the teacher-training pool for INSET. Almost all such long courses have been provided by the universities, the polytechnics, and colleges of higher education. Because of the funding device employed, long courses have been seen as national courses which, in the case of public sector higher education, required approval by the Secretary of State until 1987 and then by the National Advisory Board (NAB). Long courses offered by the universities leading to a recognized named award did not require formal approval, but their other long courses did. It is important to note that any courses which attracted pool funding had to be on open offer to teachers from any of the LEAs.

The pooling arrangements, which were introduced as a means of sharing INSET costs on the basis of enhancing the quality of the education service as a whole, have been a central feature in the development of INSET over some three decades. This is largely because of the way the pool worked. Normally the pool provided LEAs with reimbursement of 100 per cent of course fees and additional teacher travel costs together with 75 per cent of teacher replacement on full-time courses. Thus 100 per cent of the costs of teachers attending part-time long courses was refunded to LEAs and, on average, about 80 per cent of the cost of full-time secondments. This money was not a DES handout, but was part of an accounting exercise connected with the rate support grant. Authorities were net contributors to or net receivers from pool funds, according to the extent of their INSET long course activities. The extent of their use of the pool by LEAs was indeed very varied, with some authorities offering very large numbers of annual secondments, thereby making heavy demands on the pool and thus being subsidized by other LEAs. The pool was not capped, so it is not surprising that there has been a steady expansion of long course INSET over a considerable period. The total size of the pool in 1981-2 was £29.8m, in 1984-5 approximately £42.3m,[6] and in 1986-7 the pool was said to be running at the equivalent of more than £80m. This rate of growth of pool spending far and away exceeds the rate of inflation over the period referred to. Further evidence of the growth of long courses is provided by comparing the annually published DES Statistics on Teachers Attending Long Courses, which gives total numbers attending the various types of long courses offered by each institution.

While on the subject of the funding of long course INSET, it should be noted that pool funding did not cover all the cost of long courses. The fees charged by higher education institutions for long courses offered under the pooling arrangements, both in the university and public sectors, represented on average very approximately one-quarter of the total cost of the course provision. This means that about three-quarters of the cost of providing long courses was borne by University Grants Committee (UGC) or NAB funds. This is still the case.

The type of provision included within the award-bearing long course programme is well known, with each of the universities and a growing number of polytechnics and colleges of higher education offering research degrees at doctorate and master's level as well as taught master's courses. The BPhil is offered by a small number of universities, whereas the BEd for serving teachers is provided by most of the polytechnics and colleges of higher education, but few of the universities. In session 1986-7 the majority of higher education institutions offered at least one advanced diploma and some provided as many as thirteen different diploma courses. In all there were well over four hundred advanced diplomas on offer in some thirty-four universities and seventy-two polytechnics and colleges of higher education in England and Wales. It is interesting to note that over 40 per cent of these advanced diplomas were being offered in the two most northerly DES divisions.

Long award-bearing courses provide an opportunity for sustained study enabling teachers to develop their professional knowledge at a level appropriate to the needs of those likely to provide leadership in the teaching of particular subjects and senior management in schools, colleges, and LEAs. The majority of courses offered are subject to continual scrutiny in order to make them relevant to the needs of participants, as well as maintaining appropriate academic standards. The recent move towards modularizing long award-bearing courses reflects the willingness of providing institutions to try to meet current needs. This development will be referred to later in the chapter.

The Training Grants Scheme

So far this section on long courses has largely focused on award-bearing courses. However, there has been a considerable development of non-award-bearing long courses in recent years, much encouraged by special government funding. Prior to this development, the non-award-bearing programme of long courses, which included polytechnic and college certificate courses, had largely been built up by the public sector and voluntary institutions as a result of the reorganization of public sector teacher-training institutions, when the equivalent of two-ninths of staff resources was allowed for INSET activities.

The first Training Grants Scheme was instituted by the DES in 1983 (Circular 3/83) to provide direct funding of INSET in certain prescribed priority areas.[7] These were: one-term and twenty-day courses on management for heads and senior staff in schools; four types of courses, mostly of thirty days' duration, in the teaching of mathematics (heads of departments in secondary schools, teaching mathematics to the less able, mathematics co-ordinators in primary schools, and mathematics for those teachers under-qualified in the subject); one-term courses for special needs teachers in the ordinary school and six-week courses in pre-vocational education. All courses in the scheme were long courses provided by higher education institutions, and needed approval by the Secretary of State. LEAs were offered indicative allowances for each category of course referred to in the Circular, amounting to an overall total of £6m to be spent on covering 90 per cent of teacher replacement costs. Other costs, that is course fees and travel expenses, were recouped from the INSET pool funding.

Subsequent Circulars were published in 1984, 1985, and 1986 extending the Training Grants Scheme by providing additional funds and adding to the areas of priority. The 1985 Circular also extended the scheme to include INSET for further education lecturers as well as for teachers in schools. By session 1986-7 the sum allocated to LEAs for the cost of teacher replacement in schools and further education colleges on courses under the scheme had risen to £24m and covered twelve prescribed priority areas with defined subdivisions in some areas.

Obviously this earmarked funding of INSET for specifically defined purposes greatly influenced the direction of INSET. As each priority area or subdivision of an area was announced, higher education institutions were invited to submit course proposals to DES for approval, based on given criteria. In a few cases existing courses were considered, but generally the approved programme under the scheme was made up of courses newly devised by higher education colleges in response to the situation. In order to quantify this development, the INSET committee of the Universities Council for the Education of Teachers (UCET) prepared an analysis of the number of approved courses offered under the Training Grants Scheme in session 1985-6 and the split between universities and public sector/voluntary institutions, as shown in Table 1.

As can be seen from Table 1, over three sessions (1983-4, 1984-5, and 1985-6), a considerable volume of new in-service courses had been developed by higher education institutions responding to this DES funding initiative. The fact that a very large proportion of this course development was initiated by the public sector higher education

Table 1 Analysis of courses based on teacher-training Circular letter 4/85

	Public sector	Collaborative	University	Total
A Management training for heads and other senior teachers in primary and secondary schools				
Basic courses (twenty days minimum)	20	2	7	29
One-term training opportunities	13	3	6	22
B Mathematics teaching (normally thirty days)				
Mathematics co-ordinators for primary schools	51	1	2	54
Teachers of low attainers in mathematics in secondary schools	14	0	0	14
Heads of mathematics departments in secondary schools	8	0	7	15
Teachers of mathematics in secondary schools who are inadequately qualified in the subject	17	0	2	19
C Science teaching (normally thirty-five days)				
Science co-ordinators in primary schools	28	0	2	30
Heads of science departments in secondary schools	6	9	14	29
D Education as a preparation for vocational training (six-week courses)				
For schoolteachers	14	0	5	19
For school and FE teachers	2	0	1	3
E Special educational needs in ordinary schools (one-term courses)	20	0	5	25
F The teaching of craft, design and technology (CDT) (one-term courses)	13	0	3	16
Totals	206	15	54	275

Note: Numbers given represent the number of institutions offering a course in that category: some institutions offered more than one course per year.

institutions, particularly those courses for primary mathematics and science, arose largely because of the difference of funding mechanisms of public sector higher education institutions and universities.

LEAs also played an important part in the overall success of the Training Grants Scheme. Clearly the priorities chosen were relatively non-controversial and so LEAs were anxious to support this programme and to take advantage of a range of valuable INSET which cost them only 10 per cent of teacher replacement costs.

School teacher fellowships

By the early 1980s it had become clear that whereas the range of long courses on offer were appropriate for the majority of teachers, some clearly felt that they would benefit more by following a programme of work which did not lead to a named award, but enabled them to study along individual lines. A number of higher education institutions, including several Cambridge and Oxford Colleges, began to offer one-term fellowships which depended on LEAs providing 100 per cent funding of teacher replacement. The high costs involved soon became the limiting factor as to whether or not there could be the growth of fellowships which both teachers and LEA officers were keen to support.

In 1981 the DES began to consider submissions for approval from higher education institutions for fellowships which were considered to conform to what could be described as a 'course' and hence be poolable. In 1982, after consultation with the Pooling Committee, the DES issued criteria which were to be applied to the approval of proposals for teacher fellowship schemes. These criteria required: the needs served by the fellowship to have been diagnosed in consultation with teachers and LEAs; the study to be of help to the school as well as the teacher, the higher education institution offering the fellowship to have appropriate expertise and resources and, where possible, a group of teacher fellows to study together in a related field.

Further guidance was given to the institutions in Teacher Training Circular Letter 4/83 which informed them that the fellowships were to be considered an exceptional form of in-service training, the number of fellowships in any one institution should not exceed three or four, the fellowships normally to be of one term's duration, and they should focus on specific aspects of education or the subject to be offered.[8]

Fellowships were first included in the DES Long Courses Booklet for teachers advertising the 1984-5 programme when forty-four higher education institutions were listed as offering approved school teacher fellowships. The number of institutions had grown to eighty-two in the booklet listing the 1986-7 programme. The popularity of teacher fellowships under the pool funding is self-evident, both on the basis of the growth of institutions offering fellowships and from the knowledge that most institutions found the DES quota they were allowed considerably restricted the number of teachers who could be offered fellowships.

There is no doubt that this growth of the teacher fellowship scheme was another example of an INSET need which could flourish only when appropriate resources were made available, that is the pool was opened with a more flexible approach to secondments.

DES regional courses

DES regional courses were introduced in 1970 as HMI/ATO courses, later to be renamed ATO/DES courses and then, in 1977, DES regional courses. It is generally understood that they were started to initiate a programme of INSET of duration somewhere between the twenty-day long course and the typical short course of up to an aggregate of say twenty hours. They were intended to be a collaborative venture involving DES/HMI, LEAs, and higher education institutions and a means of initiating new areas of INSET.

The mechanics for funding DES regional courses were centred round the divisional inspector who bid annually for part of a global sum of money allocated by the DES for this purpose. Divisional inspectors invited the sub-regions, mostly based on universities, to submit costed proposals for appropriate programmes of INSET according to needs as identified by LEAs and teachers in the region or sub-region. The criteria for selection of successful submissions and indeed the detailed procedures of bidding, collaboration, and administration varied considerably from one division to another. It should be remembered that the funding from DES to cover lecturers' fees and expenses, course materials, and some administrative costs was only part of the overall cost of DES regional INSET. LEAs contributed substantially by paying for travel costs and all, or part of, the residential costs of teachers attending those courses involving residence. Higher education institutions also made generous contributions to the cost of DES regional courses, often by providing free lecture-room accommodation and the use of resources and, in the case of some institutions, by bearing a very large proportion of the administrative costs.

The provision and management of DES regional courses in England and Wales between 1978 and 1983 was surveyed in a report of the Association of Institute and School of Education In-Service Tutors (AISEIT).[9] This report examines in considerable detail the extent, nature, development, and management of DES regional courses; it assesses the value and effectiveness of regional courses and also raises issues concerning the planning of future regional INSET work. The report very positively confirms, both from institutional and from LEA responses, that DES regional courses have been one of the very successful INSET ventures of the last two decades. One can perhaps assume that the DES also recognized the success of DES regional courses, because of the regular increasing of the global funds made available. The aggregated returns from twelve sub-regions in the report (that is about 60 per cent of the total sub-regions) showed an increase in teachers attending DES regional courses from 3,546 in the session 1978-9 to 6,182 in 1982-3, with an increase in funds over the same period from £81,745 to £171,570.

It is interesting to note that although the subject areas covered by DES regional courses were very wide ranging, including an appreciable number of courses aimed at minority groups of teachers, the subjects which pre-dominated overall were management, science and technology, microcomputing, and special needs.

In analysing the reasons for the success of DES regional courses, I would suggest the following. They were, in most sub-regions, a genuine co-operative exercise involving DES/HMI, LEA advisers, teachers, and both organizing and teaching staff from higher education institutions. This collaboration usually extended from the identification of needs, to the planning of the courses, and often to shared teaching of the courses. They provided opportunities for teachers from one LEA to interact with teachers from another, in the context of a structured learning situation and hence promoted exchanges of ideas and good practice. They generally combined course-based work with school-based work and thus were seen as being relevant to classroom practice. Finally, they were extremely cost effective in LEA terms, particularly so because many schools were willing to support DES regional courses without receiving LEA cover for participating teachers.

Short course INSET

Whereas long course INSET provision and much of the DES regional programme has been in the hands of higher education institutions, short course provision has been much more widely based. Most LEAs provide their own - sometimes very extensive - programmes of INSET usually initiated and co-ordinated by their advisory service and frequently held in their Teachers' Centre. HM Inspectorate offer a programme of short courses for serving teachers, often held during vacations and often using accommodation in higher education institutions. Some further education colleges and most higher education institutions also contribute to the short course programme. Additionally several other agencies such as subject associations, learned societies, and teachers' professional associations provide short course programmes of INSET.

Most of the funding for short course INSET has come from LEA sources; either from the Rate Support Grant (RSG) or from council-levied rates. This funding has covered LEAs' own programmes of INSET, the running of Teachers' Centres, and financial support for teachers attending short courses provided by outside bodies. Because LEAs in practice were free to spend whatever they chose on short course INSET the variation in opportunity for teachers from one LEA to another was very considerable. It should be noted that moneys nominally included for INSET in the RSG were not necessarily used for this purpose, because it was not earmarked. Furthermore, the level of financial support offered by different LEAs was very variable and it has not been uncommon for teachers on a particular course to be receiving vastly different amounts of financial help.

Quantification of the volume of INSET take-up on short courses is very difficult to provide. The figures given in Table 2 from surveys conducted in 1979 and 1983 are taken from the 1984 ACSET Report.[10] While they show a substantial increase in the number of teacher involvements in INSET over the four-year period, there is no way of identifying the relative proportions of long and short courses.

Table 2 Number of teacher involvements in INSET

	1978-9	1982-3
INSET requiring no release from normal duties	443,000	522,000
INSET requiring release	252,000	275,000
	(4,820 FTE)	(5,530 FTE)

The figures in brackets give the full-time equivalent (FTE) teachers requiring release and these can be broken down as follows:

	Number of FTEs	
	1978-9	1982-3
Released for one year or more	1,850	2,340
Released for one term or more but less than one year	250	390
Released for less than one term	2,730	2,800
Total	4,820	5,530

The half million or so teachers attending INSET activities without release one can reasonably assume would generally be following either a short course of less than one week's equivalent duration or a part-time long course. Of those requiring release, it might be assumed that well over half would be attending short courses. This assumption being based on the proportion of FTEs for release of less than one term and the knowledge that in 1978-9 there were relatively few courses of duration between twenty days and one term.

The above figures relate to LEA returns and do not take account of INSET activities for which teachers did not make claims for financial assistance. Thus much of the INSET offered by professional associations such as the Association for Science Education and the Historical Association are not included.

By defining the level of INSET activity merely in terms of numbers of teachers attending does not give a very clear picture of the real volume of INSET taking place. For example, ten teachers attending a five day event is half of the INSET provision compared with that of ten teachers attending a two-day course. It is for this reason that UCET decided to include 'teacher hours' in their quantification of the volume of non-award-bearing INSET courses offered by the universities. The data collected by UCET, for the same two sessions as given above, representing the volume of non-award-bearing INSET (short courses) offered by the university sector can be summarized as in Table 3.

Table 3 Teachers attending non-award-bearing short courses

	No. of courses	No. of teachers attending	No. of teacher hours
1978-9	1,189	54,512	678,105
1982-3	1,409	58,542	725,987

The number of teacher hours are determined by adding together for each course the product of the number of teachers attending and the length of the course in hours. It can be seen that all three figures increased over the four-year period with the rise of the number of teachers attending courses (just under 20 per cent) being proportionately the same as both of the increases in the ACSET numbers. The 'teacher hour' figures are perhaps better comprehended by converting them into FTEs. Thus, using one teacher receiving 360 hours of INSET as one FTE, the total volume of non-award-bearing INSET provided by universities in 1982 amounted to well over 2,000 FTEs.

The INSET role of Teachers' Centres

LEA Teachers' Centres have become such an established part of the overall pattern of INSET provision that it is sometimes forgotten that very few of them are much over twenty years old. As is well known, the period of rapid growth of centres took place in the late 1960s and early 1970s particularly to foster the Nuffield and earlier Schools Council curriculum developments. During the 1980s the number of centres has become stabilized around the 500 mark, although as is pointed out in Schools Council Working Paper 74, Teachers' Centres: A Focus for In-Service Education? the number does depend on how the term Teachers' Centre is defined.[11] The inquiry, on which Working Paper 74 was based, was conducted over the period 1979-81 and estimated that of the 485 centres existing then in England and Wales, 385 were multipurpose with the rest being subject specialist centres.

In reviewing the activities of centres, the inquiry confirmed that nearly all the multipurpose centres offered a programme of short INSET courses, primary teachers made much more use of centres than secondary teachers, and the most popular courses/workshops were on primary language and reading, primary mathematics, and primary art and craft. It also informed us that on average 32 per cent of course leaders were advisers, 32 per cent teachers, 14 per cent centre leaders, 11 per cent higher education lecturers, and 11 per cent others; on average 67 per cent of courses were held out of school time, 23 per cent in school time, and 10 per cent a mixture of in and out of school time. However, perhaps the most important outcome of the inquiry demonstrated that Teachers' centres were generally very highly thought of both by senior LEA officers and by the vast majority of teachers who had used them.

In trying to characterize the distinctive role of Teachers' Centres as INSET providers, one is aware of the tremendous variations in the operation of different centres. These differences obviously depend on many factors such as the availability of finance and resources, the influence of LEA officers, the availability in the area of INSET offered by other providers, the relationships of centre leaders with LEA officers and with institutions of higher education, and the effectiveness of any machinery for INSET co-ordination. However, in comparing the overall short course INSET provision made by higher education institutions, it is generally the case that courses offered by Teachers' Centres are shorter and less specialist in nature.

The need for change

The very complex system of funding INSET which grew up over some four decades had many shortcomings including the following: an inflexibility which had led to some imbalance between long courses and other INSET activities; a lack of reliable and consistent information about the costs of INSET both within LEAs and institutions of higher education; a variability of financial provision for INSET made by different LEAs and hence a disparity of opportunities for teachers living in different geographical areas, and finally a considerable difficulty in both short- and long-term planning of INSET by LEAs and by higher education institutions.

The ACSET Report of 1984

The 1984 Report of ACSET's Teacher Training Sub-committee, The In-Service Education, Training and Professional Development of Teachers, highlighted many of the problems referred to in the previous paragraph. However, particular attention needs to be drawn to the following statement made in the report, after expressing concern that the pre-1987 funding arrangements tended to be over-supportive of long courses: 'This is not to imply any doubt on our part about the value of long courses: on the contrary we attach importance to their continuing role as a major form of INSET'.[12]

Except for one (concerned with area INSET committees) the fourteen main recommendations of the ACSET Report fall into three categories. The first is concerned with funding arrangements and includes: a general grant, paid at 90 per cent, to LEAs to cover INSET costs set at 5 per cent of LEAs' expenditure on teachers' salaries; guidance to the UGC and NAB/WAB on the importance of continuing to fund higher education institutions for INSET activities of one term or more full-time (or part-time equivalent) with the hope of greater consistency in fee levels between the universities and public sector institutions of higher education; the costs of shorter courses organized by higher education institutions to be met through fees set between fully economic fees and charging what the market will bear and, finally, some central funding of higher education institutions for development work of INSET.

The second category of recommendations relate to the school: every school is to have an agreed procedure for reviewing INSET needs and for assessing priorities for INSET; a review of every school's INSET needs to be carried out annually by senior staff; every school should make an annual submission to the LEA for the release of any teachers for whom externally based INSET is proposed; the headteacher along with senior staff responsible should ensure that school-based INSET activity is properly evaluated and that teachers embarking on externally based courses are adequately prepared, and on return encouraged to share any new insights and skills.

The third group of recommendations relate to the LEA and include: every LEA should develop clear and coherent policies towards INSET; LEAs should review their locally based INSET provision; every LEA should set a budget for INSET to cover all aspects of INSET costs and every LEA should satisfy itself that there are adequate staffing resources for each school to enable school-based INSET to take place.

These recommendations have been set out in such detail because they were in effect the starting-point of the major funding changes which have recently taken place. Generally speaking the recommendations were well received by the majority of organizations involved in INSET. Certainly those recommendations which related to LEAs and to schools were welcomed, because they all pointed into the direction of a better-structured approach to INSET planning to ensure more coherence and hence a more effective delivery of INSET. The part which was to some extent controversial relates to the funding proposals. Some members of higher education institutions were naturally reluctant to see the pool funding being abolished but others recognized that there did need to be some greater flexibility in INSET-funding arrangements. However, all parts of higher education were unanimous in opposing the recommendation that the directly attributable costs of short courses (full-time courses of less that twenty days) should be met by fee income with institutions charging on top of these costs whatever contribution to overheads the market would bear. In the first place the attributable costs are high compared with the level of fees that LEAs have been used to and second, in a time of serious financial constraints in higher education, where was the rest of the overheads which the market could not bear be expected to come from?

'Better Schools', 1985

The ACSET proposals were accepted in principle by the government in the White Paper <u>Better Schools</u>.[13] There was of course no mention there of the ACSET recommendation on the level of funding, although there is reference to an annual expenditure by LEAs on INSET for school teachers of approximately £100m, which it suggests was fairly evenly divided between teacher release and the cost of provision. What is not made clear, however, is the way this figure was arrived at. Does it represent only LEA funds or does it include DES money? If it represents the total spending on INSET, except for funds through higher education, then it is surprising that two years later in 1987 the total funding was set at £200m even though this figure does not include INSET for further education lecturers.

The only proposal not included in the ACSET report which appeared in the White Paper was the DES's intention to divide the proposed specific grant into two parts: one part to continue the existing in-service grants for national priorities and the other for locally assessed priorities.

TRIST (TVEI Related In-Service Training Scheme)

TRIST, funded by the Manpower Services Commission (MSC), was announced in March 1985 as an interim measure until the DES Specific Grant arrangements could be introduced in 1987. The scheme was offered over the two-year period 1985-7, being complementary to other INSET provision. Although TRIST had the express purpose of fostering TVEI-related in-service training for teachers of secondary age pupils and further education, its real importance was as an agenda for wider changes of INSET provision.

In the first year of the scheme, £6m was made available and this sum was increased to £20m for the 1986-7 financial year. LEAs were invited to submit proposals under the scheme for funding offered in four bands, which were related to pupil/student numbers in secondary schools and equivalent classes in further education. The LEA proposals, which had to meet criteria such as providing a balanced programme, covering a number of different areas and showing how these fitted into the LEA's overall INSET, were considered by representatives of the MSC, DES, and HMI. Reimbursement of costs of relevant training approved under the scheme was at 100 per cent. Some 10 per cent of the total TRIST funds were reserved for bids from higher education institutions to take part in innovative national and regional INSET activities. It is somewhat unfortunate that a scheme which was introduced partly to achieve better planning and a more co-ordinated approach to INSET should offer a timescale for submission which many LEAs found totally unrealistic and often led to proposals which were too hastily prepared.

From the outset it was accepted by MSC that TVEI-relatedness was to be interpreted very broadly with considerable emphasis on utilizing a range of types and methods of training. This resulted in some valuable experimentation and at least two very significant consequences. The first was a shift towards the use by LEAs of their own staff as trainers and hence away from the traditional higher education providers. The second consequence was a considerable encouragement to schools to engage in school-based INSET, because resources were being offered for this purpose. Although the ACSET Report and other writers have drawn attention to the increasing development of school-based and school-focused INSET, the real situation was that relatively few schools had begun either to arrange school-based INSET or to approach the further professional training of its teachers using a school-focused model. TRIST was undoubtedly a potent agent for change in this situation and many more schools are now becoming engaged in school-based and school-focused activities.

The evaluation programme of TRIST had three parts: the national evaluation by a partnership of the University of Surrey and Roehampton Institute of Higher Education; an evaluation of local evaluations focused on a single region undertaken by the University of Sussex and local evaluations in each participating LEA, drawn together through the DELTA project undertaken by the Cambridge Institute. All three evaluations have recently been published in a series of booklets for disseminating the outcomes of TRIST and, as well as posing a number of unanswered questions, provide a wealth of ideas and suggestions for all those with some responsibility for INSET.[14]

The LEA Training Grants Scheme

The scheme, to operate from April 1987, was announced in

Circular 6/86, published in August 1986.[15] It heralded expected fundamental changes in the funding arrangements which have and will continue to alter the nature of INSET provision considerably more than was generally expected. The new arrangements, better known as GRIST (Grant Related In-Service Training) replace in one scheme the previously separately funded teacher-training INSET pool, the Training Grants Scheme for national priority INSET, the DES regional courses programme and the TVEI-related INSET Scheme (TRIST), funded through MSC. GRIST offers every LEA an overall indicative allowance for its INSET programme divided into two parts: approximately one-third of the total for individually listed national priorities with 70 per cent funding and approximately two-thirds for local priorities with 50 per cent DES funding.

There were nineteen national priorities in the scheme: nine for school teachers, six for further education teachers, one joint between school and further education teachers, and three which were also extended to include youth and community workers. The areas followed very closely those in the 1986-7 In-Service Training Grants Scheme with additions of training in the teaching of religious education for school teachers, special needs for further education teachers, training for teachers mainly engaged in advanced further education, training to help combat misuse of drugs and training for youth/community workers and educational psychologists. However, there was one fundamental difference in the operation of the GRIST scheme for national priority INSET and that was in opening up eligible training to include virtually any INSET activity of any length which could be described as satisfying a given brief statement and commentary. Eligible training under the previous In-Service Training Grants Scheme had meant attendance on courses offered by higher education institutions, most of which had been especially designed in consultation with HMI and required DES approval. Circular 9/87, which announced the GRIST arrangements for financial year 1988-9, retained all the national priorities in the previous Circular with some reorganization. This included the breaking down of the special needs category into four separate ones: hearing disabilities, disabilities of sight, severe learning difficulties, and training for designated teachers to meet special needs in ordinary schools and also the making of a separate category from the shortage subject priorities of one-year retraining courses in mathematics, science, and CDT.

Further revisions of the national priorities are included in the 1988 Draft Circular. The previous priorities of training in the teaching of mathematics, science, CDT, and training related to industry, the economy and the world of work being subsumed into one category - training for the national curriculum: content. This category also embraces the teaching of English which had not previously been included in the national priority list. Similarly the priority which covered GCSE training and the development of records of achievement have been included in a new category to reflect recent initiatives, namely training for the national curriculum: process. Out goes the separate priority of school teachers related to the curriculum in a multi-ethnic society, although it is retained for further education teachers and in comes a brand new priority: training in the teaching of 4-year-old children in primary classes. The priority changes for further education teachers remain almost the same except that six categories are now regrouped into four.

Under the GRIST scheme for 1987-8, £200m was allocated for grant-aid, of which £70m was in respect of national priority areas. Thus, taking into account the levels of grant-aid, DES offered an earmarked grant of £114m provided LEAs individually contributed their share of the rest. The size of each LEA's indicative allocation was based on the pupil/student population for the national priority areas, but in the case of the local priorities a formula was used which also took into account the LEA's previous in-service expenditure. It appears that this previous spending was based on the LEA's use of the INSET funding pool and caused much disquiet in some quarters. Overall funding under GRIST for 1988-9 was increased by 3.5 per cent to £207m with some adjustment of local priority allocations towards an ultimate equalization basis.

SOME CONSEQUENCES OF GRIST

Many of the problems which GRIST has brought along, particularly those relating to higher education institutions, were anticipated when the DES Position Paper on the new funding arrangements was published in September 1985.[16] Bodies such as UCET, on behalf of the universities, and SCETT, on behalf of the public sector higher education institutions, recognized and warned the DES and HMI that the shift away from INSET offered by higher education would be considerable and this has certainly been the case.

The most serious detrimental consequence of GRIST funding has been the fall in the number of teachers attending one-year full-time award-bearing courses with the number of LEA-funded teachers for session 1987-8 in the university sector showing a reduction from 2,112 in the previous year to 673. That is a fall of 68 per cent. Even the part-time recruitment on the university award-bearing courses was reduced showing, for LEA-funded students, a fall from 2,771 in 1986-7 to 2,343 in 1987-8, which is a reduction of 15 per cent.

It seems most unlikely that recruitment on full-time courses will appreciably increase unless the funding arrangements are changed and indeed further reductions may very well follow in subsequent years. Although this situation is very much regretted by colleagues in higher education, the LEA viewpoint is that the high cost of secondments (variously estimated at £18,000 to £20,000 per average one-year FTE) prohibits more than a few special cases. However, these financial grounds which so considerably reduce the viability of full-time courses do not apply to those long part-time courses requiring no teacher replacement. Here the courses represent extremely good value for money to LEAs because of the high subsidy provided by the funding bodies of higher education institutions. It was certainly not intended by ACSET that there should be this huge reduction in the attendance of teachers on award-bearing courses; as has already been pointed out, the report specifically refers to their continuing role as a major form of INSET.

Long award-bearing courses have played a crucial part in the in-service education of teachers in providing opportunities for advanced study which is of particular importance in the long-term needs of the education service. In the past, these courses have been the means by which specialists have been trained to promote the development of education in a variety of roles such as advisers, inspectors, teacher-trainers, education officers, heads of schools, and heads of subject departments. It is not surprising that in planning GRIST proposals, LEA officers see the more immediate needs of schools and colleges such as the introduction of GCSE and the national curriculum as a higher priority. No doubt if more money had been made available for INSET, then the reductions in the recruitment on long award-bearing courses would not have been so severe. It is worth noting again that the ACSET recommendation on the level of INSET funding was at 5 per cent of expenditure on teachers' salaries and this would have raised a much larger sum than has been put into GRIST.

At the present time there is so little information available as to how INSET funds have been spent in the first GRIST year that one can make observations based only on limited evidence. However, it seems to be the case that relatively large amounts of the GRIST moneys have gone towards the costs of the LEA infrastructure of INSET, such as parts of advisers' salaries, administrative salaries and costs, and the maintenance of Teachers' Centres, rather than the direct costs of INSET provision. Clearly all these items of expenditure are a legitimate charge to INSET funds, but in the case of many LEAs, GRIST has provided an opportunity to make savings on items of expenditure not previously charged as INSET. The argument has been put forward many times by DES officers that GRIST does not limit LEA spending on INSET, but it has to be understood that present-day financial constraints on earmarked allocation is seen by many elected LEA councillors as a limit on spending. The fact that university secondments were down in the session 1987-8 by some 1,400 FTEs means that nearly £30m was diverted to some other aspect of INSET funding. It does not seem likely that the expansion of LEAs' own INSET provision was as high as this and hence one is probably left with the explanation of infrastructure spending.

The consequences of the failure of LEAs to support long courses adequately are becoming very serious for higher education institutions and in the longer term will result in a reduction of the resources available for INSET as well as the quality and diversity of INSET on offer. The reduction of resources arises because the level of staffing and departmental running costs in higher education institutions depends on student numbers on long award-bearing courses. Hence, the recent fall in numbers attending these courses means that schools and departments of education will either be faced with redundancies or at least a policy of non-replacement of any departing staff. This means that the whole of the higher education INSET resource base will begin to wither and what has gone will be extremely difficult to bring back.

What has been the effect of GRIST on non-award-bearing INSET? Although lack of precise information as to what has actually happened on the ground makes it difficult to assess the situation with real certainty, it would seem that many of the medium-length courses are not now recruiting so well. This problem particularly arises in the case of the six-week-type courses which were approved by DES under the original Training Grants Scheme. There are two reasons why these courses have either been reduced in length or are failing to recruit adequately on the longer version of the courses. First, under the original scheme only the approved higher education courses could be used for national priority funds, but with GRIST they are competing for the limited finance with very short events provided by LEAs themselves. Second, the universities do not receive central funding for non-award-bearing work and consequently need to charge a level of fee which is economic or at least covers the direct costs. Although public sector institutions have been receiving funding for all long courses (that is twenty-day courses or longer) they will soon be in the same position as the universities. This situation over funding is a major problem for higher education. Many LEA officers find it difficult to understand why higher education institutions are having problems in responding to the trend of focusing more INSET on specific needs, thereby switching resources from long courses to shorter ones. On the face of it, this does seem to be a straightforward issue. However, government policy decrees that continuing education should be provided by higher education at full economic rates and the UGC has found itself unable to make any exception for education departments. So higher education is put into the situation of charging fees which are seen by many LEAs to be prohibitive.

The provision of courses to replace DES regional courses seems to be very patchy. In some areas LEAs are offering a number of courses which have been arranged in collaboration with others, but over the country as a whole there does not seem to be anything like the range of such courses as was offered previously. There is clearly a boom in short courses of one or two days' duration and it seems likely that as more and more of the GRIST funds are allocated to individual schools, thus dividing available finance into relatively small amounts, this trend will continue to grow. Thus more and more INSET may become superficial and suffer from the limitations of what can be covered in a very short period of time.

All higher education institutions are responding to the 'market forces' philosophy, with its emphasis on good value for money, by attempting to sell their wares in whatever way they can. Nearly all universities have modularized advanced diploma and taught higher degree courses so that individual modules or groups of modules may be taken without following the full course. This offers two possibilities: first, teachers and their LEAs may be more attracted to enrol on a course which is more narrowly focused and less demanding in time than a full diploma or degree course, and, second, many of the modules are being offered as part of Credit Accumulation/Transfer Schemes. Teachers taking one or two modules may then subsequently take additional units which could eventually lead to an award.

Another way in which higher education is responding to the present situation is by entering the consultancy field and selling staff time to schools and LEAs, particularly in the involvement of school-based INSET, including the statutory 'Baker days'. Once again the problem in developing this work lies in the level of charges which need to be made. Schools and LEAs have been used to receiving help and advice from higher education either free of charge or at very low cost, and are in many cases now surprised that charges of the order of £200 per day need to be made for consultancy work. Some institutions of higher education have been embarrassed by individual schools suggesting services should be offered free to compensate for the help which schools give in receiving students on teaching practice. Many higher education institutions would welcome such a quid pro quo arrangement if it were made possible by the funding bodies.

The development of Credit Accumulation and Credit Transfer Schemes which allow teachers to obtain advanced diplomas and degrees over an appropriate period of time and in more than one institution has been warmly welcomed by both teachers and LEA officers. A Credit Accumulation Scheme follows as a consequence of modularizing an award-bearing course; the main issues are the length of period over which modules are deemed to be award worthy and whether or not there can be retrospective credit given for modules taken as self-standing courses. In the case of Credit Transfer Schemes, the situation is more complex. The key issue revolves around the willingness of an institution or validating body to accept a unit or units of study undertaken in another institution and the main considerations involved are the length and appropriateness of level of the unit and its coherence with the rest of the programme. Progress in setting up Credit Transfer Systems in different areas of the country is varied with some groups of institutions having established a clear pattern of working together, in some cases across the binary line, while others are only at the consultation stage. As is usually the case, this way of developing, without any laid-down structure or framework, leads to a wide variety of practice and will make it difficult to mesh different local schemes into a national scheme, assuming that such a step is desirable. In this connection UCET has recently produced some guidelines which it invites member universities to adopt in setting up new Credit Transfer arrangements at master's level.

An extension of Credit Accumulation/Transfer Schemes wholly based on higher education institutions is now developing which usually involves the addition of modules taught predominantly by LEA advisers and teachers in their own premises. However, the validation for award purposes of such modules is not readily acceptable to many universities, largely because of the problems of exercising appropriate academic controls.

It has already been suggested that many of these developments arise through necessity. That is to say, the need for higher education institutions to match perceived INSET requirements of LEAs and their teachers with available higher education staffing resources. This is not to say that the shift of INSET provision from higher education to LEAs, the need for higher education staff to spend more time marketing their INSET, the remodelling of diploma and degree courses into modules with Credit Accumulation and Transfer Schemes and the consequent problems of coherence, will or will not result in more effective INSET. Only time will tell. However, on the face of it, much of what has happened since the introduction of GRIST should result in a closer understanding of working relationships between LEA and higher education personnel. In fact, the whole question of all parties involved in INSET working together is of such prime importance that it is proposed to devote the penultimate section of this chapter on some consideration of past and present arrangements for co-ordinating INSET.

AREA CO-ORDINATION OF INSET

When Area Training Organizations based on universities were set up following the McNair Report of 1944, they were given the role of co-ordinating teacher-education in specific geographical areas. For some ATOs this co-ordination was almost entirely restricted to initial training. However other ATOs, generally those which were large providers of in-service work, eventually saw the need for setting up some formal co-ordinating arrangements. Arising from the increasing involvement of member colleges in providing INSET and the growth of provision by LEAs in the area, the ATO based on Leeds University set up a committee in 1967 to co-ordinate and promote in-service teacher-training and curriculum development within the area, having regard to the provision made by LEAs, to advise upon and organize courses as was deemed necessary. Membership of the committee included a representative of each LEA in the area (there were six county boroughs and two very large country authorities), representatives of fifteen member colleges of education, a representative from each of three neighbouring universities and an HMI assessor. In 1974 when LEAs became reorganized and in 1976, following the demise of ATOs, the committee was reconstituted to meet the needs of the changing situation. However, the work of the committee remained broadly the same and throughout the two decades from 1967 to 1987 attempted to review and initiate INSET provision offered by higher education institutions, having regard to the LEAs' own courses. The success of the committee in continuing to receive the strong support of its various membership arose from its role of fulfilling two important functions. First, the committee obtained the agreement of the DES not to approve any long course which member institutions wished to offer unless they received the positive support of the committee (an exercise which was carried out with considerable care) and, second, the committee recognized the value of planning an effective programme of DES regional courses as a real collaborative venture. From these two functions carried out effectively, the committee received sufficient support from its members to tackle many other issues, including the harmonizing of different LEA policies relating to INSET.

The 1984 ACSET Report, referred to previously, recommended that proposals be invited for INSET committees whose main function would be 'to act as "broker" between LEAs and HE institutions in promoting a match between need and provision'.[17] ACSET further proposed that some twenty committees be established with tripartite membership of teachers, LEAs, and higher education with a salaried officer to administer the co-ordinating operation. No one seemed too clear what this brokerage role involved but in any case it was not taken up in that form by DES. The 1985 DES Position Paper spoke of the case for strengthened regional co-ordination 'to ensure that HE providers are aware of and respond to needs identified by client LEAs, and to encourage collaborative responses on the part of providing institutions and LEAs'.[18] The paper goes on to identify some of the issues involved but makes little commitment in suggesting a possible structure or that specific resources should be identified for the purpose.

In responding to the DES Paper, the Leeds-based Co-ordinating Committee suggested a rationale for establishing area committees which included: the enablement of a diverse range of INSET provision to be planned for all teachers in the area; the facilitation of long-term, co-ordinated planning of regional INSET involving teachers, LEA officers, and higher education institutions, the provision of a forum for debating INSET issues across LEA boundaries so as to prevent possible insularity, the process of INSET planning to be more 'cost effective' in terms of time by obviating the need for each higher education institution to consult separately with a number of LEAs and vice versa. The advice also recommended that the size of area should be large enough to achieve the rationale previously stated, yet geographically compact enough to reflect both traditional and likely new patterns of INSET attendance and involvement, bearing in mind previous experience of collaboration and such practical issues as economical travel networks.

In the event DES decided not to take this opportunity of creating a national system of area/regional co-ordinating committees and instead left the whole question of local collaboration and co-ordination of INSET to individual LEAs. Circular 6/86 and subsequent Circulars have suggested that in considering LEA GRIST proposals account would be taken of local planning arrangements, including consultations with universities and public sector institutions of higher education. Knowing how varied the extent of these consultations are in different areas, one can only conclude that the DES definition of an acceptable consultation process has very wide limits. It is difficult to understand why since ATOs were disbanded in 1975 successive Secretaries of State for Education have failed to provide any substitute arrangements for co-ordination. Several different proposals for INSET co-ordination have been mooted since 1975, but still the nettle has not been grasped and so ad-hoc arrangements, only some of which are effective, continue to be the order of the day. It is ironical that GRIST was introduced to help organize INSET more systematically and to promote more purposeful planning, yet this linking of LEAs and higher education INSET providers is in effect left to chance.

Much of the last part of this chapter has been critical of what has happened as a result of the introduction of GRIST. I make no apology for this, because I believe that many institutions of higher education are not being allowed to make their best contribution to the overall provision of INSET. However, in looking to the future, it has to be recognized that the aims of GRIST are sound and a much more systematic approach to the planning of INSET was long overdue. The process of starting with the careful identification of need at the level of the school, the LEA, and the country; of matching provision to meet these needs and of concluding with the evaluation of the effectiveness of the INSET which results will be most welcome. What is required now is some change in the funding arrangements in order to ensure that there is a better balance of INSET provision to meet longer-term needs such as the education and training of researchers and managers as well as providing support for the more narrowly focused problems of the day. It may very well be that to accomplish these ends some form of 'top-slicing' of funds will need to be established for certain approved long courses. Perhaps this could be achieved by introducing an INSET pool!

NOTES AND REFERENCES

1   DES, Teacher Education and Training, James Report, London, HMSO, 1972.
2   Lord James, 'The James Report's Third Cycle', in R. Watkins (ed.) In-Service Training: Structure and Content, London, Ward Lock Educational, 1973, p. 12.
3   DES, Mathematics Counts, Cockcroft Report, London,

HMSO, 1982, para. 716.
4   DES, Teaching Quality, Cmnd 8836, London, HMSO, 1983, para. 86.
5   DES, Education: A Framework for Expansion. Cmnd 5174, London, HMSO, 1972, para. 62.
6   ACSET (Advisory Committee on the Supply and Education of Teachers), The In-Service Education, Training and Professional Development of School-teachers, Report of the Teacher Training Sub-committee, 1984, para. 31.
7   DES, The In-Service Teacher Training Grants Scheme, Circular 3/83, London, HMSO, 1983.
8   DES, School Teacher Fellowships, Teacher Training Circular Letter 4/83, London, HMSO, 1983.
9   C. Day, A Survey of the Provision and Management of DES Regional Courses in England and Wales 1978-1983, Report of the Association of Institute and School of Education In-Service Tutors, University of Nottingham, 1986.
10   ACSET Report, 1984, op. cit., Annex, paras 2 and 3.
11   D. Weindling, M. I. Reid, and P. Davis, Teachers' Centres: A Focus for In-Service Education?, Schools Council Working Paper 74, London, Methuen Education, 1983.
12   ACSET Report, 1984, op. cit., para. 34.
13   DES, Better Schools, Cmnd 9469, London, HMSO, 1985.
14   MSC, An Evaluation of TRIST Management, Sheffield, MSC, 1988.
     MSC, Local Evaluation of INSET: A Meta-Evaluation of TRIST Evaluations, Bristol, National Development Centre for School Management Training, 1988.
     MSC, Managing INSET in Local Education Authorities, Bristol, National Development Centre for School Management Training, 1988.
15   DES, Local Education Authority Training Grants Scheme: Financial Year 1987-88, Circular 6/86, London, HMSO, 1986.
16   DES, Proposed New Specific Grant Arrangements for the In-Service Education and Training of Teachers, Position Paper, London, HMSO, 1985.
17   ACSET Report, 1984, op. cit., para. 67.
18   DES, Position Paper, 1985, op. cit., para. 30.

SELECT PUBLICATIONS OF
PROFESSOR WILLIAM TAYLOR CBE

BOOKS

Universities under Scrutiny, Paris, OECD, 1987.

Metaphors of Education (ed.), London, Heinemann Educational, 1984.

New Zealand Reviews of National Policies for Education (with assistance from P.H. Karmel and Ingrid Eide), Paris, OECD, 1983.

Education for the 'Eighties: The Central Issues (ed. with Simon) London, Batsford, 1981.

Research and Reform in Teacher Education, Windsor, NFER, 1978.

Educational Administration in Australia and Abroad (ed. with Thomas and Farquhar) St Lucia, University of Queensland Press, 1975.

Education 1973: Perspectives and Plans for Graduate Studies (with Downey, Daniels, and Baker), Toronto, Council for Ontario Universities.

Research Perspectives in Education (ed.), London, Routledge & Kegan Paul, 1973.

Heading for Change, London, Routledge & Kegan Paul, 1973.

Theory into Practice, Cardiff, Harlech, 1972.

Policy and Planning for Post-Secondary Education, Strasbourg, Council of Europe, 1971.

Towards a Policy for the Education of Teachers (ed.), London, Butterworth, 1969.

Society and the Education of Teachers, London, Faber, 1969.

Educational Administration and the Social Sciences (ed. with Baron), London, Athlone, 1969 (Japanese edn 1970).

The Secondary Modern School, London, Faber, 1963.

CONTRIBUTIONS TO BOOKS

'Education 1836-1986; partnership and professionalism' in M. Thompson (ed.) University of London 150th Anniversary Faculty Lectures.

'Staff supply and development', in A. Paisley (ed.) Handbook of Educational Ideas and Practices, London, Croom Helm.

'Education and the Economy', in M. Stephens (ed.) Universities, Education and the National Economy.

'School to work', in D. Corson (ed.) Education for Work, Palmerston North, NZ: Dunsmore Press, 1988.

'Educational research in England and Wales', in J. Nisbet (ed.) Educational Research: The World Yearbook of Education, London, Kogan Page, 1985.

'Productivity and educational values', in G.D.N. Worswick (ed.) Education and Economic Performance, London, Gower, 1985.

'The future for teacher education', in I. Reid and D. Hopkins (eds) Rethinking Teacher Education, London, Croom Helm, 1984.

'The national context 1972-82', in R.J. Alexander et al. (eds) Change in Teacher Education, London, Holt, Rinehart, & Winston, 1984.

'Organisational culture and administrative leadership in universities', in T.J. Sergiovanni and J.E. Corbally (eds) Leadership and Organizational Culture, Illinois, University of Illinois Press, 1984.

'Innovation without growth', in T. Horton and P. Raggatt (eds) Challenge and Change in the Curriculum, London, Hodder & Stoughton and the Open University, 1982.

'Changing priorities in teacher education', in R. Goodings, M. Byram and P. McPartland (eds) Changing Priorities in Teacher Education, London, Croom Helm, 1982.

'Quality control: analysis and comment', in T.R. Bone and H.A. Ramsey (eds) Quality Control in Education, Proceedings of the Ninth Conference of the British Educational Management and Administration Society, 1981.

'Education and the world of work', in N. Dufty, W. Neal and E. Hinchcliffe (eds) Education and the World of Work, Carlton, Vic: Australian College of Education, 1980.

'Family, school and society', in M. Craft (ed.) Linking Home with School (3rd revised edn), London, Methuen, 1980.

'Education and the economy in England in the 'eighties', in

P.D. Tannock (ed.) Education Policies and Prospective Economic and Social Developments in Australia, the UK, and the Federal Republic of Germany: A Comparative View, Perth, University of Western Australia, 1980.

'Teacher education in industrializing countries', in H.B. Leavitt and H. Klassen (eds) Teacher Education and National Development, Washington, DC, International Council on Education for Teaching, 1980.

'Half a million teachers', in P. Gordon (ed.), The Study of Education, vol. 2, London, Woburn Press, 1980.

'Professional development or personal development?', in E. Hoyle and J. Megarry (eds) Professional Development of Teachers: The World Yearbook of Education 1980, London, Kogan Page, 1980.

'Education in comparative perspective: the case of teacher education', in B. Holmes (ed.) Diversity and Unity in Education, London, Allen & Unwin, 1980.

'Managing contraction', in R. Farquhar and I. Housego (eds) Canadian and Comparative Educational Administration, Vancouver, University of British Columbia Press, 1980.

'The teaching role of universities in the context of the Williams Report', in Australian Universities to the Year 2000, Conference of University Governing Bodies Australian Vice-Chancellors' Committee Occasional Papers 2, 1979.

'Accountability and values', in R.A. Becher and S. Maclure (eds) Accountability in Education, Slough, NFER, 1979.

'Power and the curriculum', in C. Richards (ed.) Power and the Curriculum, Driffield, Nafferton Books, 1978.

'Teachers and the continuous reorientation of education', in E. King (ed.) Reorganising Education, London, Sage, 1977.

'Recurrency and reform in higher education', in D.W. Piper and R. Glatter (eds) The Changing University, Slough, NFER, 1977.

'Secondary schools and social change', in I. Morris (ed.) Signpost for Education, Edinburgh, Convention of Scottish Local Authorities, 1976.

'The head as manager: some criticisms', in R.S. Peters (ed.) The Role of the Head, London, Routledge & Kegan Paul, 1976.

'Administration, planning and systems analysis', in W. Taylor et al. (eds) Educational Administration in Australia and Abroad, St Lucia, University of Queensland Press, 1975.

211

'The contribution of research to the study and practice of educational administration', in M.G. Hughes (ed.) Administering Education: International Challenge, London, Athlone Press, 1975.

'Teacher education', in Encyclopaedia Britannica, 1975.

'Policies for Higher Education: Summary Report' in Future Structures of Post-Secondary Education, Paris, OECD, 1974.

'Support for educational research and development', in H.J. Butcher and H.B. Pont (eds) Educational Research in Britain, London, University of London Press, 1973.

'The organisation of educational research in the United Kingdom' in W. Taylor (ed.) Research Perspectives in Education, London, Routledge & Kegan Paul, 1973.

'Knowledge and research' in W. Taylor (ed.) Research Perspectives in Education, London, Routledge & Kegan Paul, 1973.

'Developments in England and Wales', in D.J. McCarty et al. (ed.) New Perspectives on Teacher Education, San Francisco, Jossey-Bass, 1973.

'Further professional studies for serving teachers', in F.H. Klassen (ed.) Innovations in Teacher Education, Washington, DC, International Council on Education for Teaching, 1972.

'Research and change', in G. Chanan (ed.) Research Forum on Teacher Education, Slough, NFER, 1972.

'A secondary curriculum for the average child', in R. Hooper (ed.) The Curriculum: Context Design and Development, Edinburgh, Oliver & Boyd, 1971.

'Teacher education and urban development', in F.H. Klassen and J. Collier (eds) Crisis and Change in Teacher Education, Washington DC, International Council on Education for Teaching, 1971.

'Training the head', in B.W. Allen (ed.) Headship in the 'Seventies, Oxford, Blackwell, 1970.

'Recent research on teacher education', in W. Taylor (ed.) Towards a Policy for the Education of Teachers, London, Butterworth, 1969.

'Issues and trends in the training of educational administrators', in W. Taylor and G. Baron (eds) Educational Administration and the Social Sciences, London, Athlone Press, 1969.

'Educational goals and outcomes in England', in M. Bresslaw and M.M. Tumin (eds) Evaluation of the Effectiveness of Educational Systems, Washington, DC, US

Department of Health, Education and Welfare, Bureau of Research, 1969.

'The use of simulations in the study of comparative administration', in W.G. Walker, G. Baron and D. Cooper (eds) Educational Administration: International Perspectives, Chicago, Rand McNally, 1967.

'The social relationship', in R. Oxtoby (ed.) Staff-Student Relations, London, World University Service, 1967.

'Family, school and society', in M. Craft et al. (eds) Linking Home and School, London, Longman, 1967.

'The sociology of education', in M. Craft (ed.) The Study of Education, London, Routledge & Kegan Paul, 1966.

'Learning to live with neighbours', in W.R. Niblett (ed.) How and Why do We Learn, London, Faber & Faber, 1965.

CONTRIBUTORS

Ron Arnold is a former Senior Inspector at the DES and is currently employed in the Advisory Service of the Oxfordshire Local Education Authority.

Josephine Cairns lectures in religious education at the University of London Institute of Education.

Maurice Galton is Professor of Education and Director of the School of Education at the University of Leicester.

Brian T. Gorwood is Organizer for In-Service Education at the University of Hull.

Peter H.J.H. Gosden is Professor of the History of Education and Head of the School of Education at the University of Leeds.

V. Alan McClelland is Professor of Educational Studies and Dean of the School of Education at the University of Hull.

J. Geoffrey Mattock is Organizer for In-Service Training at the University of Leeds.

Pauline Perry is Director of the South Bank Polytechnic and a former Chief Inspector at the DES.

Robert Povey and Peter Abbotts are on the staff of Christ Church College of Higher Education, Canterbury.

Sally Tomlinson is Professor of Educational Research at the University of Lancaster.

Ved P. Varma is a former Educational Psychologist with the London Boroughs of Richmond-Upon-Thames and Brent.

INDEX